D1611547

HELL-BENT

ALSO BY JASON RYAN

Jackpot: High Times, High Seas, and the Sting That Launched the War on Drugs

HELL-BENT

One Man's Crusade to Crush the Hawaiian Mob

JASON RYAN

LYONS PRESS
Guilford, Connecticut
Helena, Montana
An imprint of Rowman & Littlefield

Lyons Press is an imprint of Rowman & Littlefield

Distributed by NATIONAL BOOK NETWORK

British Library Cataloguing-in-Publication Information available

Library of Congress Cataloging-in-Publication Data available

ISBN 978-0-7627-9303-7 (hardcover)

∞™ The paper used in this publication meets the minimum requirements of American National Standard for Information Sciences—Permanence of Paper for Printed Library Materials, ANSI/NISO Z39.48-1992.

For my parents, who taught me the value of being honest and thoughtful, patient and persistent

Contents

Prologue 1

Chapter One: They Took Everything 6
Chapter Two: Vicious, Mad Dogs 43
Chapter Three: He Will Stop at Nothing 74
Chapter Four: Enemies in Common. 109
Chapter Five: If You Looking for Trouble 135
Chapter Six: No Rock Da Boat 163
Chapter Seven: My Bare Hands 188
Chapter Eight: Love Never Fails. 214

Epilogue 242
Acknowledgments 255
Sources. 256
Notes. 261
Index. 283
About the Author 296

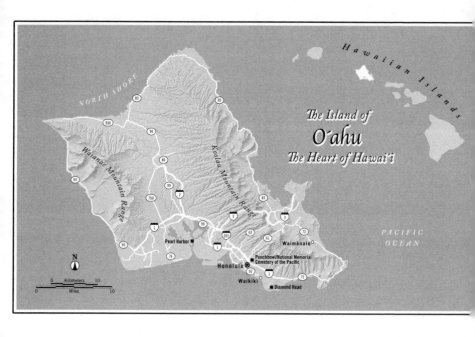

Prologue

He could have driven to the gravesite with his eyes closed.

For years Chuck Marsland made near-daily visits to the cemetery, piloting his wide-bodied Chrysler convertible up Puowaina Drive. The two-lane road remains the only way in and out of the cemetery, remarkable for how it hugs the side of an extinct volcano. Travelers on Puowaina Drive are treated to one of the more stunning vistas in Hawaii, a quarter mile or so of unobstructed panoramic views of the city of Honolulu and the Pacific Ocean.

On its own, Honolulu's skyline could be considered less than inspiring, a jumble of office towers, hotels, and condominiums generally devoid of distinctive styling or world-class architecture. Yet in its relief against the shimmering Pacific and Diamond Head, another and much larger extinct volcano that looms toward the end of Waikiki Beach, the skyline is made magnificent. But this view, flashing by at thirty-five miles per hour or so, is merely a prelude to another magnificent sight encountered by motorists on Puowaina Drive. At the top of the hill the road curves right, delivering automobiles into spectacular burial grounds within the shallow crater of the volcano.

The tranquility of the cemetery, owing as much to its position hundreds of feet above bustling Honolulu as to the lifelessness of its occupants, stands in contrast to the volcano's explosive beginning. The Hawaiian landmark was created in a single day more than seventy-five thousand years ago, when eruptions of superheated volcanic gas blew earth, ash, and rock into the air. As this stream of debris fell from the sky and scattered in the wind, it accumulated and formed a circular crater wall. The hillsides and crater then cooled and solidified, eventually becoming carpeted with tropical flora.

For centuries the hill accommodated lookouts on the island of Oahu. Long before Honolulu's high-rise hotels were built, before Hawaii became a US territory and then the fiftieth American state, Hawaiians gazed down from this landmark at open fields, fishponds, coconut groves, and the ocean. They trekked up the 578-foot-tall slope to watch for incoming ships, which promised the arrival of exotic goods and people. Until the early 1800s, Hawaiians also came to the hillside to dump the corpses of human sacrifices. It is for this reason that Hawaiians know the volcano as Puowaina, or "hill of sacrifice."

What might have mandated a sacrifice in old Hawaii? The violation of a societal taboo, or *kapu*, such as eating with the opposite sex or having physical contact with royalty, among other things. These transgressions sometimes demanded fatal punishments, and, after an execution elsewhere on Oahu, the violator's body might be brought to Puowaina. There the corpse might be burned, either in an oven or atop a large rock. Other times corpses were left to rot on the hillside. Secret royal burials were also performed at Puowaina, within the extinct volcano's shallow crater.

By the nineteenth century, after Hawaiian royalty had relaxed the *kapus*, Puowaina became a place one might look forward to visiting. The crater became popular with picnickers, and, thanks to Hawaii's King Kalākaua, in 1875 it was planted with acacia, algaroba, eucalyptus, and Inga trees. Two decades later, just as the United States took control of the Hawaiian Islands as a territory, Honolulu residents contemplated using the crater of Puowaina as a burial ground, though the idea was dismissed due to concern that the city's drinking-water supply could be contaminated by the elevated, decomposing bodies. That fear was overcome a half century later and the United States government began preparing the 116-acre crater as a national cemetery to hold thousands of soldiers killed in World War II. On July 19, 1949, the National Memorial Cemetery of the Pacific officially opened within the volcano's crater.

Few people casually refer to the hill and its burial grounds as the National Memorial Cemetery of the Pacific. Relatively few people, too, especially non-Hawaiians, refer to the hill as Puowaina anymore. To most people this landmark is Punchbowl Crater, or, simply enough, Punchbowl, so named for the gentle slope of the extinct volcano's concave interior. Inside Punchbowl are more than thirty-three thousand gravesites for those who fought in conflicts including World War II, the Korean War, and Vietnam, whether they died in battle or afterward. Many of the cemetery's original burials were World War II casualties from the Pacific Theater, including 776 victims of the Japanese aerial attack on December 7, 1941, that targeted the US naval base at Pearl Harbor, situated just ten miles away.

Rectangular grave markers dot the lawns that cover the crater. Each marker displays the barest details of a life etched in stone: name, place of birth, duration of life, religious affiliation, and military rank. A walk among these markers reveals that the dead within the National Memorial Cemetery of the Pacific came from nearly every place in America: Massachusetts, West Virginia, Arkansas, Idaho, Arizona, and so on. Many soldiers did not reach their twenty-fifth birthday. Some grave markers only read "Unknown."

Exotic and attractive trees are found in Punchbowl, including golden trumpet trees, a breadfruit tree, monkey pod, plumeria, and Chinese banyan—whose thick trunk resembles a mass of fused and intertwined snakes, making it seem as if the tree's chaotic root system has been partially exposed above ground. Overshadowing this tropical, and sometimes quite colorful, foliage is the thirty-foot-tall stone statue of Lady Columbia that looms opposite the cemetery entrance at the end of the Chinese banyan tree–lined central boulevard. Standing on a carved stone ship's prow at the top of a grand staircase, Lady Columbia is the centerpiece of the Honolulu Memorial, which was installed in 1964 to honor those who went missing in action or were buried at sea during fighting in World War II, Korea, and Vietnam. Beneath Lady Columbia is an inscription excerpted from a letter written in 1864 by Abraham Lincoln to Lydia Bixby, a Boston widow thought then to have lost five sons in the American Civil War.

THE SOLEMN PRIDE
THAT MUST BE YOURS
TO HAVE LAID
SO COSTLY A SACRIFICE
UPON THE ALTAR
OF FREEDOM

It was later clarified that Bixby likely lost just two sons in battle. These deaths still would have earned her the sympathy of Marsland, who once remarked to the cemetery's director that he "belonged to a fraternity no parent wants to join"—those whom had lost a child. Yet there was little fraternal in the way Marsland grieved for his son, Chuckers. Marsland, who grieved constantly, grieved alone.

When Marsland rounded that curve into the cemetery each day, he drove down the central boulevard toward Section T, located opposite the cemetery entrance, along the east side of the Honolulu Memorial. Parking close to the foot of the memorial's staircase, Marsland would exit his car and walk onto the lawn of Section T, heading for Site 140. There lay the grave of his son, Charles F. Marsland III.

Sometimes Marsland sat down on the lawn beside the grave. Other times he stood, his tall, rail-thin figure conspicuous among the sea of flat stone markers. Cemetery employees and other regular visitors bore frequent witness to Marsland's graveside presence, though the privacy they always afforded him made his one-sided conversations inaudible. From afar you could only see him speaking to the grave, his words carried off by the wind.

There's no knowing exactly what was said, but Marsland did disclose to friends at least one promise he made his dead son. Charles F. Marsland Jr. vowed to find the people who killed his beloved Chuckers. He was hell-bent on bringing them to justice.

CHAPTER ONE

They Took Everything

It's not a good sign when a policeman shows up at your front door. It's even worse when it's the chief who's knocking.

Francis Keala did not have to go far to reach the home of Charles Marsland. The neat, single-story house on Poipu Drive was just a mile from Keala's own home in the tranquil Honolulu neighborhood of Hawaii Kai. The chief had been there many times on account of his friendship with Marsland. Their boys went to school together and were close friends as well. The men shared a boat, which they used to take the boys swimming, diving, and fishing. Police Chief Keala and Marsland, a lawyer for the city of Honolulu, worked together plenty, too, any time the department faced a legal problem. The men were so close that Marsland had asked Keala to be his son's godfather.

But unlike past visits, today's house call would not be a happy one. Marsland would soon greet Keala at the door and suffer through the worst day of his life. The man had already endured some doozies. During World War II, Marsland had commanded an infantry landing craft in the Pacific theater, participating in the invasion of the Philippines as American forces sought to regain control of the islands from the Japanese. After the war, in Boston, the young lawyer went through a bitter divorce that resulted in his return to Hawaii and his family being split in two. About the same time as his island homecoming, Marsland's father died.

Yet none of this heartache and tragedy was sufficient preparation for the morning of April 17, 1975, when Marsland answered the door to hear the most heartbreaking news a parent can hear: His child was dead. Through sobs Chief Keala revealed the news that Marsland's nineteen-year-old son Chuckers had been found lifeless that morning in Waimānalo, a rural area on the other side of the Koolau Mountains, about ten miles away from the Marsland home. Chuckers had been shot multiple times in the head and chest, left on the side of a desolate road.

"As soon as I saw Francis, I knew something was terribly wrong, because he was crying," Marsland later wrote. "When he told me that Chuckie was gone, something inside me died, too."

A motorist had discovered Chuckers's body that morning at daybreak, near the Waimānalo intersection of Hihimanu and Nonokio Streets—back roads, off the main highway that circled the island, running through farmland that abutted the Koolau Mountains. Because of this out-of-the-way location, as well as the probability that Chuckers was killed very early in the morning, it was unlikely anyone witnessed the murder, save the killer or killers. Nearby residents had, however, heard multiple gunshots.

Whoever killed Chuckers certainly wanted him dead. An autopsy performed later that day confirmed Chuckers had been shot twice in the chest with a shotgun at close range, with pellets entering his heart. If that had not been enough to kill him, at least four gunshot wounds to his head were. They had been delivered into his face from a handgun fired at point-blank range.

There wasn't much for the police to recover from the murder scene. A large comb and hairbrush were found on the roadside, but detectives could only speculate if these beauty products belonged to the victim or the killer or killers, or were just litter that had already been on the ground when the murder occurred. Beyond the comb and brush, there were just some empty shotgun shells and Chuckers's body, punched through by bullets and shotgun pellets.

Chuckers had been well dressed, sporting garb typical of the 1970s disco scene. He wore a blue leisure suit, with a blue and white long-sleeve, button-down shirt underneath. On his feet were blue socks and white boots. Around his throat was a Puka shell necklace, and in his pockets were packs of gum and cigarettes, as well as some loose change and a paycheck. Two gold rings were on his fingers. Such attire was appropriate for his job as a doorman, or bouncer, at one of Waikiki's most popular nightclubs, the Infinity. Chuckers had worked a shift there until the club's closing at four in the morning. Two hours later he was found dead.

Like his father, Chuckers was tall and lean, standing six feet, two inches tall and weighing 177 pounds. He had recently moved out of his father's home in Hawaii Kai, where he had lived for nearly eight years following his parents' divorce in Boston. Marsland said he returned to Hawaii with his eleven-year-old boy because he wanted his son to feel "the sand beneath his toes." To Marsland's satisfaction, Chuckers embraced life by the sea and was fond of water sports. Also living at the Marsland home was Marsland's girlfriend, Polly Grigg.

For high school Marsland sent Chuckers to his alma mater, Punahou School. Protestant missionaries to Hawaii founded the private school in 1841 to educate their children. A decade later the school opened to all races and religions. Since then Punahou School had developed into one of the most well-regarded schools in Hawaii, if not the United States. Alumni of the school include President Barack Obama, golfer Michelle Wie, actress Kelly Preston, eBay founder Pierre Omidyar, and Hiram Bingham III, a US senator and explorer of the Inca city of Machu Picchu.

Chuckers's enrollment at Punahou School, from which he graduated in 1973, was not the only sign of an upper-crust life in Hawaii. Marsland was a member of the Outrigger Canoe Club. There, during the summer, Chuckers would practice canoeing during the week in preparation for weekend races. He could also use the club to surf, riding across the same shoreline as famed Hawaiian surfer and Olympic swimmer Duke Kahanamoku, who was once also a club member. When Chuckers was old enough to drive, Marsland bought his son a Chrysler convertible to match his own. Now Chuckers could cruise Oahu himself.

The island was a mesmerizing place to explore. Two mountain ranges run north to south on Oahu, covering much of the island's six hundred square miles. On the western, or leeward, side of the island are the Waianae Mountains. On the eastern, or windward, side of Oahu are the Koolau Mountains, which are frequently cloud covered and prone to heavy rainfall. The Koolau Mountains are magnificent for their severe climb up out of the earth; the dark, moody hues of green that cover their steep slopes; and the fact that the mountains run the length of the island.

Standing in Honolulu, one's back to the ocean, one gazes upon the Koolau Mountains knowing that for all their beauty, they are landmarks that conceal and obstruct. The mountains divide the Windward Coast from the rest of the island and form a natural inland barrier to Honolulu, a city that otherwise sprawls in every available direction, pushing up against hillsides, into valleys, and against the sea. The mountainsides of the Koolau Range are steep and carpeted in thick tangles of plants. These slopes are not easy to explore, and some ridges and peaks are outright treacherous, better reached by helicopter than foot. Gazing upward through a mist at the lush and cloud-obscured Koolau Mountains, it seems there exist parts of Hawaii that cannot be easily known, if known at all.

But those untrod slopes stand in contrast to the rest of Oahu, which is more easily accessible. Within three hours one can circle nearly the entire island by car, so long as traffic cooperates. Beginning in Waikiki and heading south along the water, one drives past imposing Diamond Head, through the wealthy Honolulu neighborhoods of Kahala and Hawaii Kai, before coming upon Hanauma Bay, where snorkelers crowd the water to view coral reefs and other ocean wildlife. Continuing along the highway, leaving behind Honolulu's sprawl, one passes another imposing extinct volcano, Koko Crater, and other popular sights, including an ocean blowhole that spouts water up out of a rock when waves crash below. Then comes Sandy Beach, popular with body surfers, and Makapuu Point, upon which sits a picturesque lighthouse high above the rolling Pacific.

Curving around to the windward side of the island, the road clings to the Koolau Mountains before entering rural Waimānalo and then the towns of Kailua and Kaneohe. Then one begins a stunningly scenic trek along the gorgeous remainder of the Windward Coast, flanked nearly the entire way by mountains on one side, ocean on the other. An hour later one can arrive at the quaint and isolated North Shore, famous for massive wintertime waves and shrimp trucks, before circling back between the mountain ranges for the return to Honolulu.

Who lives on Oahu and the Neighbor Islands? A hodgepodge of people. Hawaii is one of the most ethnically diverse places in the country, with significant populations of Caucasians and Asians, including citizens with Japanese, Filipino, Chinese, and Korean ancestry. Native Hawaiians themselves make up just a small portion of the islands' population.

In 1982, native Hawaiians comprised 19 percent of the state's population and were outnumbered by both Caucasians and residents of Japanese descent. Pure Hawaiians made up less than 1 percent of the population, with that population continually declining due to intermarriage and interbreeding with other races. A growing population, on the other hand, was the number of kamaainas, or long-term residents of the islands who did not possess Hawaiian blood. Though these people called Hawaii home, they would not refer to themselves as Hawaiian, that descriptor being reserved for people with native bloodlines. Marsland, for example, was at least a third-generation kamaaina, literally translated as child of the land, on account of his Norwegian grandfather having emigrated to Hawaii in the nineteenth century.

Upon learning of Chuckers's death that April morning, one of Marsland's first calls was to Chuckers's girlfriend, Cathy Clisby, who was at the couple's apartment in Waikiki. Upon being told of her boyfriend's murder, Clisby began crying and screaming, "Chuck's dead!"

Friends and family streamed to the Marsland home that day to offer condolences, clogging Poipu Drive with cars. Among the visitors was Chuckers's friend, Eric Naone, who had just seen his buddy early that morning, as the Infinity nightclub was preparing to close and Chuckers was finishing his shift. Naone offered to help at the Marsland home by moving some of the other guests' cars. He greeted Mr. Marsland in the garage. To Naone, Marsland looked visibly depressed.

Marsland confirmed such an observation with his words.

"They took everything away from me," the grieving father told Naone.

For those who do not live on the islands, it can be hard to imagine any serious crime occurring in Hawaii. Popular culture and travel advertisements have conditioned outsiders' minds to think of only the most conventional, and peaceful, tropical imagery when envisioning Hawaii. When someone mentions Hawaii, the mind inevitably conjures images of pineapples, hula girls, luaus, and leis. Perhaps a ukulele is playing in the background.

Throughout the twentieth century, Hawaii was subject to much embellishment, with popular culture focusing narrowly on the more romantic aspects of the islands, usually some combination of the above-mentioned objects combined with sun, surf, sand, and sexy skin-baring women. Hit songs and movies extolled the pleasures of the Hawaiian Islands. In 1937 Bing Crosby starred in the musical *Waikiki Wedding*. It was Crosby, too, who crooned the seemingly immortal version of "Mele Kalikimaka," which appears on radio airwaves each holiday season, promising a Hawaiian Christmas that will be "green and bright, the sun to shine by day and all the stars at night ..."

In the 1960s Elvis made three pleasant-sounding films in Hawaii: *Blue Hawaii, Girls! Girls! Girls!,* and *Paradise, Hawaiian Style.* A few years later popular American television shows such as *I Dream of Jeannie* and *The Brady Bunch* filmed special episodes in Hawaii. When Alice, the Brady family's housekeeper, steps off the plane in Honolulu, she is the beneficiary of such over-the-top Hawaiian hospitality that she has trouble seeing through all the leis piled around her shoulders, neck, and head.

In the essay "Lovely Hula Hands," whose title refers to a "famous and very saccharine" song by the same name that "embodies the worst romanticized views of hula dancers and Hawaiian culture in general," Hawaiian scholar Haunani-Kay Trask laments such mass-media depictions of the islands, particularly since the media have helped boost a tourism industry in Hawaii whose effects she finds destructive and insufferable. Hawaii's modern history, Trask argues, is one of appropriation.

"To most Americans, then, Hawaii is theirs: to use, to take, and, above all, to fantasize about long after the experience," writes Trask. "Just five hours away by plane from California, Hawaii is a thousand light years away in fantasy. Hawaii, as an image of escape from the rawness and violence of daily American life, is mostly a state of mind."

Even when crime was depicted in Hawaii, it was fantastical. Popular television shows *Hawaii Five-O* and *Magnum P.I.* thrived by presenting wrongdoing on the islands in distorted fashion. The fictional crime shown in these long-running television series tended to be atypically exotic, involving international spies, jewel thieves, kidnappings, and whatnot. Both programs, too, featured bachelor protagonists defined by their unwavering dedication to uncover mischief and mayhem in Hawaii. That's not to say that people didn't enjoy such drama—both were extremely successful, long-running productions.

Hawaii Five-O originally aired from 1968 to 1980 and was then resurrected in 2010 with a new cast and crew. On the original show, actor Jack Lord played uncompromising detective Lieutenant Commander Steve McGarrett, who was part of a special state police force. McGarrett, perched high atop the Ilikai Hotel in Waikiki in the show's opening credits, seemed to watch over all Hawaii. On *Magnum P.I.*, which aired from 1980 to 1988, actor Tom Selleck portrayed Thomas Magnum, an easygoing, Ferrari-driving private investigator living on a huge waterfront estate.

None of this media, of course, was obligated to document the reality of Hawaii. That was part of the fun, for viewers to indulge in a dreamy, tropical existence that seemed available to anyone willing to hop a jet and ride halfway across the Pacific. Nonetheless, taken together these fanciful depictions were overwhelming, becoming the popular portrait of the islands. Consequently, Hawaii's presentation to the world was largely a skewed one, with little attention paid to the islands' inequities and darker societal elements.

So for the many tourists who began jetting to the islands in the 1960s and the decades to follow, Hawaii seemed a paradise, indeed. They came to see the state's beautiful beaches and valleys, indulge in its unique and relaxed culture, and enjoy its year-round temperate weather, which usually consisted of sunny and comfortably breezy, seventy-something-degree days. Most of all they came to ignore problems while on vacation, both their own and those belonging to Hawaii.

In the early days of jet tourism, one frequent visitor gushed that you could step off the plane and smell wild ginger. Then the scent of ginger, she said, was replaced by jet fuel and car exhaust, as so many people were coming to see Hawaii. By 1980 more than four million people were visiting each year. Some of these visitors stayed permanently. From 1960, the year after Hawaii earned its statehood, to 1980, the population on the islands grew by 50 percent, to almost one million residents.

No matter their ultimate destination in Hawaii, nearly all these people first landed at the international airport in Hawaii's capital, Honolulu, on the island of Oahu. Half the state's population lives on Oahu, though it is only the third largest of the state's eight major islands. These eight islands, from smallest to largest, include Kahoolawe, Niihau, Lanai, Molokai, Kauai, Oahu, Maui, and Hawaii (also known as the Big Island). The cluster stands alone in the middle of the Pacific Ocean, in its own time zone, nearly three thousand miles from California and nearly four thousand miles from Japan.

One cannot easily ignore this geographic isolation. Everywhere in Hawaii, beachside or mountaintop, there is a nearby vantage point from which to stare out on the endless ocean. The vast Pacific, in which one can spy humpback whales off the shore during the winter and early spring, reinforces the fact that the traveler is far, far from home. It is easy for an outsider to think of the islands as a parallel world, bound to nowhere else, free of global concern.

Hawaii's unique and exotic trees, its pleasant and relatively unchanging weather, its cultural quirks . . . all indicate a place untethered, devoid of the more common sights and rhythms found on the earth's continents. Hawaii proudly exists alone, its landscape merging with none other.

Hawaii's people, however, have merged with others, ever since the 1778 arrival of English explorer Captain James Cook, who is credited along with his men as being the first Europeans to visit the Hawaiian Islands. Upon making landfall, Cook and his crews traded with the Hawaiians and enjoyed warm relations, but soon left to explore the North Pacific in search of a Northwest Passage—a sea route across the top of North America connecting the Atlantic and Pacific Oceans. Unable to cross the Bering Strait, Cook returned to Hawaii a year later. This time he was killed, supposedly stabbed after he and his men skirmished with Hawaiians over a stolen boat. Though Cook's time in Hawaii was brief, and ultimately bloody, the sea captain's visits were significant for alerting the wider world to the existence of the islands. For the first time since Polynesian sailors arrived to the islands from the Marquesas and then the Society Islands centuries earlier, Hawaii was once again a destination.

About the same time as Cook's visit, the legendary warrior Kamehameha the Great began his deadly conquest of the islands, beginning with his home island of Hawaii and then in 1795 expanding to Maui, Molokai, and Oahu. By 1810 Kamehameha's conquest was complete, and he ruled the islands until his death in 1819. His royal successors would be far less adept in maintaining Hawaiians' independence and prosperity in the face of outside influence and immigration.

Among those crashing the shores were Protestant missionaries from New England, some of the first outsiders to make Hawaii their home and slowly wrest control away from its royalty and natives. They first set sail from Boston aboard the *Thaddeus,* enduring a five-month journey. Upon making landfall in 1820, they proceeded to not only introduce Hawaiians to Christianity, but also written language and the printing press.

Merchants, too, began regularly visiting Hawaii, eager to trade ironware, liquor, and luxury goods for Hawaiian sandalwood, and, when that ran out, Hawaiian land. American, British, French, and Russian visitors competed with each other for influence over the islands' inhabitants, finding Hawaiians to be willing and generous trading partners and hosts. Meanwhile, the Hawaiians had been dying in droves, the native population depleted by famine, inter-island warfare, and, most significantly, diseases, including many brought by visitors and immigrants, like syphilis, gonorrhea, pneumonia, cholera, influenza, and smallpox. More than 300,000 Hawaiians are thought to have existed when Captain Cook landed on the islands. A little more than a century later, the 1890 census counted 34,436 pure Hawaiians.

While the native Hawaiian population declined, Hawaii's immigrant population boomed. In the late nineteenth and early twentieth centuries, tens of thousands of immigrants from China, Japan, Korea, and, later, the Philippines came to work on Hawaiian sugar plantations, which increasingly formed a significant part of the island economy. A much smaller number of immigrants also came from across Europe to work on the plantations, including laborers from Portugal and Scandinavia.

Hawaiians not only lost their health and population advantage, they lost their land. Sweeping changes to property laws in the nineteenth century resulted in Hawaiians more or less relinquishing native land to Hawaiian royalty, chiefs, and foreigners. As famed Hawaiian entertainer Don Ho once quipped, this chapter of Hawaiian history began when Protestant missionaries taught natives to pray.

"We looked down to pray, and when we looked up all our land was gone," said Ho, whose own ancestry mirrored the islands' multiculturalism, with Hawaiian, Chinese, Portuguese, Dutch, and German bloodlines.

Then, at the end of the century, the Hawaiians lost their sovereignty. It began with the Bayonet Constitution in 1887, in which *haole*, or foreign, planters and businessmen forced King Kalākaua, under threat of harm, to agree to a new constitution severely limiting the Hawaiian monarch's power. Six years later, in 1893, some of these same men, with the help of armed American forces, toppled the monarchy entirely when Queen Liliuokalani, sister to the late King Kalākaua, yielded to the insurrectionists in an effort to avoid bloodshed. She assumed this shift in power would be temporary, that the US government, upon learning of the insurrection, would restore her to the throne. The queen's assumption was wrong. The Hawaiians would not reclaim power.

By 1898 Hawaii had been annexed by the United States and made a territory. By 1959 Hawaii was America's fiftieth state, and on the cusp of a tourist- and real estate–inspired economic boom. Yet the passage of time and the influx of so many visitors and capital did not heal all wounds. Native Hawaiians, in particular, were bothered by the past and present changes affecting their islands. The 1970s saw a wave of activism regarding the alleged abuses against Hawaiians, including the overthrowing of the Hawaiian monarchy nearly a century earlier. Demonstrations were staged in protest of policies seen as detrimental to Hawaiian heritage and property, with some activists calling for the United States to return Hawaiian land to native Hawaiians outright, or at least pay reparations. Others sought lesser concessions, and, to some satisfaction, in 1978 the Office of Hawaiian Affairs was created to better the lives of native Hawaiians.

Yet this hardly mollified all the critics. What's more, the racial tension and anger over the alleged culture-corrupting influence of mass tourism were compounded by a problem on the islands that bothered every ethnic group: widespread crime. Like much of the rest of the United States, Hawaii's violent crime rate had been climbing. The 1970s was easily the most murderous decade in modern Hawaiian history, and in 1975 homicide detectives in Honolulu had much more than the murder of Chuckers Marsland to consider. Just halfway through the year the Honolulu Police Department was overwhelmed with twenty-eight murder cases, half of them unsolved. This midyear murder count was greater than any full-year total in the 1960s.

Unsolved murders were all too common in Hawaii, mostly due to a thriving criminal underworld that profited from illegal gambling. In the 1960s gambling was wildly popular throughout the Hawaiian Islands, especially among Asian-American populations in the state. While other ethnic populations, including native Hawaiians, gambled as well, it was predominantly Hawaiian residents of Asian descent, sometimes known locally as *Pakes*, who controlled the games. On Oahu there were games available in almost every pocket of the island, including cockfights that drew hundreds of people in rural areas like Waianae and Waimānalo, card and dice games in Chinatown, and floating casinos that moved around apartments in Waikiki and other parts of Honolulu. The casino-type games took cues from Las Vegas, offering patrons food and drink, nude girlie shows, and the use of professional craps tables in exchange for a ten-dollar admission fee.

For some men, extortion of gambling operators was a surer bet for making money than playing games of Monte, craps, or poker. By threatening harm, crime lords could exact weekly fees from the gambling operators, who would rather grumble over a protection payment than suffer violence. These weekly payments amounted to a few hundred thousand dollars in annual income for the crime lords, though the cash flow could be diminished by police gambling raids and competition from other gangsters.

Extortion was a dangerous game. Infringements on one's turf, as well as the occasional refusal of payment, required swift and brutal retribution. As underworld battles raged, victims in Hawaii's criminal underworld included people who were shot, stabbed, strangled, slashed with a sword, beaten, bombed, burned, and pickaxed. One man was said to meet his end by being dropped into a shark tank, though others countered that he was actually cooked in swill and then fed to pigs. In any case, he was no longer around.

No operator stayed atop the criminal underworld for long. One crime boss, George Soon Bock "Yobo" Chung, rose from lowly burglar who broke into homes while families attended funeral services to a suspected murderer who demanded ten-thousand-dollar protection fees at a time from men who ran gambling games. He was shot dead in a Chinatown gambling hall in 1967, executed after being picked out of a group of forty men forced to line up against a wall. Another crime lord associated with Chung, John Sayim Kim, was badly mangled by a car bomb six months earlier. Deposed, Kim then carved out a minor role in the underworld on the Big Island, where he walked with a limp.

Each attack, whether a shooting or car bomb, engendered more violence. As a result of the tit-for-tat gangster warfare, bodies began piling up. So much so that when Francis Keala became Honolulu's new police chief in 1969, he was compelled to confront the problem. Whereas his predecessor had claimed Hawaii's underworld was composed of disorganized crime, Keala espoused a different belief. Through secret, regular briefings held at the police department throughout 1970, Keala informed more than three hundred of Hawaii's civic leaders, law enforcement officials, politicians, judges, reporters, and news editors about the depth of organized crime in Hawaii.

At thirty-nine years old, Keala was the youngest chief in the history of the Honolulu Police Department and its first to have a college education. Beyond the challenges of organized crime, Keala, like police chiefs across the country, had to handle broad social unrest in the 1970s, including antiwar demonstrations and a counterculture fond of marijuana, an illicit crop that was well suited to be grown in Hawaii's tropical climate.

Keala's presentation on organized crime was startling for its particulars. He disclosed the names of the local crime syndicate's alleged leaders, showed photographs of these men, and detailed their arrest records and suspected crimes. Keala's briefings impressed his audiences, including the media. In a subsequent series on organized crime by the *Honolulu Advertiser*, the newspaper gravely warned, "The crime syndicate is here, in force." Its existence, the paper went on, was far more of a threat to the "real Hawaii" than pollution, traffic jams, tourism, or even hippies.

What especially alarmed the newspaper was not just the existence of organized crime in Hawaii but signs that mob activity in the Aloha State might become more entrenched and more powerful. While still lacking the permanence and sophistication of mainland criminal networks, the Hawaiian underworld had undergone rapid growth during the turmoil of the 1960s, evolving from a collection of street gangs to a more centralized, and

HELL-BENT

profitable, leadership structure. The fear was that this new organization—as well as the increasing amounts of money it collected from gambling, prostitution, and narcotics—would attract a takeover from the mafia on the American mainland. Then Hawaii would never be able to rid itself of the mob.

Though plausible, this concern overlooked the fact that the local underworld was extremely resistant to any intrusion from off-island mobsters, no matter the benefits of their extra muscle, money, and political connections. As one insider described the situation, "The only way the mainland Mafia could take over is come in and kill about ten people and I'm not sure they could do it even then. There is a strong anti-haole feeling, especially in the local mob."

This antipathy to outsiders was so strong that in 1969 it spurred a drastic reordering of the underworld ranks. There was a new leadership structure, Police Chief Keala told his audiences. The Hawaiian Syndicate had been born.

At least that's what the newspapers called the criminal organization. Its members referred to themselves as The People, The Company, or The Family, sometimes referring to each other as "bruddah." Others knew the Syndicate gangsters as "the boys." By any name the gang was, in the eyes of its founders, more than a way to make money—it was a way to compensate for two centuries' worth of economic and political injustices perpetrated by outsiders against Hawaii's native population. Gathered in September 1969 in a home in the small community of Laie on Oahu's Windward Coast, the founding members of the Hawaiian Syndicate voiced their frustrations with the status quo of the underworld, which seemed to mirror the marginalization of natives in the islands' legitimate economy. In particular many people felt, fairly or not, that whites and Japanese Americans in Hawaii had enriched themselves at the expense of others.

As Roy Ryder, one of the Syndicate's founders recalled, the Syndicate was formed "to make things good for the state of Hawaii, our Hawaiian people.

"The Orientals had everything for years," said Ryder, an admitted killer and Syndicate crime lieutenant. The Syndicate wanted "to move in on the Orientals and take control of all gambling and illegal things in the State.

"[To] get it for our people," Ryder said.

Personal resentment also played a part in the Syndicate's formation. Wilford "Nappy" Pulawa, who had previously worked as a strong-arm man for crime boss Earl K. H. Kim, complained to his associates that Kim "gave him the bone. Took all the money and gave him what's left."

Though much of the Syndicate's membership had Hawaiian blood, its first leader was of Samoan heritage. Alema Leota was born on Oahu in 1928 to two Mormon immigrants from American Samoa who settled in Laie, which was home to a small Mormon population and the first Mormon temple built outside of Utah.

Leota had a violent bent and was known as a brawler. One of his first known brushes with the law occurred in the summer of 1951, when he and his younger brother Reid assaulted two tavern owners after being asked to curb their use of profanity. The young Leota men cut the face and blackened the eyes of one proprietor and broke the jaw of the other owner, who was sixty-two years old.

Soon after that the Leota brothers, who police described as having a "wild hatred for Negroes," were arrested for threatening a black man. As the police arrived, Reid Leota, who was armed, told them, "If you guys had come five minutes later there might have been four dead Negroes."

A few months later the police did come too late, and, indeed, one black man was dead. On January 29, 1952, the Leota brothers fought with thirty-nine-year-old Charles Nelson at a pool hall on Smith Street. Alema Leota chased Nelson outside and beat him over the head with a cue stick. When Nelson fell to the ground, Reid Leota stomped the man repeatedly, bruising his lungs, breaking his ribs, fracturing his skull, and rupturing his heart. Nelson died the next day.

Reid Leota was convicted of second-degree murder and sentenced to twenty years in prison for killing Nelson. Alema Leota received a ten-year sentence for his role in the attack. At about the same time, Alema was sentenced separately for selling marijuana to an undercover federal agent. At the marijuana sentencing, Federal Judge J. Frank McLaughlin took stock of the man in his courtroom, whose reputation for administering beatings went far beyond the crimes in which he was actually charged.

"You are one of the worst criminals I have ever had before me," said the judge. "You are vicious."

Leota was contrite.

"If you could look into my heart," he told the federal judge, "you would know that now all I want to do is be good and serve my family, community, and my country."

Though he'd eventually try to make good on that pledge by mounting an unsuccessful campaign to become governor of Hawaii, Alema Leota slid back into the underworld following his release from prison. He worked as a strong-arm man beside Pulawa, helping collect money from gambling operators and bookies. By 1969 Leota was on top of the underworld, living in a plush Waikiki apartment and regularly enjoying Honolulu's finest restaurants and nightclubs.

Leota's ascent was enabled, in part, by the Asian kingpins who preceded him having been sent to prison, pushed aside, or killed. Leota was among those questioned about the Chinatown shooting death of "Yobo" Chung, though the murder ultimately remained unsolved. Another potential suspect questioned by the police was Pulawa, Leota's top lieutenant and the most feared man in the Hawaiian Syndicate, whose alleged actions rattled underworlds near and far. Some said Pulawa earned the nickname "Nappy" because of the appearance of his hair. Others said it was because he fancied himself as powerful as Napoleon.

In 1968 a gambler from the mainland was nearly choked to death at the Honolulu airport when he was suspected of cheating locals in craps games by using loaded dice. Soon two Mafia hit men from Rhode Island arrived in Honolulu to avenge the attack on their comrade. They went looking for Pulawa specifically, until the Honolulu police intercepted the hit men and advised them to go home where it was safe. Such counsel was sage advice. A few years later two other mobsters from Las Vegas arrived in Honolulu to settle a score with the Hawaiian Syndicate. The mobsters were returned to Sin City stuffed into a trunk, chopped into pieces. Attached to the trunk was a note that read, "Delicious, send more."

It was not long before Pulawa replaced Leota as head of the Hawaiian Syndicate, though this transfer of power between the men in 1970 was accomplished, perhaps surprisingly, without the spilling of blood. With the feared Pulawa on top, the Syndicate was then able to extort even greater amounts of money. Few people dared not to pay. An exception, at least for a brief spell, was a small gang of black pimps in Chinatown who refused to pay tribute to crime lords for running a prostitution ring. Then the charred torso of one of these black gangsters was discovered in the city trash incinerator in June 1969. It took police a month to identify the remains as belonging to forty-seven-year-old Richard "Dickie" Johnson, but even then they weren't sure whether Johnson had been burned alive or killed before being incinerated. In any case the blacks began paying.

The Syndicate's taxing of even this fringe black gang in Honolulu demonstrated the thoroughness in which they had begun operating and the significance of revenues from prostitution, which had been outlawed locally in 1944. Given the large tourist and military populations on Oahu, as well as a robust local demand, prostitution was a booming business in Honolulu, especially downtown and in Waikiki, where prostitutes lined beachfront Kalākaua Avenue from sundown to sunup. These women charged about thirty dollars a trick and, according to reports, were expected by some pimps to gross at least two hundred dollars a night, which was either an exaggerated, or exhausting, rate of work. However many tricks the women turned, as much as 40 percent of their earnings were paid to the Syndicate. Those who didn't pay were beaten or, in some cases, killed.

The criminal underworld rotated the stock regularly, pushing women to travel internationally through a sort of prostitution circuit. The girls typically started their tour on the East Coast of the mainland and then moved to cities farther west, the mob spiriting them out of town and into a different legal jurisdiction as soon their arrest record grew and prosecution loomed. From Washington, D.C., the prostitutes might move to Chicago, then Los Angeles before arriving in Hawaii, where they worked under the supervision of local gangsters. Once the women drew a few busts on Oahu or the Big Island, they were flown to Guam and then, finally, to Japan. In 1970 the Hawaiian Syndicate was estimated to earn as much as three million dollars in fees annually from prostitution.

Drug trafficking and distribution was another moneymaker for the Hawaiian underworld. Hawaii's position as a Pacific crossroads meant that many illicit substances passed through its ports, and residents. Drugs in Hawaii were remarkably potent and pure, and therefore popular. The purity was owed to the fact that for drugs like heroin and cocaine, Hawaii was often the first international stop in the journey to the mainland, meaning the product had not yet been diluted, or cut. Heroin seized at the Honolulu airport in the 1970s was consistently found to be 90 to 100 percent pure.

By 1975 much of the heroin coming through Hawaii came from Southeast Asia's so-called Golden Triangle, which encompasses parts of Laos, Myanmar, and Thailand. The majority of it arrived undetected in the luggage of airline passengers. Security personnel were unable to thoroughly search the baggage of the forty-two thousand passengers who landed and departed each day at Honolulu International Airport, which in 1977 was the second-busiest American airport with 129 flights a day. In addition, some Asian heroin was allegedly stashed inside the cadavers of American servicemen killed in Vietnam, and unpacked by medical clerks who processed the bodies as they were being shipped home for burial.

The cargo coming into Hawaii's seaports was scrutinized even less. Containerized cargo, in fact, was hardly inspected at all in Hawaii in the 1970s. Furthermore, the US government judged it too tall a task to patrol all the personal watercraft arriving in Hawaii, including sailboats suspected of smuggling cocaine from Mexico and South America via Tahiti. Peruvian surfers who traveled to Hawaii for surfing competitions also were known by police to smuggle cocaine.

For marijuana, Hawaiians took care of themselves, using the islands' advantageous climate and soil to grow potent strains like Maui Wowie, Kona Gold, Puna Butter, and Kauai Electric, sometimes in booby-trapped fields. In the late 1970s an estimated fifty thousand to eighty thousand pounds of marijuana, or *pakalolo* as it's known locally, was exported from the Big Island each year. The Syndicate, however, received only a small yield from the marijuana trade, with much of the money split among small, independent farmers.

The Hawaiian underworld made additional money trafficking guns to Japan and peddling pornography. Gangsters also resold pilfered jewelry, as well as stolen home appliances, sometimes offering the bulky goods for sale at municipal golf courses. And they demanded tribute money from bar owners, threatening to start brawls and destroy taverns should there be no payment. They even muscled in on local fish markets, setting inflated prices for seafood. But no matter all these revenue streams, whether drugs, guns, hookers, petty crime, or pornography, the Syndicate depended on one activity above all for its survival: gambling.

Under Pulawa's leadership of the Syndicate, gambling revenues increased dramatically, though business practices remained crude. During his reign, one of his terrorizing lieutenants, Henry Huihui, called a meeting of bookies and gambling game operators to inform them that they owed 20 percent of their earnings each week, and that the Syndicate expected them to keep daily gambling records. Before the meeting concluded, Pulawa required that each gambling operator sign a contract agreeing to these demands. The gamblers were then given the contract on which to affix their signature: just a blank piece of paper.

Collections were made on Wednesday, when one of Pulawa's henchmen visited the men and received envelopes full of cash. To keep track of payments, each envelope was marked with letters or numbers that identified the gambler paying tribute, whether Tramp, Hotcha, Blackie, Nobu, Freckles, Chocolate Joe, or any of the other scores of gamblers in Hawaii cowed by the Syndicate into paying. The money was then delivered to Pulawa and his lieutenants in a high-rise apartment in Honolulu, where the cash was spread across a bed and counted, organized into piles of two hundred dollars. The haul was substantial, with Pulawa's bagman—the boss's top money collector—claiming to have accumulated eight hundred thousand dollars from thirty-three gamblers over fifteen months in the early 1970s. During football season the Syndicate collected an extra thirty thousand dollars each week due to the popularity of parlay sheets, in which gamblers made a series of bets on games in hopes of securing a large payout, should all those bets succeed. Of course the biggest winner was always the Syndicate, who correctly bet that gamblers would rather cough up a portion of their earnings than suffer beatings. The rare gambler who refused to pay was quickly made to fall into line. On at least one occasion, Pulawa sat calmly in an apartment, a gun in his lap, while Huihui beat a gambler in front of him—a scene seemingly cut straight from a movie. Other gamblers were assaulted by Syndicate lieutenants in bathrooms, emerging from the toilet stalls beaten and bloodied. As Pulawa, speaking in the Hawaiian Pidgin commonly used on the islands, told one Japanese gambling operator: "If no pay, shake 'em down. If not, push the head in toilet."

Beyond the handsome Huihui, who was known as both an extremely amiable and extremely pugnacious man, Pulawa's gang of lieutenants included the boyish-looking Alvin Kaohu (known as "Blue Eyes"), Bobby Wilson, and Ryder, a former classmate to Pulawa at Honolulu's Roosevelt High School, where Ryder was a football star. After high school Ryder played football while briefly attending the University of Hawaii—very briefly.

"I only went to one class," said Ryder. "I'm not too sharp."

In high school, he explained, "girls did my homework. I went for play football, that's all."

The Syndicate was a tight-knit bunch. In addition to their work in the underworld, Pulawa and Kaohu played golf twice a week. Ryder said he and Pulawa were nearly inseparable. Some of the Syndicate members shared apartments, each with their own room, in addition to having homes that housed their wives and children. Ryder said he left his "first family" to join The Family, or Syndicate, upon its formation.

"I give up my family," said Ryder, sounding very much the football jock. "In this thing you don't give 100 percent, you give 110 percent."

Ryder and his fellow lieutenants were paid several hundred dollars a week by Pulawa for their work. No doubt this helped sustain their friendship, although some gangsters groused about Pulawa being greedy, especially compared to his predecessor, Leota. But it was fear, not generosity, that was essential to Pulawa's grip on the Hawaiian underworld. The crime boss kept an arsenal of at least thirty guns stashed around Oahu, said Ryder, who cleaned the weapons. Among the firepower were shotguns, automatic rifles, pistols, grenades, and silenced handguns. Few dared cross Pulawa.

"Nappy was the quiet but deadly and brutal kind of guy," said one former prostitute intimately familiar with a number of the Syndicate members. "Of all the gangsters that I was around I was the most uncomfortable in Nappy's company."

Syndicate members in Honolulu would routinely invite women to accompany them on business trips to the Neighbor Islands. Partly this was to provide cover and give the appearance of couples or a group of friends on a holiday. Partly this was so the men could enjoy themselves in the evenings. The women, for their part, earned some money, went shopping, and enjoyed drugs and alcohol. Generally the ugly side of Syndicate business was avoided during these excursions, but there were exceptions.

"Where other of the crews, they protected the women pretty much—if stuff was going to jump off, it wouldn't be around the women. With Nappy you never knew," says the prostitute. "You never knew what was going to set him off."

Those who wanted to stay on top, and alive, killed rivals at the slightest provocation. Sometimes there was no provocation, and killings were just precautionary, to remove someone who could become a threat. In Hawaii's underworld there was little room for half measures or mercy. Once you started a job, you finished it.

"They used to say, 'If you knock them down you're going to have to kill him.' That was their credo, if you will," said retired FBI agent Ray Hamilton, who worked in Hawaii for twenty-four years. "If you hit somebody and knock them down . . . that was an indicator that guy was going for the big ride."

Yet not everyone feared the Syndicate. Outside of the underworld, out of sight of the savage beatings and out of earshot of the warnings to turn someone into "fish bait," Pulawa and his crew enjoyed a certain degree of Robin Hood popularity among fellow Hawaiians. As a US congressional committee reported in 1978, local gangsters had "their roots in Hawaii where local culture demands a great deal of loyalty, eliminating the possibility of producing informers. They also enjoy a good rapport and popularity with the public, many of whom apparently are envious of the 'get rich quick' status of local people."

To some locals the local crime syndicate was a visible and rare example of Hawaiians succeeding economically. For too long, these locals felt, the Hawaiian people had been marginalized in their own land, trampled on by others, especially the Caucasians and Japanese Americans who dominated island business and politics. The Hawaiians' dearth of prosperity during the islands' latest economic boom—attributable to development and tourism—was nothing new, as the natives felt similarly exploited or ignored a century earlier when wealthy white businessmen established profitable sugar plantations among the islands and overthrew the Hawaiian monarchy.

Moreover, its illegal acts could be seen as a general form of protest and rebellion, the Syndicate's brazenness a message that foreigners had no right to tell Hawaiians what they could and could not do in their own homelands.

"A lot of the organized crime was just saying, 'Fuck it,' to the haole government," said David Bettencourt, a longtime criminal defense lawyer in Honolulu who represented Syndicate member Huihui. "It wasn't really anything that organized. It was just saying, you know, 'We'll make liquor when we want to, we'll gamble when we want to, we'll have cockfights when we want to.'"

Huihui said he met Pulawa during protests over the removal of forty families living in Oahu's Kalama Valley, where developers planned to build new homes and a golf course. Protesters arrested in the valley, however, don't recall either gangster joining their cause, though some do remember some fearsome-looking men offering them guns to defend the valley, even displaying to them an arsenal packed into the trunk of a car. The protesters declined the weapons.

Members of the underworld joined in other Hawaiian activities, too. Huihui, along with at least one underworld contract killer, belonged to groups protesting the US Navy's use of the small, unpopulated Hawaiian island of Kahoolawe as a bombing range. Pulawa's lieutenant Wilson led a Hawaiian canoe club on Kauai. Pulawa was known to pontificate about aspects of Hawaiian culture and the virtues of hiring young Hawaiians and putting them to work. He, like other members of the underworld, also donated money to Hawaiian canoe clubs, musicians, and Hawaiian nationalist and renaissance movements.

Pulawa, said Hawaiian singer Danny Kaleikini, is "a very nice man, a very intelligent man. He is a philosopher. He reads a lot. He cares."

In perhaps the greatest example of Pulawa identifying with Hawaiian history, in 1972 he asked a sketch artist to draw him with the helmet of Kamehameha the Great atop his head. The comparison is not too far-fetched. Kamehameha conquered the Hawaiian Islands; Pulawa conquered the Hawaiian underworld. Both were bloody endeavors.

The Syndicate's interest in Hawaiian causes coincided with its investment in legitimate businesses on the islands. These investments were designed to both launder money and claim a legitimate piece of the growing economic pie for themselves. They engaged Charles Kauhane, a former speaker of Hawaii's territorial House of Representatives, to help buy real estate, giving cash in paper sacks to the representative of thirty-two years so that he could convert it to cashier's checks. The Syndicate made down payments to purchase the $1.3 million Cooper Ranch on windward Oahu and the Grand Hotel in Anaheim, California. Both deals fell apart. Pulawa attempted to build an eight million dollar, eighteen-story complex in Honolulu that would feature a nightclub, spa, and office space. The Syndicate leader purchased property for the project, commissioned an architect, and tried to contract Hawaiian entertainers to perform at the complex. It never came to fruition. Pulawa also was involved in small businesses that included a cleaning company, a theater booking agency, and an automobile painting firm.

Underneath these efforts at legitimacy and the victimization status gangsters embraced by wrapping themselves in the cloak of the Hawaiian rights movement, the Syndicate was a highly predatory organization. Like many of the commercial and political interests in Hawaii controlled by other ethnicities, the Syndicate profited at the expense of someone or something else. In mild cases a business owner was extorted for regular tribute payments. In extreme cases people were killed, though it wasn't always apparent.

Since the 1960s, when assorted Asian gangsters competed for influence in Hawaii, the underworld controlled by Leota and Pulawa had seemingly become less violent. But Gene Hunter, whose reporting on the Syndicate for the *Honolulu Advertiser* made him a runner-up for the Pulitzer Prize, wrote in 1970 that the decline in shocking gangland killings was misleading. The Syndicate had simply wised up.

"At this point, the syndicate apparently was growing more cautious," wrote Hunter in his landmark series of articles on organized crime in Hawaii. "Disappearances—especially of known underworld characters whose absences might never be reported to police—create fewer headlines than do bodies left lying in the streets."

Among those who disappeared were gamblers Dennis M. "Fuzzy" Iha and Lamont C. "Monte" Nery. Each went missing following the murder of Harry Otake, who was found strangled in the trunk of his car in February 1970. Otake was a commercial orchid grower who grossed more than one hundred thousand dollars a year at his four-acre farm in Kaneohe on the Windward Coast of Oahu. He began growing orchids as a hobby, but soon was supplying more than a thousand vanda leis a day to local florists and thousands of vanda blossoms to restaurants and nightclubs to use as garnishes and table decorations.

Otake also administered gambling junkets to Las Vegas, which, in contrast to so much other gambling activity on the islands, was completely legal. Here's how it worked: Local junket guests were invited to buy round-trip airfare from Honolulu to Las Vegas for, say, five hundred dollars. Then the junketeers were given nearly that same amount back in the form of chips to Las Vegas casinos, not to mention free food and lodging at a casino. In essence junketeers were being given a free trip to Las Vegas. At least that's what junket operators like Otake might have argued. Of course many people who took a trip to Las Vegas gambled more than the amount given to them in free chips, which meant the casinos made money.

The junket operator profited by making a commission for each person he put on a plane to Las Vegas. Additionally, junket operators profited through commissions made by collecting IOUs from gamblers who had returned home to Hawaii in debt to the casinos. It was thought that Otake might have been robbed of more than ninety thousand dollars that he had collected in debts. Suspicion among law enforcement and the underworld soon fell on Iha and Nery for the robbery and killing.

The Syndicate was allegedly angry about Otake's death, since it deprived them of revenue. Otake, like other gambling operators, had been making regular payments to organized crime members in order to operate his business, as much as a thousand dollars per junket or flight. Whoever killed Otake, in other words, had stolen from the Syndicate. Just weeks after Otake's body was found, Iha and Nery went missing. Meanwhile the Nevada Gaming Commission temporarily halted all junkets from Honolulu to Las Vegas due to the publicity surrounding Otake's murder and the casinos' growing desire to distance Nevada's gambling industry from underworld violence.

Four years later the commission acted again to draw a line between the state's gambling industry and Hawaiian organized crime, naming Pulawa and his lieutenant Kaohu to the commission's so-called black book, or list of persons prohibited from entering Las Vegas casinos. This list, which had not been updated since it was created about fifteen years earlier, already contained the names of some of America's most notorious mobsters, including Sam Giancana, a Chicago underworld boss and member of La Cosa Nostra. Pulawa and Kaohu, found to be "of notorious and unsavory reputation," were blacklisted due to testimony from a number of men who had applied to the commission to run junkets to Las Vegas from Hawaii.

In response to this testimony, gaming commission chairman Peter Echeverria said, "This Hawaiian Syndicate must be one of the cruelest in the world. I have tremendous concern about any spillover into Nevada gambling."

Or, as commissioner Clair Haycock fretted during the commission's August 1974 meeting after hearing testimony from Harold Fong, the US attorney, or top federal prosecutor, for Hawaii: "You have painted such a bad picture. I think the Hawaiian Islands is the world's most wonderful spot. It is my very favorite place. I am wondering what is becoming of your paradise over there?"

By this time Pulawa's reputation had caught up with him back home as well, attracting the attention of state and federal authorities there. Since 1972 the Honolulu Police Department and the Internal Revenue Service had been working together to develop a case against the Hawaiian Syndicate. In March 1973 Pulawa, Huihui, Kaohu, Leota, and Wilson were arrested and charged with conspiring to defraud the government of income tax revenue owed in relation to extortion schemes that allegedly earned one million dollars from 1969 to 1971. As he recalled in a memoir, when the defendants assembled in federal court, Judge Samuel King looked at the "five local boys" standing before him and thought to himself: They look like the front line of the Los Angeles Rams.

Yet it was not their size and strength that was most threatening to the judge.

"They might have looked like professional football players at first glance," King wrote, "but there was something else: a coldness in their eyes that could give you chills."

Among the government's witnesses at trial were former Syndicate bagman George Ekita, who made the weekly collections of tribute money, as well as gamblers who testified of being threatened or assaulted by Syndicate gang members. Former Syndicate lieutenant Ryder, who was also charged with the gang members, was among those who agreed to testify for the government, detailing the crimes he and his colleagues allegedly committed as leading members of the Hawaiian underworld. It was an astonishing betrayal, given the sacrifices Ryder had previously made for his criminal friends. Ryder testified how he left his first family for the Syndicate and then started a "second family" with the former girlfriend of another gang member. When he had a son, he named him Alema after the former Syndicate leader Alema Leota. The same child also has Pulawa's Hawaiian middle name, Ryder said on the stand, though he couldn't remember exactly what that name was.

Ryder explained to the jury that he was kicked out of the Syndicate when Pulawa blamed him for bungling the hiding away of two men who, upon Pulawa's orders, had allegedly killed a rival gang member. When Pulawa later threatened the life of one of Ryder's friends, entertainer and fellow government witness Sherwin K. "Sharkey" Fellezs, Ryder decided to testify against his former friends and gang members. In exchange the government paid him a monthly stipend of $925 and relocated him and his second family to the mainland, where they could be better protected.

Despite Ryder's cooperation and all the years of investigation, the federal government still came up short in proving a conspiracy. Before the case even went to the jury, the judge dismissed the charges against Leota. On the defense side, Brook Hart, the lawyer for Huihui and Wilson, conceded that wrongdoing had occurred and that Pulawa was even a "crime lord."

"What they did agree to do, and horribly so, was extort money," said Hart. "We're not here to suggest they're angels. They're clearly not."

But any wrongdoing, Hart argued, did not include conspiring to defraud the government of tax income, which was the only criminal charge hanging over the men. Such a deliberate crime was "too sophisticated" for these men, said Hart. "What we have here is a lot of people running around at Mr. Pulawa's instruction."

The government knew the chances of conviction were iffy. One IRS criminal tax investigator put the odds at fifty-fifty. As the lead criminal tax investigator, Clifford Scott, admitted, criminal tax cases "are a little unusual, because you never really know if you have a crime until the jury says so. They're different from a robbery or a murder, where you know you have a crime. With tax cases, you just can't say that. It's a constant process of searching for indications, for pieces of evidence, to justify all the expenses."

On February 16, 1974, despite the government's claim otherwise, a jury said there was no crime, acquitting the Syndicate members. Vindicated, the defendants walked out of the courthouse that afternoon. As they climbed into cars and began driving away, Honolulu police swarmed the area. Pulawa, Huihui, Kaohu, and Wilson were promptly arrested again, this time charged by the state with murder, kidnapping, and conspiracy. Also charged in the killings was Pulawa's girlfriend, Dannette Beirne Leota, who had once been married to Alema Leota's late brother, Reid. All of the accused pleaded not guilty.

Two months earlier, the Syndicate members soon learned, their former colleague Ryder had led police to the remains of Iha and Nery, the men suspected of robbing and strangling Harry Otake, the junket operator and orchid grower. As Ryder admitted to police, he and the other Syndicate members killed Iha and Nery and buried them in a shallow grave on Mokuleia Beach on Oahu's North Shore. Months after telling the police about the executions of Iha and Nery, Ryder repeated his story for a jury weighing the murder, kidnapping, and conspiracy charges against the Syndicate members.

According to Ryder and other witnesses, Pulawa, Kaohu, and Wilson all gathered at Nery's tenth-floor apartment in Waikiki before dawn one morning in February 1970. Nery wasn't home, but the Syndicate members encountered his roommate, gambler Clarence "Japan" Handa. The men waited with Handa for Nery to return, passing part of the time by cutting the apartment's phone line. Handa, a slight man who made regular payments to the Syndicate, complained about the phone and how people might think something was amiss should they call the apartment and get no answer. Pulawa was so moved by Handa's grumbling that he had Kaohu phone a friend at the local telephone company to ask for a repair. Now the gangsters were awaiting two men as dawn approached: Nery and the telephone repairman.

The telephone repairman arrived first, at about three in the morning, and knocked at the door. Inside the apartment Pulawa, Kaohu, and Wilson all pulled out their guns. Learning it was the phone company employee on the other side of the door, they put the weapons away and allowed the repairman access to the apartment.

While the repairman was making the fix, Nery arrived home. He sat down with the gangsters at the kitchen table and had a beer, apparently oblivious to his guests' ill will. As soon as the repairman left, the gangsters' guns came out again, pointed at Nery's head. After searching Nery for weapons, the gangsters tied their captive's hands with the electric cord from a coffeemaker and then interrogated him. His belongings were thrown into trash bags. Handa pleaded with Pulawa to release his friend.

Pulawa denied the request, saying that Nery "gotta go."

"Monte is no damn good," he said of Nery. Then Pulawa threatened the life of Handa and his girlfriend, forbidding them to talk about the abduction.

The gangsters then readied Nery for transport across the island to Laie, where Pulawa's girlfriend had a home. As they left the Waikiki apartment, Pulawa instructed Handa on how to respond to any inquiries about Nery.

"Just tell them he take a trip," said Pulawa. "Stay out of this business. You got nothing to do with it."

In the home of Pulawa's girlfriend, the gangsters promised to set Nery free so long as he helped them lure Iha. The only catch, they told Nery, was the two of them had to immediately take a flight off Oahu and never return. Nery, still being held at gunpoint, took the bait. He had no choice. He phoned Iha at a gambling game in Honolulu and asked that he meet him immediately at a restaurant called the Crouching Lion because he was having car trouble. To sweeten the offer, Nery told Iha he had a pair of "haole wahines" with him.

Iha came to the Crouching Lion. But instead of finding Nery and two damsels in distress, he encountered members of the Syndicate, including the newly arrived Ryder. Iha was asked to take a ride, and he agreed. In the car he tried pulling a gun, but, according to Ryder, he and Kaohu "just beat the hell out of the guy and put him on the floor." They taped Iha's hands together as they drove back to the house in Laie.

The day passed. After sunset the gangsters, save Kaohu, who had to work a shift as a paramedic, piled into two cars and drove with their captives along the North Shore. Each gangster carried a pistol except Pulawa, who kept a machine gun in his arms. Packed inside the car trunks were buckets, lime, shovels, and a pick. When the cars reached Mokuleia Beach, Pulawa ordered the cars to pull over alongside the isolated strip of sand.

"Put 'em here where the Pake stay," said Pulawa, referencing a rival Asian gang member he and Huihui had allegedly previously killed and buried nearby.

Iha and Nery, now naked except for the tape that bound their wrists and gagged their mouths, were marched in darkness onto the beach. While Pulawa's girlfriend allegedly stayed behind in a car as a lookout, Ryder and Wilson took turns digging a large hole in the sand. Iha and Nery were made to watch the making of their own grave.

Suddenly Iha sprinted toward the water about twelve yards away. The large wintertime swells on the North Shore can be dangerous for the most able swimmers and surfers, never mind a man with his wrists bound together. Nonetheless Iha judged the sloshing ocean a safer bet than keeping company with his captors.

He didn't even get his feet wet. Iha had only taken a few steps before Wilson allegedly smashed a shovel across his head, knocking him unconscious.

The hole finally excavated, Pulawa ordered Nery to get in. Nery stepped calmly into the grave and knelt.

"You make this one," Pulawa said to Wilson. Gun in hand, the Syndicate lieutenant stepped into the grave behind Nery. He placed a jacket over himself and Nery to muffle the noise and hide the muzzle flash. Wilson then shot Nery four times in the head.

Next was Iha, whose unconscious, shovel-beaten body was thrown into the grave. Pulawa gave an order this time to Ryder, who felt around in the darkness for Iha's head. Finding it, he fired two bullets into it. Then the men splashed the dead bodies with lime and ocean water, covered Iha and Nery with sand, and obscured the gravesite with brush before driving away to the home of Pulawa's girlfriend, where they enjoyed dinner. Or so said Ryder, who, in exchange for his testimony, was given immunity from prosecution for his role in the alleged kidnappings and murders.

It was a dramatic account by Ryder, but before the defense could rebut the prosecution's version of events, Judge Walter Heen declared a mistrial on the grounds that, in regard to the conspiracy charges, the statute of limitations had lapsed. To the dismay of prosecutors, the whole case would have to be retried.

The defendants, however, were relieved. Some of the men, who had appeared in court in either golfing attire or aloha shirts, then gathered in front of a statue of Kamehameha the Great outside the courthouse to discuss their feelings about going free, at least for now.

"We're happy about it, to the point where we can go back to our families and our jobs," said Huihui, whom Pulawa had appointed spokesman. "But we're unhappy because we had no opportunity to present our side of the case, which we think would have resulted in an acquittal by the jury."

No matter the acquittal on federal tax charges and the more recent murder mistrial in state court, the government persisted in their pursuit of Pulawa. In April 1975 the Syndicate leader again went to trial on another set of federal tax charges. Whereas a year earlier he had been acquitted with fellow Syndicate gang members for conspiring to defraud the government of tax income, this time Pulawa alone was charged with tax evasion, or failure to pay the income tax he owed. From 1969 to 1971, the government alleged, Pulawa made more than nine hundred thousand dollars and owed at least half that in taxes. Pulawa, on the other hand, filed joint returns with his wife that said they earned $16,791 in taxable income during those three years and owed just $863 in taxes. For most of the time, claimed Pulawa, he was unemployed, with his wife being the family breadwinner.

The federal government, under the direction of a special federal organized crime strike force attorney named Michael Sterrett as well as US Attorney Fong, produced some of the same witnesses who had appeared in the first tax trial, establishing that Pulawa captained an expansive extortion network and collected hundreds of thousands of dollars from gamblers. Moreover the government documented the lavish lifestyle enjoyed by Pulawa and how it did not square with his and his wife's stated income.

Pulawa, who took the stand in his own defense and testified in a voice so raspy it reminded some, perhaps fittingly, of actor

Marlon Brando's performance in *The Godfather*, was questioned by Sterrett as to how an unemployed man and father of three was able to afford at least ten recent golfing trips to the Neighbor Islands.

Pulawa said his friends always paid for him.

Why would they do that, asked Sterrett?

"They must like me," said Pulawa.

In 1972 Pulawa, his wife, and two friends enjoyed an all-expenses-paid trip to Munich to see the Olympics. Why, asked Sterrett, would a gambling junket operator have given you four round-trip tickets to Germany?

"Because," Pulawa said, "he remembered he did not give me anything for my birthday."

Pulawa's right-hand man, Kaohu, testified for his friend and said that they never kept any of the money they collected, but gave it to others for safekeeping. Once enough money accumulated, said Kaohu, they were going to invest it and create jobs for themselves and the community. Unfortunately they never got to that point.

The jury was skeptical of these kinds of explanations. When Pulawa's wife claimed to have saved thousands of dollars from her jobs as a pharmacy clerk and theater cashier in order to buy investment property in California, several jurors laughed out loud. Pulawa was convicted of tax evasion and of signing false tax returns. It may have taken a few years, but the government had finally gotten its man.

For all the talk of murder, deception, and intimidation during the trials of the Hawaiian Syndicate, there were at least a few light moments, including a handful remembered fondly by defense lawyer Hart. It was during the jury selection of one of Pulawa's tax trials that Judge King listened to one woman say she was willing to serve on a jury except that she was planning to leave for Maui the next day.

"Oh well," quipped King. "Here today, gone to Maui."

During one of the Pulawa trials, Hart was amused to see a trial transcript in which a witness's name was grossly misspelled. Instead of Royale Kamahoahoa, Hart said the court reporter listed the witness as Peerless Mahoho.

Lastly, also during jury selection for one of the Pulawa trials, Hart was questioning a potential juror who claimed she would not be a good juror because she had trouble with the English language.

How long, Hart asked, have you spoken English?

"Since grade school," said the woman.

What about before then?

"I don't know, I guess baby talk," she said.

Hart howled. The rest of the courtroom erupted in laughter, too, including Pulawa, who, according to one newspaper reporter, "usually sits stone faced behind his black mustache."

The sentencing of Pulawa by Judge King was a more solemn affair. Taking into account all the witnesses who claimed to have feared for their life when being beaten and extorted, King told Pulawa, "The community is afraid of you."

"It does seem to be," said King, "that if there ever was a case for applying the maximum term possible, this is it."

Pulawa was then sentenced to prison for twenty-four years. At the time, it was the longest known sentence in the United States for tax evasion—longer than the eleven-year sentence gangster Al Capone had received in 1931, as well as the fifteen-year sentence Los Angeles mobster Mickey Cohen had been given in 1961. Pulawa soon left Hawaii for federal prison on McNeil Island in Washington's Puget Sound.

The conviction was a significant victory for federal prosecutors. Finally, it was felt, a blow was struck against organized crime in Hawaii.

"There were people saying the case would never get to trial and if it did there would never be a conviction because of the fear that [Pulawa] generated," said Sterrett. "I personally was very proud of that jury for standing up to him."

Still, some locals refused to believe in Pulawa's guilt. When eighteen-year-old golfer Randy Barenaba won the National Public Links Championship on Kauai in 1975, two months after Pulawa's conviction, the young man choked up at the awards ceremony and said there is one man he hoped would hear about his victory.

That man, said Barenaba, is "Mister Nappy Pulawa."

"They put the wrong man away," said Barenaba, who, despite being many years Pulawa's junior, had taught the alleged Syndicate leader to golf. "They put the wrong man away."

Nonetheless, the conviction of Wilford "Nappy" Pulawa in the spring of 1975 was a seminal event in Hawaii's criminal history. The underworld churned in his absence, with Pulawa's former lieutenants, and others, vying for power. It was during this upheaval that Chuckers Marsland was murdered, which sparked even more strife among the lawless. Upon Chuckers's murder a new antagonist to Hawaiian organized crime was born. His name was Charles Marsland, and he had a score to settle.

CHAPTER TWO

Vicious, Mad Dogs

Almost immediately the trail went cold. Days passed, then weeks, without an arrest for the killing of Chuckers Marsland. In the aftermath of his death on April 17, 1975, the police searched Chuckers's apartment, questioned his coworkers, and interviewed his friends. Despite these efforts, the police learned few clues to the murder.

Coworkers told police that Chuckers seemed fidgety as he finished his shift at the Infinity. He strangely asked his colleagues for their pau drink, which was the free alcoholic beverage an employee earned from the club at the end of the night. Something was obviously bothering Chuckers, but he confided this anxiety to no one.

The police made notes of the men and women Chuckers spoke with in his last hours, knowing that his work in a nightclub often brought him into contact with patrons who were members of the Hawaiian underworld. They also found the murder victim's car parked in Waikiki, making it likely Chuckers got into another automobile that took him around to the other side of the island, where he was killed. The assumption, then, was that Chuckers knew his killers. Otherwise why would he enter the car, unless forced to do so? But this was guesswork, and that wasn't enough to make a solid case.

The lack of progress began to exasperate Charles Marsland. As he told his son's friend, Eric Naone, Chuckers was "everything" to him, his only son, his namesake, and the only consolation to Marsland's failed marriage in Massachusetts. When Marsland had split with his wife a decade or so earlier, each parent had taken custody of a child. Marsland kept the boy; his ex-wife Jane was to raise the younger girl, Laurie Jane.

Charles Marsland had originally gone to Massachusetts to attend college. The only child of deep-sea diver and underwater demolition expert Charles F. Marsland and schoolteacher Sadie Marsland, he had been born in Honolulu on April 11, 1923. One of his grandfathers, who emigrated to Hawaii from Norway, worked on Oahu's Ewa plantation in the late nineteenth century and also served as a member of King Kalākaua's royal guard. Marsland was fiercely proud of his family's history on the islands and their status as a kamaaina family. According to a friend, Marsland "bristled at any questioning of his local credentials."

Like his son after him, Marsland attended the prestigious Punahou School for high school—swimming, running track, and playing football. He was noticeably handsome and well dressed—characteristics that would remain consistent his whole life. During his senior year in 1940, the school yearbook, the *Oahuan*, remarked that Marsland "has made quite a reputation for himself as a dancer de luxe and a number one good sport. Charlie's amiable grin has been a contributing factor in making him quite a popular fellow."

After a stint at the University of Hawaii, Marsland enrolled in Tufts College in Medford, Massachusetts. There he also joined the Navy Reserve Officers Training Corps, becoming a crack rifle shot. On account of this military training, Marsland would not get to enjoy campus life in New England for long.

At the end of Marsland's first semester, Japanese planes bombed Pearl Harbor in Hawaii, prompting the United States to enter World War II. Marsland eventually found himself back in the Pacific, though he was not home in Hawaii but sailing the ocean to help invade the Philippines. Lieutenant Marsland served as an executive officer, or second in command, on a ship carrying infantry, before himself becoming a commanding officer. Photos from his voyage show his often bare-chested crew as they island hopped the Pacific after coming through the Panama Canal.

At least one college admirer missed Marsland's handsome face and friendly disposition. The naval officer kept a photo sent to him from Debbie, a young woman who posed in a skirt and sweater alongside a gate at Tufts College in January 1945. On the back of the photograph she apologized for not wearing less:

Chuck-
Sorry darling, but it's too cold for a bathing-suit
Aloha nui loa!
Debbie

At war's end, possibly to the disappointment of Debbie, Marsland remained in the Pacific with the Navy, working as a discipline and prison administration officer based at Pearl Harbor. About seven years after first starting college, Marsland returned to Tufts and then graduated in 1949. Next came enrollment at Northeastern University School of Law in Boston, where he graduated three years later. Within a year he was hired as a legal assistant in the office of the attorney general of Massachusetts. By 1953 Marsland was named an assistant attorney general, investigating and prosecuting cases involving gambling, organized crime, and murder. He found the work thrilling, especially when his office coordinated massive stings. As Marsland fondly remembered:

We'd go out and set up entire cities. We'd bring in state troopers from the western part of the state that nobody knew and put them in these cities to set up all of the gamblers and bookies. (The state troopers) would pass themselves off as roofers.

Then we'd go in with three hundred or four hundred war-rants and start knocking people over. Once we went in it was like rats fleeing a sinking ship, running to Florida. It was fantastic! It was an absolute ball.

In an office dominated by Irish Catholic prosecutors, the Protestant Marsland seemed to fit in just fine, at least most of the time. The exception was the day he and some of his colleagues earned an audience with a bishop. As Marsland later recalled to friends, he stood at the front of the receiving line, eager to make a strong impression. When the bishop arrived and casually offered his ringed finger for a customary kiss, Marsland misunderstood the gesture and seized the bishop's outstretched hand, squeezing with a vigor that was the hallmark of Marsland's legendary and crushing handshake.

Besides committing an unfortunate faux pas, Marsland injured the bishop. As he shook the outstretched hand, bones could be heard cracking. The bishop winced.

It is imagined that Marsland was gentler at home. By 1953 he had married, his bride the former Jayne Watts, a talented enter-tainer who became one of Boston's first female television person-alities, working as a popular weathergirl for WBZ-TV under the name Jane Day. Judging by Day's reputation, Marsland had done well for himself. His wife was not only a widely described beauty, but cheerful and clever. Among her calling cards was her famous "thought for the day," which accompanied her daily weather fore-cast. Another was her ability to write important weather infor-mation on a glass wall for her viewers—using both hands at the same time. People loved her, with some fans meeting her at events sponsored by department stores to obtain her autograph.

"No announcer," one newspaper columnist wrote, "can make the advent of awful weather sound sunnier than Jane Day."

Within a few years of marriage, the young couple moved to the South Shore community of Hingham, just south of Boston, and began a family. Their son, Charles F. "Chuckers" Marsland III was born in 1955. A daughter, Laurie Jane, was born two years later. Despite the demands of small children, the Marslands kept an active social calendar, helping promote and partake in local dances, plays, fashion shows, and charitable events.

At this point in his life, Marsland was ascendant. He had survived the war and reintegrated into society, securing work as a prominent prosecutor in his new home of Massachusetts. He had married a stunning and charming wife who was adored by thousands of television fans. He had become a father to a baby boy and girl. Next up, of course, was a political run.

In 1958 Marsland resigned his position in the attorney general's office and began work in private practice. He set his sights on becoming district attorney for Plymouth County, hoping to unseat the incumbent, a fellow Republican. But Marsland fell short, earning about 42 percent of the vote in the Republican primary.

A bigger disappointment would follow, as his marriage broke up. It is unclear what prompted Marsland and his wife to split, though some of Marsland's acquaintances cite infidelity as the cause, and that Marsland claimed to have punched his wife's lover. Upon returning to Hawaii with Chuckers in 1967, Marsland hardly ever spoke of his family life in Boston. Given the sensitivity of the situation, few friends dared to ask him much about the particulars behind his departure. They knew, though, that Marsland's relationship with his daughter suffered during this turn of events, and that father and daughter spoke infrequently after their separation, despite Marsland's attempts to contact her. Friends to Marsland say that this estrangement caused him great sorrow. Upon the death of Chuckers, he had in effect lost both of his children.

As for Marsland's former wife, at some point Day became romantic with Jack Campbell, the owner of a radio station in Plymouth, Massachusetts, where she had begun working. Campbell was also a close friend of the Kennedy family, raising money for US Senators John F. and Edward Kennedy. In 1963 Campbell and his radio station employee, Day, were among Massachusetts notables who traveled to Washington to attend the funeral services of President John F. Kennedy. At this time Day also went by the name Jane Marsland. Day and Campbell would eventually marry.

In Hawaii Marsland, too, found love again. Shortly after arriving back in Honolulu, he began dating Polly Grigg, an interior designer who worked for Sheraton Hotels. Elegant and accomplished, Grigg was eventually named a vice president with design responsibilities for Sheraton hotels across Asia and the Pacific. Grigg had moved to Hawaii after her husband died from injuries sustained in World War II. Like Marsland, she had a son from her marriage.

The couple spent many weekends bodysurfing and enjoying Oahu's beaches with another couple: Phil and Joan Hester. Marsland and Phil Hester both worked at First Hawaiian Bank, where Marsland was a trust officer and Hester's boss. The two men forged a fast friendship, spending every lunch hour exercising at the local YMCA. Marsland was popular with the entire office, in fact, as Hester recalls colleagues being impressed with Marsland's legal career in Boston.

The Hesters remained friends with Marsland and Grigg even after Marsland passed the Hawaiian bar and left the bank to return to legal work, being hired as a deputy attorney general for Hawaii. A year later, in 1971, Marsland the lawyer became deputy corporation counsel for the City and County of Honolulu, handling civil legal issues and lawsuits. Oftentimes this work involved the Honolulu Police Department, requiring Marsland to defend policemen from complaints of brutality, as well as to ensure the department's compliance with federal requirements to better integrate and promote women in the police force.

Marsland made the most of this position, earning a reputation as an aggressive advocate for the city and a friend to the police force. In one case, Marsland suspected a surfboard rental company of defrauding the city by not paying appropriate fees for the use of a city-owned building on Waikiki Beach. As retribution, and despite a federal judge's order not to interfere with the company's assets while it underwent a bankruptcy, Marsland sent six police squad cars and a number of trucks to the building early one morning. After having the police break the surfboard company's locks and cart out its belongings, Marsland turned the building over to a rival concessionaire. The company complained about the "commando style" operation, but Marsland was unmoved. It would not be the last time his actions flew in the face of a judge, and it may have been the beginning of a habit.

All the while, Marsland's son Chuckers was maturing into a man. By all accounts Marsland doted on his son, wanting the best for him. Yet, like many parents, he struggled to be consistent with discipline. At times Marsland was observed to be overly strict with Chuckers. In other instances Marsland was more a friend than father, acting in a manner one might expect with no mother in the house.

"He was a good, caring dad . . . liked to kid around with his son, maybe kind of pushed the envelope a little bit and maybe say some off-color things, but nothing mean or really nasty," said Mark Keala, a friend and classmate to Chuckers and a son of the Honolulu police chief. "He didn't come across as being like a real hardass to Chuck."

When Chuckers was a teenager, Marsland enrolled him in Erhard Seminars Training, a self-actualization course popular in the 1970s. Marsland had previously completed the course himself and was so impressed with the experience that he insisted Grigg and Phil and Joan Hester take the course with Chuckers as well. Self-control was a significant focus of the seminars, so much so that participants were not allowed to leave a session to use the bathroom. Though that particular rule seems silly to her now, Joan Hester recalls the seminars favorably. Not only did the training have a positive transformative effect on her, she says, she and her husband enjoyed the company of Chuckers and Grigg.

"It was wonderful," said Hester. "It brought us all closer together."

Joan Hester and her husband noticed the blossoming of Chuckers's personality during those seminars, discovering him to be quite attractive and funny.

"We became very fond of Chucky at that time. He was kind of a neat kid," said Hester. "He was a beautiful, very handsome young man."

For most of his teen years, Chuckers bounced around Oahu playing sports, joining pickup basketball games, or racing in the ocean at the Outrigger Canoe Club. And while he was a neat kid to Joan, Chuckers's own friends describe him as a little bit of a misfit, never exceedingly popular or smart, but nonetheless cheerful enough to always keep company with a small group of buddies. Such friends were willing to tolerate Chuckers's major flaw: a tendency to exaggerate and boast.

"As he got older he wanted to try and fit in more and more. He would embellish a lot of things, relationships, people that he knew and so forth," said Keala.

"Typically you roll your eyes, because you know that's kind of who Chuck was, a little over the top . . . wanted people to know him, wanted people to like him," continued Keala. "When he would tell his stories, you know, in high school, his stories were always a little bit bigger and a little bit wilder than the story would actually turn out to be. That was kind of his nature."

At home it was much of the same. Grigg confided to a friend that she felt Marsland had spoiled Chuckers, and that the boy incessantly bragged about his well-to-do mother in Boston. Grigg said Chuckers was "just so full of himself you could hardly listen to him when he got to be a teenager."

Toward the end of high school, Chuckers's body filled out. Mentally, too, he had seemed to mature, at least from the perspective of his proud father.

"From an awkward, raw-boned teenager," Charles Marsland wrote in a letter, "he had developed a poise, maturity and grace far beyond his years. He spent a part of each day in either the gym or the water, and his shoulders and chest matured from raw strength to being incredibly powerful."

Suddenly Chuckers was less inclined to tolerate slights from others, fighting back when he was pushed around during athletic contests. As his buddy Jon Andersen recalled, Chucky became somewhat of a "wise guy," no longer willing to be picked on or intimidated. An acquaintance of Chuckers's from Waikiki's late-night scene gave the same assessment, claiming Chuckers "changed from a real nice guy to a tough-guy type.

"He was a hard-as-nails, shove-around type of guy," said the acquaintance.

Among those who could no longer boss Chuckers around was his father. The two were said to quarrel more often as Chuckers got older. By age nineteen, Chuckers's desire for independence was so strong, he moved out of the house and started living with his girlfriend, Cathy Clisby, and roommate Alexander Pedi.

Clisby, who was originally from Canada, had moved to Honolulu with a girlfriend after finishing high school in Washington State. She found work in Honolulu restaurants and bars, eventually becoming a cocktail waitress in Waikiki. It was through her job that she met Chuckers, though she knew him as Chuck. It was not long before they began sharing an apartment at the southern end of Waikiki, close to Diamond Head, just a few blocks from the beach.

"I adored him. He was a great guy," said Clisby. "Very, very personable."

The two spent lots of time together, often dining for breakfast early in the morning after finishing work at separate nightclubs. Then they would head home to sleep.

"Him and Cathy were sweethearts. Both tall, super looking
... they were a couple madly in love," said Pedi.

The couple was serious enough to discuss moving together to
California, where Chuckers had been offered an athletics scholarship to Pepperdine University. In high school Chuckers had
been a star volleyball player, helping Punahou capture its first
state title in 1972.

"He had a lot of potential," said his high school coach, Chris
McLachlin. "He was a great leaper and had all the talent to be an
outstanding college volleyball player."

Before enrolling at Pepperdine, Chuckers began taking
classes at the University of Hawaii and nearby Chaminade University. He also took a night job at the disco, seemingly in no
hurry to leave for California. Instead he was happy to live and
work in Waikiki, where he could enjoy nightlife, relax on the
beach, and spend time with his girlfriend.

Chuckers's position as a doorman at the Infinity disco sometimes demanded a tougher and more vigilant disposition. How
else to manage drunks and customers who wanted to fight on
the dance floor? And with lines out the door and three hundred
people inside listening to live music, the management appreciated an employee who could resolve a problem quickly.

"He liked the situations where he had to manhandle some
badasses at Infinity," said Pedi. "He loved being a doorman over
there. He liked to flex his muscles."

The Infinity Club opened beneath the Sheraton-Waikiki
Hotel in 1974, the club's plum and purple interior swarmed by
attractive waitresses. These women, known as Dolls, dressed in
outfits that consisted of little more than heels, stockings, and
skimpy one-piece bathing suits that rode high on the women's
legs. The Infinity's Dolls bore a resemblance to the more famous
Playboy Bunnies and Penthouse Pets who worked at clubs in
other parts of the country. They were also subject to strict house
rules. The Dolls could not sit with a customer, but were allowed

to "perch" at the bar. They also were not allowed to bend over, but instead had to "bunny dip," or crouch down. Overseeing these women was Carmen Pirics, who herself had worked as a Playboy Bunny and Penthouse Pet.

"Infinity sells a little sex in a way that looks good but different from anything around," Pirics said when the club opened. "We show a lot of flesh."

As a doorman and host, Chuckers was charged with seating and supervising guests. His boss, manager Paul Bowskill, said Chuckers was always punctual, well mannered, and hardworking. He liked to smile, he recalled, and was sometimes mischievous.

At this time, Bowskill said, the Infinity was one of a handful of popular Waikiki nightclubs. In the 1970s Waikiki was the best place in Honolulu to find entertainment, for locals and tourists alike. Whether in search of music, a movie, a good restaurant, or a good time, Waikiki was it. As Pedi recalled:

> It was a cowboy show. It was disco at its finest. You had the nightclubs. I was a regular John Travolta. I was out there boogying and getting what I could get. Had money in my pocket, wearing a tuxedo and having a good time. It was great, it was wild. Drugs rampant, huge. Cocaine. Pot. Thai stick was out there for a while. There was all kinds of stuff. Hash oil, oh my god . . . We all had our dashikis and our razor blade chains around our necks. Bell-bottoms and our jumpsuits.

But not everyone shared such enthusiasm for the entertainment district. As writer William Helton reported in 1971:

> Here lies Waikiki, four hundred and fifty acres of concrete and humanity crunched between an Army fort, a park, a canal, and the ocean . . . It mixes in all the ingredients of an urban

eyesore in the middle of a paradise: Easy money for thugs and
prostitutes, a festering jungle for dope addicts and pushers,
traffic madness, parking frustrations, and gallons of noise.

Supplying much of this noise were the nightclubs. Just down the street from the Infinity was the Polynesian Palace, where the Hawaiian hunk Don Ho crooned his hit "Tiny Bubbles" to two sets of sold-out shows six nights of the week, packing more than five hundred people inside for each show. Described by *People* magazine as a "swarthily handsome" combination of Wayne Newton, Don Rickles, and Charles Bronson, Ho's biggest fans were his "grandmas"—blue-haired women who could not resist the heartthrob and his naughty sense of humor. These older fans stormed the stage after each show to receive an open-mouthed kiss from the lusty singer.

"I kiss grandmas because they're clean. I haven't picked anything up from a grandma yet," Ho once said. "Besides, Grandma don't yell rape; she appreciates."

One time Ho kissed a grandma passionately, and her teeth came out. Another time he delivered a kiss of death to an elderly fan, who expired in his embrace.

"She was the most beautiful grandma I ever kissed, ever held in my arms," said Ho. "So I gave her one of my real suck 'em up kisses. Afterward, I felt this jerk against my chest."

Ho then went backstage with the dead woman's husband and helped him call the couple's son to deliver the bad news.

"Don't worry about it," the son told Ho. "She probably died happy."

During his long entertainment career, Ho made television appearances on *The Brady Bunch, Batman,* and *I Dream of Jeannie.* He performed and socialized with a bevy of celebrities who included Frank Sinatra, Bob Hope, Elvis Presley, and Jackie Kennedy. He even threw the former First Lady into a swimming pool in Honolulu while Secret Service agents glared.

Ho was married to his high school sweetheart, with whom he had a large family. Yet he spent most nights in bed with two showgirls he kept as girlfriends, unapologetic about his overactive libido and unconventional relationships. He met girlfriend Patti when she was nineteen, and Liz when she was seventeen. Years later they were still with him, and his wife was still happily living in their large family home. Then there were all the other young women who came though town to enjoy him perform, both onstage and in the bedroom. Oftentimes they didn't even wait until the show ended to take off their clothes. As *The Don Ho Show* entertainer Sam Kapu recalled:

> One night, I felt there was somebody standing behind me. I turn around and I see two twenty-something-year-old girls. One's got a bottle of champagne. The other's got glasses and both of them are completely naked. I said to them, "What're you going to do?" They said they were going to go out and pour a glass of champagne for Don. So when Don finished the song, they go out; one is on one side of him and she puts the glasses down and the other one pours the champagne.

The action could be just as lively backstage. Ho's dressing room in the Polynesian Palace was a popular hangout for friends and acquaintances of the singer, not to mention a necessary stop for many politicians and Hollywood celebrities. One of Ho's friends, John Defries, said that "second to the State Capitol, Don's dressing room attracted all types. The place was a beacon and he was a consummate host." Among the regular visitors were a number of Hawaiian gangsters, including Eric Naone and Ronnie Ching. Both men were fixtures of Waikiki's late-night scene, and both were muscular and intimidating. Naone, an unemployed Vietnam veteran who claimed to have hopes of becoming a policeman, was so strong he was reputed to lift and press a homemade barbell consisting of manhole covers welded to each end of an iron rod. His personality was alleged to be as cold and hard as the metal he lifted.

"Eric Naone was not a pleasant individual. If you was on the wrong side of Eric Naone, look out. He was frightening," said Christopher Evans, a Honolulu lawyer who defended Naone. "He was one of the entourage for Don Ho. He was a muscle guy, he was the arm, he was protection. You just didn't want to be on the wrong end of Eric Naone, believe me."

Naone and Ching would wander Waikiki during darkness, patronizing various nightclubs, usually dressed in heavy leather coats. One of their regular stops was the Infinity, where they'd stop to chat with their friend, Chuckers Marsland. Of the two gangsters Naone was a closer friend to Chuckers. They played softball together on weekends and hung out at bars. On a few occasions Naone, who was a few years older than his buddy, was invited to eat at the Marsland home with Chuckers and his father.

Having a friend as strong and fierce as Naone was convenient for Chuckers in his work as a doorman. When certain guests would become boisterous at the Infinity, Chuckers would not hesitate to drop Naone's name. Naone did not mind and was glad to back up a friend, especially since Chuckers had been threatened by a Samoan clubgoer who had previously tangled with Naone.

That altercation had started when a gang of five or six Samoans jumped Naone. Following the assault, Naone swore revenge. To facilitate the payback, he and some friends had a sit down with the Samoans in which Naone proposed fighting them again, two at a time, until he had run through the whole gang. The Samoans supposedly refused.

Not to be denied retribution, Naone kept tabs on the Samoans, eventually finding them one evening at the Infinity nightclub. By Naone's own admission, when a Samoan named Nico approached Naone and asked for a match, Naone said nothing. Instead of a match, he launched a flying karate kick, hitting Nico in the lower stomach and sending him staggering backward. Nico left the club without retaliating, at least not that night. Such was the rough-and-tumble landscape in Waikiki for street toughs.

On another occasion Naone, Ching, and another man entered the Infinity and motioned for Chuckers to join them in the bathroom. A few minutes later they reemerged, with Chuckers's buddies quickly leaving the club. Noticing the strange interaction, Chuckers's manager, Bowskill, asked what was going on. Chuckers promptly unbuttoned his coat, revealing three handguns tucked into his belt. The gangsters had asked him to hold them, perhaps because police were nearby.

Bowskill expressed disapproval and told Chuckers to inform his father about the incident. It was common knowledge among the club employees that Chuckers's father was a prominent attorney for the city and familiar with many members of the police force. Chuckers had made sure that information was well-known.

The next day, when Chuckers reported for work, Bowskill asked him if he had indeed told his father about holding the guns.

"Yeah," said Chuckers.

"What did he say?" asked Bowskill.

"He said, 'Next time, give them a roll of duct tape,'" said Chuckers, implying that his father meant the gangsters could conceal the guns themselves in the bathroom, taping them behind a toilet or under a sink.

Curiously, Marsland did not caution his son about the dangers of associating with gun-toting gangsters. He did not insist he quit the nightclub. He did not, apparently, worry about his boy's safety. Indeed Marsland later boasted of the "devastating consequences" suffered by the few nightclub patrons who resisted Chuckers and how his son did not suffer a single scratch or bruise.

For some time Chuckers lived between two worlds: the law-enforcement community and the law-breaking community. He often bragged about knowing cops and criminals alike, whether his father and their family friend, Honolulu Police Chief Francis

Keala, or underworld figures like Naone and Ching. Such a role suited the attention-seeking teenager perfectly.

"Chuck, he wanted to be perceived as someone that was important . . . to be known as someone, or as someone who had information. Or as someone who was, you know, who was worth getting to know," said Mark Keala, the chief's son.

If Marsland wasn't alarmed at Chuckers's interactions with gangsters, it might have been attributable to the fact that Oahu was a small island and it was inevitable that one would occasionally brush up against less-savory characters, especially at night in Waikiki.

"It was easy to run into the wrong people during that time period," said Mark Keala. "It wasn't surprising that Chuck could find the wrong people, and especially as a bouncer. It seemed to be the type of job you would have if you were looking for trouble or trouble would find you."

Chuckers's girlfriend, Clisby, said that given the frequency with which nightclub employees encountered members of the underworld, it was only natural to become friendly with some of these people.

"You really didn't think anything of it because it just seemed like it was a normal thing. This what was going on in the world," said Clisby. "You knew who they were. You saw a lot of, um, you know, prostitutes or johns who were your friends. You weren't involved with them, [but] we all would party together because being in the bar business you knew everybody, and everybody knew you."

So normal, in fact, that Clisby was not even particularly awestruck when Chuckers told her that Ching and Naone killed people for a living, though neither man had been convicted of such a crime. Better to befriend alleged killers, one supposes, than make enemies with them. Besides, who else could stop by the police chief's office in the afternoon and then rendezvous with underworld hit men at night. Aside from a few vice cops, no one but Chuckers.

"He sort of felt that he was pretty much invincible," said Bowskill.

"Like a Greek god. Invincible," said Chuckers's roommate, Pedi. "He thought he was above everything."

So invincible, in fact, that Chuckers did the unthinkable one evening. Declaring Ching to be too "rowdy," he ejected him from the Infinity. Other club employees went out of their way to avoid such a confrontation with the gangster. Bowskill said that when Ching was in the club, he usually appeared high. He was also cold, beady-eyed, and unfriendly. Everyone knew his reputation as an underworld hit man.

"He looked like a guy you didn't want to mess with," said Bowskill. "You were always cautious when he was in there. It was like a time bomb and you got the feeling he could go off at any time."

When Chuckers told Ching to leave, the gangster did not explode in a rage. He was, however, visibly angry. As Ching left, he snarled he was going to "get" Chuckers.

❦

In the weeks before he died, Chuckers Marsland was noticeably nervous. At home in his second-story Waikiki apartment, he'd peek out the window while talking to Clisby, checking to see if someone was lurking outside, worried that he was being followed. He told Clisby he was thinking about sleeping at his father's house for a few nights, until he felt safer. He obviously felt in danger, but disclosed no reasons for his paranoia. In hindsight Clisby thinks he might have been protecting her, sparing her from knowing too much.

That, apparently, was Chuckers's problem: He knew too much. And he had a big mouth. In the underworld such a combination can get you killed very, very quickly.

There are a couple of theories about why Chuckers ended up on the side of an isolated stretch of road outside Honolulu with bullets in his head. Each of them involved him tiptoeing too close to Hawaii's underworld. His father believed Chuckers was an innocent victim, targeted by gangsters because he had overheard, or witnessed, something incriminating. Calling the murder "completely senseless," Marsland hypothesized that gangsters feared Chuckers might relay whatever he witnessed to the police.

"A lot of the underworld people who went in there knew his relationship with the police chief," said Marsland, who also added that every clubgoer knew Chuckers was his son, too.

It is perhaps predictable that a parent would absolve his child of wrongdoing, finding it hard to imagine any offense that would justify his son being shot to death in the darkness. Despite the occasional fight and Chuckers moving out of the house shortly before his death, Marsland and his son were extremely close. The two men talked constantly.

"[Chuckers] would get up every morning, lay on the couch, make himself a cup of coffee and stay on the phone for a good hour," said Pedi. "I found out later it was his father he was talking to. Every morning."

Chuckers also visited his father at his office three or four times a week and attended some of his trials. On weekends they scuba dived and had dinner together, sometimes inviting Marsland's mother, Sadie, a former teacher on Oahu who had an outsize reputation on the island as a schoolmarm.

"Everybody interacted really well. It seemed like a very, very loving family," said Clisby, who often tagged along, witnessing firsthand the strength of her boyfriend's relationship with his father.

"We spent a lot of time out at his house with his dad," said Clisby. "[They were] just regular, everyday guys enjoying life . . . They got along famously. They were very, very close."

But beyond Chuckers's loved ones, others were not as willing to pardon the young man's sins. Not only did these people disagree with Marsland's statements that Chuckers was "a likeable kid" who "got along with everybody," some seemed to believe Chuckers got what he deserved.

If there was indeed fear that Chuckers was talking to the authorities about crime in Waikiki, this concern was well-founded. In one instance Chuckers had told his father and Chief Keala about an illegal gambling game operating on one of the top floors of his apartment building. This game was so well attended that Pedi, Chuckers's roommate, had trouble finding a parking space on the street when the gambling was in session. Shortly after Chuckers mentioned the gambling game to his father and Chief Keala, the police raided the game. It's unknown if anyone in the police department compromised the confidentiality extended to Chuckers and exposed him to gangsters as the police's source.

Others believed Chuckers was killed over a cocaine debt, though there is dispute over whether Chuckers sold drugs, let alone used them. Some high school acquaintances remember him as a dealer at Punahou School, though their recollections lack specifics. Chuckers's close friends from high school don't recall him peddling anything. But a coworker at the Infinity, Joseph Kama Jr., said he once saw Chuckers and Ching snort a foot-long line of cocaine in the office of the nightclub. Ching sold cocaine to Chuckers in the men's bathroom, too, said Kama, and Chuckers would sometimes duck into the restroom to get high.

"That's when he popped it out and did his trick," said Kama, a security guard. "When he would come out, he would be blowing his nose."

Eventually, said Kama, Chuckers ran up a debt with Ching that he was unable to pay. Ching, on the other hand, said that Chuckers bought cocaine from Naone. According to Ching, Chuckers became panicky in the weeks before his death because he had begun buying yet more cocaine from a rival gangster. Chuckers was afraid Naone might find out.

Such allegations don't square with others' impressions of Chuckers. Bowskill doesn't recall Chuckers sneaking into the bathroom regularly at the Infinity, nor does he remember him ever displaying any other sign of cocaine use. Clisby says she never saw Chuckers use cocaine. In fact she said he only used marijuana once or twice. And Pedi, their roommate, said he never saw Chuckers use or deal cocaine from their apartment. Yet Pedi was always impressed with the amount of cash Chuckers kept in his wallet.

"If he was, I didn't know about it. No one was knocking on our door. He never brought it home," said Pedi. "If he did, he was doing it out of the club."

Lastly, some wonder if the explanation for the murder was much more straightforward: Chuckers angered someone and paid a heavy price for his misstep. Naone told the police that his Samoan nemesis could have possibly attacked Chuckers out of retaliation for their previous dispute and Naone's flying karate kick. Others wonder if a patron turned away from the club door had sought revenge. Chuckers routinely denied people admission because they were intoxicated or underage. Then there was Ching, who had vowed to "get" Chuckers for ejecting him from the Infinity. On the same day that Chuckers's body was discovered in rural Waimānalo, Ching visited the Infinity and suspiciously told Kama, the security guard, "You don't know nothing."

In any case it seemed to all boil down to loose lips and poor associations.

"The rumors were that he was talking too much. Saying too many things. Talking to his dad," said James Koshiba, a prominent Honolulu attorney whose criminal defense clientele made him familiar with the Chuckers Marsland murder case and other intrigue in the Hawaiian underworld.

Koshiba continued:

I heard, too, that [Chuckers] was kind of a dandy. Pushed his weight around once in a while. He may have just stepped on the wrong toes. It didn't take too much in those days to have some sort of action or retaliation taken. There were lots of killings during that time. With a person like Ronald Ching, who really had no reservations or scruples about taking a life, you're treading on very dangerous waters, boy. It wouldn't take much. Just an insulting remark, an offhand remark, that might be enough for somebody like that.

Ching's friend Naone was not much different. Naone's daughter Erica described how her father thrived in the islands' "favor economy" and would regularly collect what he believed was owed to him by friends and acquaintances, whether free meat, limousine rides, or valet parking and a reserved table at the Royal Hawaiian hotel in Waikiki. Few had the courage to deny Naone these demands, no matter how many years, or decades, had passed since Naone performed the original favor, which was usually something criminal or strong-arm related.

"He felt entitled to a kind of attention and service that isn't normal and he was furious when he didn't get it," said Erica Naone, who was born in 1981, six years after the murder of Chuckers Marsland. "He was very sensitive to slights, and if he felt like he wasn't being absolutely respected he was really, really insulted and upset."

His temper, which was awe inspiring, could be triggered in an instant.

"It was totally terrifying to do anything with him, because there was no predicting when it would turn . . . It was so sudden and it didn't always make sense," Naone's daughter said. "I know that he loved us, and he was terrifying, and you just had no idea which one you were going to get."

As a child, Erica Naone said, she was subjected to constant screaming from her father, provoked by things as minor as holding a mop handle incorrectly. The more Naone screamed, said his daughter, the more nervous she would become. Her nervousness then gave way to crying, which made her father scream even

louder as he promised to truly "give her something to cry about."
Sometimes young Erica began sputtering apologies, which infuriated her father to the point that he once grabbed ahold of her
lips to stop them from moving, squeezing her face until she began
bleeding.

Such physical abuse, however, was rare. Instead, Erica Naone
said, her father relied primarily on intimidation to achieve his
goals. She could not recall a time when her father did not terrorize children and adults alike:

*In my head, he seemed like he could grow . . . It seemed like he
could expand, he was wider and taller, and he would get very
scary. The veins on his neck and head would stand out, and all
his muscles would be flexed, and his eyes would be wide open
and really terrifying. I have really vivid memories of being
in a room and he's taking up the entire doorway. It felt like he
could hardly fit in the doorway, it's completely blocked with
all his muscular bulk, [and he's] screaming.*

The emotional toll of this type of intimidation was devastating.
"I wished that he would hurt me physically because that
would be better than being scared to the level I was scared," said
Erica. "Please, break my bones, [just] don't keep doing this."

Ching and Naone were fearsome thugs, that much was clear.
Yet for all the notorious reputations, rumors, and theories surrounding Chuckers's death, evidence of their involvement was
hard to come by. As time went on, and despite Chief Keala's direct
involvement in the Honolulu Police Department's investigation,
no arrests were made for the murder of the young man. In the
days after Marsland's murder, the police interviewed Chuckers's
coworkers, as well as Naone and Ching, who had both visited
Chuckers just before the Infinity closed. Neither was formally
a suspect, and both denied having any knowledge of who killed
Marsland. But as noted in a police report, Chuckers's girlfriend

told investigators "she wouldn't be surprised if Eric [Naone] or one of Eric's friends was responsible," given their reputations as gun-toting, underworld killers.

The same day of the murder, Naone met with police to clear his name. He told a detective he had been with Ching most of the evening and early morning in Waikiki and how they had encountered their friend Chuckers. After they said good-bye to Chuckers, they drove with another friend, Gregory Nee, to Kaneohe, on the other side of the island, so Naone could obtain a change of clothes from his mother's house. Around daybreak, Naone said, they returned to Waikiki.

As the detective wrote of the interview, Naone

knows that Ching is considered a police character but mentioned that he is still a personal friend. He has never seen him do anything wrong and whatever Ching does is Ching's business as long as he isn't implicated one way or another. He knows that Ching and [Chuckers] Marsland always got along and wouldn't encounter the thought of Ronald Ching having anything to do with the demise of Marsland.

Hours later Ching was interviewed by the police. He said little of value. The detective wrote:

Although being very cordial and sincere, Ching would not give this writer an oral statement. He only agreed to what Eric Naone stated. He also refused to take a polygraph test. This writer refused to let him know what Naone's statement actually was.

He went on to say he doesn't appreciate the police hasseling [sic] him on the streets because that's where he makes his living and it appears the police coupled with their exploits seem to deter his normal life and movement. He does not

want to get on the bad side of the police and is willing to
come in and talk, requested the police have more tact on their
approach to him.

———

Five days after Chuckers's death, on April 22, 1975, the young man's funeral was held at Central Union Church in Honolulu. Known by its congregation as the "church in the garden," the tall, grand New England–style stone church was built in 1924 at the corner of Beretania and Punahou Streets. No matter the intensive development of Honolulu in the twentieth century, the church's campus has remained a lush and grassy tropical garden.

Inside, too, the church proves a serene and beautiful sanctuary. Its painted white interior is flooded with sunlight streaming through the church's many side windows and glass-paned doors. During nice weather, which occurs often in Honolulu, these doors are left open, allowing for a comfortable breeze to drift across congregants as they worship. Above the altar is a message chosen by the former Reverend Albert W. Palmer, who presided over the church in the 1920s: "Love Never Faileth." Those words are the Apostle Paul's, taken from Corinthians 13:8, which says "Whether there are prophecies, they will fail; whether there are tongues, they will cease; whether there is knowledge, it will vanish away."

"Love," on the other hand, "never fails."

Friends and family packed the church to remember Chuckers's life and mourn his death. There were more than two hundred visitors—so many that the funeral service had to be moved from a chapel to the main church. Some of those who attended recall Chuckers lying in an open casket, which seemed to be an unusual decision considering that Chuckers had absorbed gunshot wounds and shotgun blasts to his head and chest. The dead man's distorted appearance upset some of these friends.

"You could tell there was a lot of makeup," said Chuckers's high school friend Jon Andersen. "It was gruesome. I've only been to a couple of those in my life and I don't like to do that."

Alexander Pedi echoed those sentiments, complaining that the deceased Chuckers bore little resemblance to his athletic roommate. Chuckers's face was reconstructed awkwardly; his formerly strapping chest was concave; and his hair, normally curly and wild, had been pasted to his head.

"It was the worst thing in the world," said Pedi.

Clisby, however, recalls her boyfriend appearing peaceful in the casket. She had chosen the clothing Chuckers would be buried in, selecting one of his favorite suits and ties.

"He looked great," she said. "He looked like he was just sleeping."

Marsland, too, thought his boy appeared princely.

"Chuckie's casket was the same azure blue as the waters we dove so often. He appeared to be softly sleeping, and there was a light lace canopy over the opening," Marsland wrote. "He was surrounded by leis and bouquets. I kissed him goodbye for the last time and prayed for him."

Also among the large crowd of mourners were Ching and Naone. They had been picked up and driven to the funeral by their mutual friend, Nee. The twenty-year-old, who had driven Ching and Naone across the island the same morning Chuckers had been killed, worked as a doorman at the Polynesian Palace. Nee, who was only an acquaintance of Chuckers's, had not planned on attending the funeral. His friends, however, needed a ride and persuaded him to attend.

"If it had been strictly up to me," Nee said, "I wouldn't have gone."

When the three men entered the church, Nee said, people were crying. He, Ching, and Naone did not stick around for long.

"We went up to the casket and paid our respects and we left," he said.

Burial followed at the National Memorial Cemetery of the Pacific. Though Chuckers was not a veteran, the nineteen-year-old was considered a dependent by the US military, entitling him to burial in the military cemetery within Punchbowl Crater on account of his father's service in the Navy. Chuckers's coffin was placed in Section T, Site 140, about eight or nine feet underground. Such depth was necessary to accommodate Marsland, should he wished to be buried there, too, as well as any future spouse.

Marsland did wish to be buried with his boy, but not quite yet. First he had work to do, including discovering who had killed Chuckers. Unfortunately for the grieving father, the police were proving useless in this task. This disappointment compounded Marsland's grief, which was already profound.

Following Chuckers's death Marsland invited Clisby to come live with him and his girlfriend. Clisby stayed in Chuckers's room and was invited to dinner each night. Marsland was clearly "devastated" by the loss of Chuckers, said Clisby, though at home his grief did not give way to anger. Clisby remembered Marsland as soft-spoken and compassionate, without exception. She stayed in his home for a few months.

"I never saw a huge change in him," said Clisby. "[He was] a gentle giant. He was just a great human being to me."

Yet others saw Marsland's grief begin to take a heavy toll.

"Everything had been knocked out of him," said friend Joan Hester. "Chuck really took it so hard. It just changed him so badly then . . . I think he lost heart and everything."

In his own words Marsland referred to Chuckers's murder as "savage, senseless insanity" and its aftermath a "nightmare."

I can't yet feel grief or sorrow—only a stabbing, remorseless pain that won't stop. Wherever I look there are memories of him—big, handsome, laughing, and so alive, happy and enchanted with life . . . He left me the richest legacy of

*beautiful memories any human ever received. He knew I
loved him more than life itself, because, thank God, I saw
nothing unmanly in telling him so. And I know he loved
me for the same reason and in the same way. One day we'll
meet again. I am only sorry that it was not my lot to be there
first—to greet him.*

Beautiful memories did not stem the tide of anger that kept
washing over Marsland. He grew increasingly frustrated by his
son's murder investigation, causing his friendship with Chief
Keala to fray. The tension between the men reflected an extreme
change in Marsland's perception of the Honolulu police. Shortly
after Chuckers's death Marsland had deemed the local department "one of the finest in the nation" and praised the detective
division for its nonstop investigation of his son's murder. Furthermore Marsland lauded Keala as an honorable friend.

"It was the measure of the man that he came to tell me personally [of Chuckers's death]," wrote Marsland. "Not only is he
one of my closest friends, but he loved, thought of, and treated
Chuckie as his own son."

But friendship counted for little in the absence of arrests.
When Marsland eventually began his own personal investigation
into Chuckers's death, the tension between the old friends was
exacerbated. Keala resented Marsland's efforts and deemed them
detrimental to the official investigation. At a meeting in Keala's
office, the men traded sharp words. Marsland was unsympathetic
to the absence of witnesses and lack of hard evidence associated
with the murder. He wanted justice for his son, plain and simple,
and was willing to go to nearly any length to obtain it. At this
point for the distraught Marsland, justice was synonymous with
revenge.

Tucking a pistol beneath his coat, he ventured out late at
night onto the streets of Waikiki, intent on questioning anyone he thought might know details about Chuckers's death. The

well-dressed fifty-two-year-old was out of place in Waikiki, especially at night, when the discos raged, prostitutes crowded the sidewalks, and members of the underworld caroused about town. Nonetheless Marsland persevered, slowly gathering clues and gossip concerning Chuckers's murder.

Among those he interviewed was Pedi. Marsland invited him to his office, and despite having previously met his roommate's father, Pedi was nervous about the impending conversation. When the men talked, Marsland was tight-lipped about the information he had already collected, mentioning only that he thought a woman might have helped lure Chuckers into the car that took him to his death. Otherwise he grilled Pedi, looking to learn any facts that might have escaped his attention.

"His father was obsessed, totally obsessed," Pedi said of the interview. "He was focused on one thing and one thing only, to find out who killed his son."

During this investigation, too, Marsland claimed to have met with a man who told him the names of a handful of people allegedly involved in the murder. If Marsland would pay twenty thousand dollars, this man said, he would "take care" of these people. As proof of a job well done, the man offered to place a finger from each victim in Marsland's mailbox. Marsland declined the offer.

Marsland also sought answers about his son's murder in the spiritual realm. He consulted a number of psychics, including a sister of his long-time girlfriend. Like Pedi, this sister characterized Marsland as nothing less than "obsessed" with finding his son's killers. In 1975 she conducted a message for Marsland, writing it down in secretarial notebooks. This message urged Marsland not to seek vengeance but instead to think and remember his son in positive terms, and to foster his own healing through the embrace of love and light. The message read, in part:

> *Prolonged grief is guilt and [Marsland] must cleanse himself*
> *of this . . . The only way he can help his son is by releasing all*

of the negative hate concerning the death. Thinking of his son only in the light, the death is not an end but the beginning of a new life on a different plane . . . The moment he releases Chucky in love and continues to think of him in the light of love, both of them will receive the benefits of the divine . . .

These kinds of divine benefits were of no interest to Marsland. He wanted names. He wanted to know upon whom he must exact revenge. But the psychic message was clear about the folly of that approach:

If you Charles Marsland continue on the course you have been on, you will be a victim, too, as surely as your son, not of death, but of the forces of evil that these people are on. You must free yourself by your own mind, releasing them to their fate and accepting good for you and for your son.

What happens to them is of no importance to you and can serve no purpose in your life. You are not on earth to live anyone's life but your own. Your son was a joy to you. Let him remain so by holding him in the light rays of love. You must now live as light possible to you, acceptive to love and light and giving the best of yourself to every situation, for you have been through a great trial and suffered much. Be kind and tender to all, for you have much to give, but most of all be sensitive to the cleansing rays of light and love and receive these rays.

Marsland would have none of it. More than a year after Chuckers's death, Marsland's fury was undiminished, his outrage unabated. He dismissed the message and further pursued his own investigation, compiling a short list of men he wanted to confront about their alleged involvement in his son's murder. These men either proved elusive, or, perhaps, Marsland believed that anything less than a formal interview with these suspects would be useless to police and prosecutors. Abandoning the idea of vigilante justice, Marsland put away his gun and turned to his lawyer, Frank O'Brien, for help in finding the men. O'Brien obliged his client by devising a creative legal solution.

In September 1976 Charles Marsland filed a wrongful death suit against ten unknown defendants, listed as John Does One to Ten, which sought more than eight hundred thousand dollars in damages for the loss of Marsland's son. Part of the motivation for the lawsuit was an impending deadline, as Hawaii law set forth a two-year statute of limitations for wrongful death civil actions. More important the filing of the lawsuit allowed for O'Brien to depose individuals with supposed knowledge of the crime. In other words Marsland could confront the men on his short list.

"We were acting like our own little investigative police force," said O'Brien, who concedes that the legal maneuver was a bold one. "Back in those days we got away with it. . . . I'm always willing to take a whack at something. There wasn't any downside."

Though the gambit cleared legal hurdles, it ultimately had little value. Among the men Marsland was most interested in having deposed was Chuckers's friend Naone. Another was Ching. The reputed hit man, however, would yield nothing.

The gangster came to the deposition accompanied by his lawyer. Ching refused to answer any questions, repeatedly invoking his Fifth Amendment rights. For the length of the short meeting, Marsland stared hard at the man he had been told killed his son. Ching's countenance was no more pleasant.

"[Ching] looked like a mean, nasty son of a gun," said O'Brien. "He wasn't happy to be there."

Thwarted, Marsland pivoted again, deciding to restart his career in criminal law. In 1976 he sought, and obtained, a transfer from Honolulu's civil law department to the city prosecutor's office. Given his experience combating organized crime in Boston, Marsland would be counted on to handle a heavy caseload.

He only hoped that this caseload might one day include the men who killed his son.

"Somehow, some way, two or three vicious, mad dogs ended his life. It was more than one, because no one could have done it on a one-up confrontation," Marsland wrote to his daughter in Boston less than two months after Chuckers's murder. "There's a lot of answers to be found, and few leads to work with . . . The case will break—but it's going to take time—and I'll see whomever did it in hell."

CHAPTER THREE

He Will Stop at Nothing

Having a major role in prosecuting suspects did not relieve Charles Marsland of his frustration concerning crime in Hawaii. If anything it made it worse. Now the grieving father did not have one brutal crime on his mind, but many. Rather than distract him from his own suffering, these cases affirmed to Marsland that something was rotten in Hawaii. It could be absolutely maddening to obtain a conviction in the Aloha State.

The challenges Marsland encountered in Honolulu as a deputy prosecutor are well illustrated by his experience prosecuting Wilford "Nappy" Pulawa and other underworld thugs in 1978 during a retrial of the Syndicate members for the murder and kidnapping of Lamont C. "Monte" Nery and Dennis M. "Fuzzy" Iha. Convicting Pulawa and his associates would not be easy. More than eight years had passed since Iha and Nery were allegedly killed, and four years had passed since the first murder trial of the gangsters had ended in a mistrial. To complicate matters, none of the prosecutors who handled the first trial were working with Marsland to retry the case.

Things went awry before the new trial even started. During pretrial hearings Pulawa tried to head off the charges by claiming that, as a citizen of the "sovereign nation of Hawaii," he was not subject to the laws of the United States. Before presiding Judge John C. Lanham, Pulawa's lawyer read a letter explaining

Pulawa's rationale, but said he would not formally file the letter as part of a legal motion, since the filing would acknowledge the court's legitimacy.

"This court is the creation of a governmental entity which has taken possession of the lands, waters and people of the sovereign nation of Hawaii illegally, immorally, contrary to the laws of the nations, contrary to good conscience, and contrary to everything just," said Pulawa's lawyer, Hayden Burgess. "Mr. Pulawa calls upon the court's good conscience to quit the present proceeding."

Without a formal motion, Lanham responded, he could make no ruling.

Hiring Burgess was a curious decision by Pulawa. Whereas the Syndicate leader had relied previously on the foremost criminal defense attorneys in Hawaii to defend him on tax and murder charges in federal and state courts, in choosing Burgess he picked a lawyer just two years out of law school. Even Burgess was perplexed. As he said to Pulawa during their first meeting at McNeil Island Federal Penitentiary, "Eh brah, why me? You've got all these other attorneys, very good attorneys. I have not handled a single murder case previously. I have only one prior criminal trial facing a jury."

Pulawa replied that he knew he could get another hotshot haole or Korean attorney, but why not pick one of his own people?

"What good, what permanent effect does it have for the Hawaiian people? Once my plane lands, the media will be there. Because I sell newspapers, I'm supposed to be a big name," said Pulawa. "Why should I have someone else standing next to me other than a Hawaiian? If the last thing I do on this earth is push someone else forward, then I want it to be a Hawaiian."

Pulawa's argument against the legitimacy of the American government in Hawaii found sympathy among his many friends and supporters. They crowded the courthouse when Pulawa was returned to Honolulu from McNeil Island Federal Penitentiary, bedecking the smiling defendant with flower leis, playing live Hawaiian music, and performing hula dances as the retrial began.

Peter Carlisle was a young, newly hired deputy prosecutor at the time. He remembers being confused by all the hoopla in the usually sedate and solemn halls of justice.

"Does this happen frequently?" he wondered aloud, above the music, to his trial colleagues, prosecutors Charles Marsland and George Yamamoto.

"No," they said, "and it shouldn't be happening now."

Judge Lanham soon forbid flower leis from being passed out in the courtroom, but he couldn't stop Pulawa's supporters from gathering outside the courthouse, where they conducted a ceremonial reading of Pulawa's words. Since going to federal prison, Pulawa had begun taking political science courses and learning Hawaiian history as president of the prison's Aloha Club. As Pulawa wrote:

> I, Wilford Kalaauaia Pulawa, a Hawaiian, strengthened and supported by the spirits of my ancestors and love of my people and by the prayers of peoples throughout the world, affirm my citizenship in the sovereign nation of Hawaii and acknowledge no legislative superior to Hawaii but God. I hereby protest the continuing foreign occupation and rule of the United States of America in Hawaii. In the over 80 years of American occupation the American government allowed the unlimited infiltration of its citizens into our lands, flooded our territories with American troops, ran our educational system, dictated our lifestyles and imposed American laws upon the Hawaiian people. This American tyranny must end and the reign over the destiny of the Hawaiian people be returned to the Hawaiian people. To this end I pledge my breath of life.

Or, as he succinctly put it in another letter to Hawaiians: "It's all take, take, take, with very little give. Hawaiians became displaced persons in their own homeland. It's intolerable."

Pulawa demonstrated his commitment to the belief that American courts in Hawaii were illegitimate by refusing to be sworn in on the witness stand and by conspicuously refusing to rise when Judge Lanham entered and exited the courtroom.

The judge seemed not to take personal offense. Though he refused to dismiss the charges, he did sympathize with some of Pulawa's arguments, saying the overthrow of the Hawaiian monarchy in 1893 was "less than honorable." Nonetheless, "we are all Americans" and "we've got to move ahead together." The trial of Pulawa, Henry Huihui, and Bobby Wilson would proceed, said Judge Lanham, though defendants Alvin Kaohu and Dannette Beirne Leota would be tried at a later date.

The matter of the court's legitimacy settled, the prosecution then confronted a number of challenges associated with their case. One obstacle was that, following the mistrial, a police detective had improperly turned over the remains of Iha and Nery to their respective families, who each had them cremated. The absence of this bodily evidence allowed defense lawyers the opportunity to cast doubt that Iha and Nery were actually dead. Compounding that problem was a claim from Nery's former girlfriend, who insisted she spent a morning with Nery when he was allegedly already murdered.

More troublesome was former Syndicate lieutenant Roy Ryder who, after leading police to the sandy grave of Iha and Nery and fingering Pulawa and others in the original murder and kidnapping trial, was now refusing to testify in the retrial. It wasn't enough for Ryder that he had been paid more than thirty thousand dollars by the government for his testimony and given immunity for his confessed crimes, which included murdering Iha. Ryder said that he understood the immunity agreement, which was never recorded, to include immunity from any future crimes he committed, too. The government balked at this interpretation of their deal and fought vigorously to compel Ryder to testify. He was the only eyewitness to the alleged murders who was not a defendant, and he was critical to their case.

After much back and forth, the prosecution reaffirmed Ryder's immunity for past crimes. With that resolved, Ryder agreed to testify, though there was a catch: He retracted his testimony from the first murder trial. Pulawa, Huihui, Wilson, Kaohu, and Pulawa's girlfriend had nothing to do with the murder of Iha and Nery, Ryder said in court. They weren't even there. Instead, said Ryder, it was he and another gangster, George I. "Fat Man" Arashiro, who had shot Iha and Nery.

Ryder also retracted his testimony regarding the formation of the Syndicate and its aim to overthrow Asian gangsters. He had just drank beer and chatted with Pulawa, Huihui, Kaohu, and Wilson, he said, and never formed a criminal network with them. Then Ryder retracted this retraction and said indeed he and these men comprised the Syndicate, though it was only he who had murdered Iha and Nery.

More cynical minds looked suspiciously on these statements. Ryder's supposed accomplice, "Fat Man" Arashiro, was dead, having been shot by a girlfriend two years after Iha and Nery were killed. Blaming past crimes on dead men was a common, and convenient, underworld tactic. Moreover, the cynics said, Ryder kept changing his story regarding the formation of the Syndicate so as not to contradict previous testimony he had made in federal tax trials and thereby inviting the wrath of Uncle Sam. All the reversing and hedging by Ryder infuriated the Honolulu prosecutors.

"It's bullshit. You can't retract," said prosecutor Yamamoto. "Once you said it, you said it."

Judge Lanham, however, disagreed. In a decision upheld by the Supreme Court of Hawaii, Lanham ruled that under Hawaiian law, prosecutors could not present Ryder's original testimony to the jury but instead must rely on his most recent statements on the witness stand. During the trial this resulted in intense questioning of Ryder by prosecutors. In one heated exchange with

Yamamoto, Ryder said he decided to retract his original testimony and set the record straight after surviving a serious medical operation. In a fit of anger, Ryder stood up on the witness stand, lifted his shirt, and bared his stomach to the courtroom.

"This is it, pal," said Ryder, revealing a surgical scar on his abdomen. "Right here."

One juror later remarked that she was grateful the scar was not on Ryder's posterior.

Ryder also taunted the prosecutors for other unsuccessful trials and claimed his previous testimony was all fabricated and orchestrated by their predecessors in the prosecutor's office.

"The more I talked the more you guys liked it. I rehearsed this for months with you folks," Ryder said on the stand, holding a transcript of his testimony four years earlier. "All this thing in here are false, planned by you folks and me."

Marsland countered that Ryder's statements constituted an "incredible and bizarre lie."

"Roy Ryder," Marsland told the jury, "went to school to play football and went to court to tell a lie . . . and he fumbled both."

A fumble or not, Ryder's testimony did not help the prosecution. Having few other witnesses, the government's case fell apart well before it went to the jury. For lack of evidence or testimony tying them to the crimes, Judge Lanham acquitted Huihui and Wilson of all charges and then acquitted Pulawa of the two murder charges and one kidnapping charge. What began as a trial involving eleven felony counts against three accused murderers was now a trial involving a single felony kidnapping charge against Pulawa. Then Judge Lanham instructed the jury that they could convict Pulawa of the lesser, misdemeanor offense of unlawful imprisonment if they felt the evidence only pointed to him detaining Nery and not actually kidnapping, or taking him away from his apartment.

On February 1, 1979, a jury found Pulawa guilty of unlawful imprisonment. Typical of his courtroom behavior, Pulawa did not acknowledge the verdict while it was read. Instead he stared down while scribbling in his notepad. He was said to be writing a book.

"Nappy is always his happy self," said his lawyer, Burgess. "Nothing fazes him."

Prosecutors were hardly satisfied with the verdict. At most Pulawa could face an additional year in prison for the conviction.

"I feel like I just kissed my sister," said Marsland.

It got worse. It was soon discovered that Lanham should never have advised the jury they could convict Pulawa on the lesser charge. The statute of limitations for unlawful imprisonment had expired seven years earlier. Lanham duly voided the guilty verdict, essentially acquitting Pulawa. Then he made some rulings regarding Kaohu and Leota's retrial that also disappointed the prosecutors, to which Marsland said, "The only comment I have is unprintable."

Still, Pulawa remained imprisoned for his federal tax offenses, though his twenty-four-year sentence had since been reduced to fifteen years behind bars. During his absence from the underworld, Huihui and Kaohu were said to be feuding and killing off each other's henchmen. Yet Pulawa's former lieutenants denied any bad blood between them and said they were, in fact, friends. Despite these claims, Kaohu was accused in the late 1970s of hiring five men to kill Benny Madamba, a gambler on the Big Island who was said to have switched his allegiance to Huihui.

Even if Huihui and Kaohu were at war, it was over a significantly reduced fiefdom left behind by Pulawa. Huihui and Kaohu were nothing more than "street fighters," according to one police source, extorting small-time gambling operators and battling over a severely fragmented underworld. Some sources claimed, too, that Alema Leota was receiving a "pension" from the Syndicate in return for his consultation with a number of new crime lieutenants. Huihui, Kaohu, and Leota all denied these allegations.

These turf battles, to the extent that they were happening, were viewed by others as distractions from a more menacing form of organized crime that operated clandestinely, with the tacit permission, if not outright support, of many political leaders in Hawaii. This more sophisticated organization, the thinking went, made more money than the Syndicate members and rarely got their hands dirty. In a series of investigative newspaper articles in 1978, *Honolulu Star-Bulletin* reporter Jim McCoy examined the underworld:

> *The fighting goes on at the lower levels where the field-grade officers of crime battle for control of revenues from narcotics, gambling and extortion operations. Sources both in and out of law enforcement have suggested to the* Star-Bulletin *that the real leaders and beneficiaries of this activity sit untouched by the bloodshed and—so far—beyond the reach of prosecution.*

Despite McCoy's significant detailing of underworld activity, these "real leaders and beneficiaries" of organized crime were not mentioned by name.

In 1978, too, the Hawaii Crime Commission published their own report on the local underworld, claiming that since 1962 organized crime was responsible for at least sixty-one murders, eighteen attempted murders, and five disappearances in Hawaii. More difficult to quantify was the damage perpetrated by organized crime against Hawaiian society. The commission claimed that gangsters made a mockery of an honest and earnest way of life.

"The situation falls into a category that approaches treason," said the report. "By forming an organization outside of ordinary society, operating in contempt of law and morality, organized crime subverts the process of government for which Americans have made the greatest sacrifices."

Where organized crime is prevalent, as it most definitely was in Hawaii, the report argued, many people beyond gangsters are complicit in wrongdoing. Some of these people have been corrupted and profit from its existence. Others have been terrified into submission. Others still are blind to it. In any case few people attempt, or have the ability, to thwart organized crime.

Behind it all is a leader, someone who bridged the underworld with surface institutions and persons recognized as legitimate. This leader established links between those in positions high and low, and wielded influence through the use of money, violence, and power. Most impressively this underworld leader did it while hiding in plain sight. According to the report:

> *The main actor is the individual, or the handful of individuals, who is clever and sophisticated enough to develop ties with the captains of street crime, exerting influence over them, but insulating himself from implication in blatant criminal activities. At the same time, the organized crime leader skillfully creates the illusion of leading a law-abiding life and ingratiates himself with powerful and respectable personalities.*

Who was this main actor? Who was so clever and versatile, comfortable among gangsters and governors, killers and kings? With Pulawa's brutal reign over, who was in charge of the underworld in Hawaii?

The crime commission's report, at more than a hundred pages, failed to mention a name.

—•—

Seven miles southeast of Maui is Kahoolawe, the smallest of Hawaii's eight main islands. Though believed to have been occupied by humans for more than a thousand years, in more modern history it has been sparsely inhabited, if inhabited at all. Over the last two centuries, livestock has constituted its most robust population, with thousands of goats, sheep, and cattle grazing on ranches established in the mid-nineteenth century, following the forty-five-acre island's use as a penal colony. These hungry beasts denuded the island of its vegetation, prompting Hawaiian officials, in an effort to stem the subsequent erosion, to designate Kahoolawe a forest preserve in 1910. Persistent goats, however, prevented the reemergence of forest, eating any shoots they encountered, leaving the soil bare. And so, bit by tiny bit, Kahoolawe's red soil continued to drift off its cliffs and into the ocean.

In 1918 Kahoolawe reverted to ranchland. This time the cattle population was capped and the goats slated for destruction. As the hunting began, the feral animals bounded across Kahoolawe's sun-scorched earth and down its steep ravines in attempts to avoid the slaughter. No matter the goats' speed and scrap, scores and scores were dispatched. A correspondent for the *New York Times* chronicled the killing in 1922:

> *With every known make of gun they were hunted down . . . hundreds of spoiled carcasses bore mute testimony to the incessant warfare being waged . . . A thousand unwritten animal tragedies took place. Grand old billies, with their dignity of flowing beard and spreading horn, on guard to protect their diminishing flocks, at the sharp crack of a rifle would go hurtling over the perpendicular cliffs into a shark-infested sea. Nannies, heavy with their unborn kids, could not keep up in the drives and were pulled down by dogs; kids with calm topaz eyes and ears like slender leaves ran, bewildered into the very legs of the man who was the destructive spirit of their world.*

Yet the goats would not be vanquished completely. When the hunters left and the gunfire subsided, the surviving goats went back to grazing and mating, quickly restoring their stocks across Kahoolawe. In 1941 the US Navy gained control of Kahoolawe and began using it for bombing practice, with ships, submarines, and aircraft all firing on the ill-treated isle. Still the goats would not go away. Despite an order from the secretary of the Navy to keep Kahoolawe's hooved population below two hundred head, the state of Hawaii said that at one point in the late twentieth century, there were fifty thousand goats on Kahoolawe.

Whatever the number, by the 1970s Kahoolawe had been reduced to an eroding isle of barren, sunbaked hardpan littered with goats and unexploded ordinances. Also dotting the marred landscape were a few historic Hawaiian ruins, including *heiau*, or temples. The disregard shown to these sacred sites, and moreover the disregard shown to Kahoolawe entirely, exasperated some Hawaiians. In a little more than a century, a beautiful island had been stripped bare, then made into a bombing site.

In 1976 activists began occupying the island for short periods of time to protest the mistreatment. Their visits usually lasted a few days or weeks—however long it took military patrols to discover them and make arrests. Among those who traveled to Kahoolawe during this time were Kimo Mitchell and George Helm, who was a musician and the leader of the newly formed grassroots activist group Protect Kahoolawe Ohana. During a trip to Kahoolawe in March 1977 with one other companion, Helm and Mitchell disappeared, supposedly after together trying to paddle a surfboard back from the island to Maui in very rough seas. Family members found their disappearance suspicious, doubting the men would attempt such a risky crossing. Also bewildering was the apparent sabotage and scuttling of a boat that was to be used to pick up the men. Rumors circulated, including one theory that Helm and Mitchell did not drown but were killed. Helm had supposedly been investigating land-use decisions in Hawaii and the influence of organized crime on local government. According to his brother Adolph, Helm was on the verge of exposing significant corruption.

Helm was not the only one talking about such malfeasance. A month before Helm disappeared, television reporter Scott Shirai of KHON-TV claimed that the "godfather" of Hawaiian organized crime was a member of a state board and tied to a pending criminal case regarding heroin. Shirai did not identify the person, did not pinpoint to which state board he was referring, nor, to many observers, provide any proof of his claims. If true, however, Shirai's report would affirm the whispered speculation that had been going on for years within Hawaiian political circles, namely that a well-known businessman and confidante of both Governor George Ariyoshi and his predecessor, John Burns, was connected to organized crime.

Less than a week after the report, State Representative Kinau Kamalii and Honolulu Mayor Frank Fasi, who was challenging Ariyoshi for governor, called for investigations of the alleged godfather. Neither politician mentioned the man's name. Their appeals yielded no immediate results.

Four months later an unlikely source dared speak his name. In just its fourth issue, a free alternative newspaper on Maui named the *Valley Isle* published allegations that Hawaii's godfather was said to be Larry Mehau, a former Honolulu policeman turned Big Island rancher and businessman. Additionally the newspaper printed interviews in which Mehau was said to have threatened Helm at Honolulu's Gold Coin restaurant, supposedly in response to Helm's activism on land issues.

"You'd better stop talking about me," Mehau allegedly said to Helm. "If I have to break your ass, I'm gonna."

The newspaper's claims caused an uproar. While a number of news outlets reproduced or broadcast the *Valley Isle*'s allegations, others dismissed the paper's credibility, putting little faith in the investigatory abilities of a newspaper with no paid editorial staff and whose previous journalism included profiles of Hawaiian musicians and a Maui potato chip maker. The paper's reporting for the godfather story relied on a number of anonymous sources, offered no proof of Mehau's involvement with organized crime, and offered no proof that Helm was murdered. Still the paper stood by its story.

"Even though we didn't have any evidence that would convict anyone, we did have overwhelming information that we felt should be known by the people and investigated by Hawaii authorities," said *Valley Isle* publisher and coeditor Rick Reed. "We were simply providing a transmission vehicle for information that had been simmering for some time."

In the wake of these allegations, a number of people defended Mehau's integrity. Governor Ariyoshi derided the "wild charge" and said he had "no questions about Mehau's background or integrity." Moses Kealoha, a fellow member of the state land board who was with Mehau during a visit to the Golden Coin restaurant, confirmed that Mehau spoke to Helm but denied that any threat was made. Instead, he said, the men were friends and asked each other for favors. Hawaiian police chiefs, too, came to Mehau's defense, claiming Mehau's associations were nothing out of the ordinary.

"Anybody who grew up in the state has friends who are criminals and who are policemen," said Kauai Police Chief Roy K. Hiram. "He has many friends in both areas."

Since Mehau was a former policeman who had often courted informers during the course of duty, the police chiefs argued, it made even more sense that he'd be familiar with less-desirable characters.

"Larry always did have a rapport with persons who may have been engaged in criminal activity, but this certainly does not mean he was involved with them," said Maui Police Chief John San Diego, who worked alongside Mehau when they served on the vice squad of the Honolulu Police Department.

Another police chief's comments, however, were more difficult to parse. Following the *Valley Isle*'s allegations against Mehau, Representative Kamalii and State Senator D. G. Anderson met with Honolulu Police Chief Francis Keala for ninety minutes to discuss the supposed godfather. According to Anderson, Keala cleared Mehau of any wrongdoing.

"[Keala] described Larry's position this way: He said whenever there's a gang war or fighting between factions and they want to talk it over, they call Larry and ask him to help arrange a truce. He is used as a mediator," said Anderson. "I understand, too, that even the police on occasion have asked him to intercede and bring peace to some situations."

Kamalii left their meeting with a different impression.

"If that isn't aiding and abetting the underworld, what is?" she asked. "What is a godfather?"

Mehau himself kept mum. His only response to the reports, at least in the short term, was the filing of a fifty-one million dollar libel lawsuit against thirteen defendants, including the *Valley Isle*, KHON-TV, State Representative Kamalii, and other media entities. The lawsuit accused the defendants of failing to verify the accuracy of their reports and causing harm to Mehau's reputation and emotional well-being.

Despite the lawsuit the *Valley Isle* continued to run stories concerning Mehau and his perceived links to organized crime. Whether the charges the *Valley Isle* had leveled were true or not, the newspaper had picked a fight with a formidable opponent. Mehau, who weighed as much as three hundred pounds, had a reputation across the Hawaiian Islands for incredible strength and toughness, as well as for having friends in the highest of places. In his youth he was a four-time amateur sumo champion who trounced Japan's top wrestlers. His endurance was awe inspiring: Mehau trained in part by performing hundreds of squats each day with his wife and high school sweetheart, Beverly, sitting on his shoulders.

Mehau was born in Hilo on the Big Island to a Hawaiian mother and haole father. His father, who was an executive with one of the Big Five sugar companies in Hawaii, had another family and was not a part of Mehau's life. Initially the distance was because Mehau's father ignored the boy. Later it was because Mehau rebuffed his attempts at reconciliation, still angry at his

father's earlier absence. Mehau said he ultimately regretted taking such a tough, unforgiving stance.

"I was stupid," he said. "I wish now I would have seen him
before he died."

When Mehau was a sophomore in high school he moved
to Honolulu to be educated at Kamehameha Schools, a private
institution dedicated to children of native Hawaiian ancestry.
According to his classmate and teammate Don Ho, Mehau's
oversize presence was felt immediately on campus, especially on
the football field:

> *He was like [Arnold] Schwarzenegger, in ultimate shape.*
> *His presence made everyone around him serious, because he*
> *was serious. My impression was here was the Hawaiian*
> *who could be King Kamehameha. The chief of war. He was*
> *the toughest guy in the school. You respected him because you*
> *knew he could tear your head off.*

Mehau graduated from Kamehameha Schools in 1948 and
then briefly attended the University of Hawaii before becoming
a policeman back on his home island of Hawaii. A year or so later,
he moved again to Honolulu because of an illness in his wife's
family. Mehau then sold roofing material before being hired by
the Honolulu Police Department.

"I loved being a cop," said Mehau. "It's a great life. It's excit-
ing. You get to help people."

Cops also get to apprehend people. Mehau was quite good
at this. In a year during which he led the morals squad in the late
1950s, he made 224 arrests and charged 199 others. In eleven
months as gambling squad sergeant, Mehau raided 485 gambling
games and arrested 4,126 people. Occasionally things got rough,
especially on the metro squad, which Mehau also led for a time,
breaking up gambling games, corralling rowdy soldiers, sweeping
the streets of prostitutes, stopping gang fights, and shaking down

thugs for illegal weapons. Mehau was said to give trouble to only those who asked for it. But when he did—watch out, because he helped them find it quickly. Beyond being a sumo champ who was offered a thousand dollars a week to wrestle professionally in Japan, Mehau had earned black belts in karate and aikido. His strength and toughness were legendary.

During a martial arts demonstration in 1957, Mehau broke bricks in half with karate chops. Not satisfied to break one brick at a time, Mehau then tried to knock through two bricks taped together.

"They wouldn't break cleanly. All they did was crumble," a newspaper reporter wrote of Mehau's performance. "Sgt. Mehau, determined man, kept smacking them until spectators' stomachs began turning over and Deputy Chief Arthur Tarbell made him stop."

Later during the demonstration Mehau stretched out between two chairs while others placed a three-hundred-pound stone eight inches thick on his stomach. Another man swung from above with a nine-pound sledgehammer.

"Sgt. Mehau didn't even grunt," the same reporter wrote. "After several sharp blows, the rock broke in two. Sgt. Mehau walked away unharmed. He didn't even stagger a bit."

On the street Mehau was just as imposing, once punching through a windshield in pursuit of a suspect who had locked himself in the car. Another time Mehau confronted a large, muscular man who was walking downtown with a pool stick in his hand, shoving passersby out of his way.

"Do you intend using that pool cue stick on somebody?" Mehau asked in a quiet voice.

The man growled at Mehau and pounded the stick in his hand.

"I think maybe you'd better give me the stick," said Mehau, extending his own mitt.

There was no answer. Mehau gave the bully one last chance.

"If you plan to use the stick," Sergeant Mehau told the man, "maybe you'd better use it on me."

"Glad to," said the public menace as he lifted the pool stick in the air, preparing to strike the policeman. In the blink of an eye, however, Mehau had thrown the man to the ground, causing the pool stick to roll harmlessly out of his hand and into a gutter. The man did not immediately get up.

Such encounters were par for the course for Mehau and his fellow fearless members of the metro squad, who cruised Honolulu in unmarked cars and wore unofficial plainclothes uniforms of aloha shirts and slacks. The men reveled in their reputations as some of the toughest men in Hawaii, though some citizens and tourists accused them of brutality.

"I really used to feel like I could fight ten regular guys and not get hurt," said Mehau, who once disarmed a gang of twenty-four gamblers with two other officers, throwing some of his adversaries through windows. "Well, I might get hurt but I could not lose."

In his ten years as a policeman, Mehau did much more than keep the peace. He taught other officers self-defense and aikido and also trained the Honolulu Police Department's K-9 division, voluntarily dropping rank from lieutenant to sergeant to work with German shepherds and Doberman pinschers. When dignitaries came to Hawaii, Mehau was regularly ordered to provide protection, serving as a bodyguard and escort. He was part of the security detail for a visit by President Dwight D. Eisenhower and, at other times, drove cars carrying Vice President Richard Nixon and President Lyndon B. Johnson. Mehau says Johnson repeatedly asked to ditch his Secret Service agents and the rest of the security escort and have Mehau drive him across Oahu like he was a normal person. Such demands made the Texan a challenging charge.

"I'm not saying he was a bad guy," says Mehau, "but you'd think he was a stevedore, what comes out of his mouth. And his wife was tougher than him."

Mehau also guarded the chancellor of Germany, the presidents of Indonesia and Korea, the Shah of Iran, and royalty from Nepal and Thailand. These assignments were granted him in part because of Mehau's strength and street savvy, but also due to his impressive deportment and charm. When Pat Nixon accompanied the vice president to Hawaii, Mehau gifted her a pineapple. Madame Chiang Kai-shek of China received mangoes from the Hawaiian policeman.

"Police sergeant Larry Mehau knows his place," noted one observer. "It's close to princes and presidents, premiers, kings and queens."

Celebrities, too, for that matter. As a policeman in Honolulu, Mehau once gave a ride along to actor Marlon Brando, which perhaps some thought fitting, given both would become known, accurately or not, as godfathers. Years later Mehau was seen in the company of Hollywood stars Jill St. John and Robert Wagner when giving them a lift to the airport on the Big Island.

For all the acclaim as a strongman and earnest policeman, Mehau's record had a few blemishes, mostly on account of excessive force by either him or the police officers he commanded. In 1958, while a sergeant in charge of the gambling squad, Mehau was suspended for ten days and transferred out of the vice division for his unconventional tactics with informers. After an eight-week investigation, his superiors found nothing illegal in his actions and indeed touted his "outstanding" record as a policeman. Yet they did find some of Mehau's relationships to informers improper, including the "loose handling" of payments to informers and being "unduly familiar" with one informer to the point that Mehau allowed him to join in on police gambling raids.

Mehau stood by his performance, and ultimately the deputy chief of police was satisfied that any missteps were the product of Mehau's "zealous efforts to achieve new heights in vice arrests."

"In weighing the factor of having vice characters as familiars," said Deputy Chief Arthur M. Tarbell, "it must be realized that all vice officers are, of necessity, thrust into association with unsavory and often criminal types."

These criminal associations would dog Mehau for the next three decades, even as he stopped patrolling the underworld. Mehau retired from the Honolulu Police Department in 1963 with a disability pension due to broken bones in his wrist. He and his wife moved back to the Big Island to begin a quieter life. Of all things, the supercop and sumo champ left police work behind to become a cattle rancher.

———

In the wake of Chuckers Marsland's death, Chuckers's father overhauled his life, transforming from doting father to hard-nosed and relentless prosecutor. Chuckers's friends in Waikiki, on the other hand, did not amend their ways. In fact, rather than view Chuckers's murder as a cautionary tale, friends like Eric Naone and Ronnie Ching became more enmeshed in the criminal underworld.

A month after Chuckers's murder, Naone had been hired by the Hawaii Teamsters. Officially he was a business agent, but the husky Naone was often observed acting as a bodyguard for the Teamsters president. Naone only spent four months with the Teamsters before quitting and heading to California in August 1975. At the end of the month, he was arrested in Los Angeles as part of a failed plot to kidnap a former Las Vegas showgirl and actress named Corrine Heffron. According to police a bandana-clad Naone and another man wearing a gorilla mask robbed and assaulted Heffron, her husband, and a friend at gunpoint outside their Bel Air home. The husband was tied up and Heffron, who once posed for *Playboy* magazine under the name Lari Laine, was put in the trunk and driven away. The police soon caught up with the car, however, arresting Naone and freeing Heffron. The gorilla impersonator escaped, but the police also arrested the Heffrons' friend, Hershey Entin, accusing him of being part of the kidnapping plot.

Entin had previously lived in Hawaii, once working in Waikiki as an unpaid errand boy for Don Ho. The entertainer expressed incredulity that Entin could have committed such a crime.

"He's basically a good kid," said Ho. "If he did what they say he did, he must have gotten a sudden brain tumor or something. He was a good kid all the time he was with us."

Naone was sent to prison after pleading guilty to a charge of first-degree robbery associated with the case. A jury, meanwhile, acquitted Entin of kidnapping and robbery charges, despite Naone's testifying against him as a witness for the prosecution.

Naone's hard times did not stop there. Two months after being sentenced for the robbery charge in July 1976, he pleaded guilty to buying ammunition, which federal law prohibits felons from doing. As Naone's lawyer explained, Naone had not bought two boxes of bullets and four holsters for himself, but as a favor to a general in the Philippines, whom he admittedly did not know.

Such an explanation was greeted with doubt. A spokesman for the Philippines said that if the military needed ammo, the government bought it directly from a manufacturer. The federal prosecutor in the case labeled Naone's story "preposterous," and Federal Judge Sam King, too, shouted in court, "That's incredible!" Dismissing claims from Naone's attorney that the ammo purchase was an honest mistake and a technical violation, King said, "When someone with a criminal record buys ammunition, it is assumed he is up to no good—that's why the law is there." Naone was sentenced to an additional eighteen months in prison.

Ching, meanwhile, had his own run-ins with the law resulting in prison time. In 1977 he began a stint in federal prison for illegally possessing firearms and explosives, serving much of this time at the federal penitentiary in Lompoc, California. At the time the prison was a high-security facility, containing some of the country's most violent criminals. Life behind bars in Lompoc was not pleasant, even for the street-hardened Ching. He worked as a prison medic, tending almost daily, by his own account, to fellow inmates who had been stabbed within the prison. He later lamented that prison offers no hope of rehabilitation, but instead seems to make criminals worse. Ching also complained that there were no federal prisons in Hawaii.

"We the only US citizens gotta go overseas to do time. Our family come to visit, they no can come visit unless they get at least a thousand bucks and that's only going last you two, three days," said Ching. "That's really being deprived . . . there's no way that the welfare going ever help or the federal government going assist in that. Uncle Sam them guys, they no give a fuck, you know, they shown us that, so ah, fuck them too . . . whatever going happen we going do the time."

Should Ching have been incarcerated closer to home, he might have been visited by any number of family members. Ching supposedly had thirteen siblings and half siblings, of which he was the fifth oldest. He was born January 13, 1949, in Honolulu to parents who separated four years later. His father, who was married four times, worked at a quarantine station for animals. His mother, who was married twice, was a housewife. Despite the large family a psychologist noted his childhood featured "a significant pattern of isolation and defective interpersonal relationships."

Ching lived with his father until he was thirteen years old, then went to live with his mother. He dropped out of high school just two months into the eleventh grade, claiming he "wanted to be free." He had been suspended from class a number of times, did not study, and admitted to falling in with the "wrong crowd." At age sixteen he was arrested twice within two months for stealing cars. As an alternative to being placed on probation, he joined the Navy in 1966, enlisting for a four-year term. Things did not go swimmingly as a sailor. He lasted less than ten months in the Navy.

At boot camp in San Diego, Ching complained of frequent nightmares that interrupted his sleep. During the daytime he was nervous and felt butterflies in his stomach. A Navy doctor noted that Ching said he felt like he was going to "tear something (or someone?) apart." The doctor's premonition that Ching could hurt others was correct, as later medical reports noted Ching had a tendency to get into fights and once beat someone so badly the victim had to be hospitalized.

From boot camp Ching transferred to Adak Naval Air Station in Alaska's Aleutian Islands. He became homesick, continued to be nervous and anxious, and threatened to go AWOL. Ching said he felt like he was losing his mind. He disliked the Navy because, "I can't smile and I can't have fun."

Months later he obtained a two-week leave and returned to Hawaii. It was not a happy homecoming: He was taken to the emergency room at an Army hospital after cutting his wrist in a halfhearted suicide attempt. During a subsequent psychiatric evaluation, Ching refused to make eye contact, bit his fingernails constantly, and seemed to be on the verge of tears.

In December 1966 Ching was honorably discharged from the Navy for "reason of unsuitability." He had been diagnosed with a schizoid personality, meaning he had solitary habits and appeared indifferent to others. Navy records indicate this diagnosis was manifested by "immaturity, impulsivity, irresponsibility, defective interpersonal relationships, depression and egocentricity."

Ching had entered the Navy as a slight young man, standing less than six feet tall and weighing 150 pounds. Upon his discharge he became bigger, nearly doubling his size and growing strong. The increased size made him more intimidating, as did other changes in his physical appearance. His body was increasingly covered in tattoos. On his left forearm was a large shark he called "Jaws," which appeared unusually friendly, as well as the words "Born to Lose." On his right forearm was tattooed a rabbit. For his wardrobe Ching favored hiding behind aviator sunglasses and loose-fitting aloha shirts.

The effect was a cool, unfriendly look that reinforced Ching's reputation as the most feared gangster in Honolulu's Chinatown, a downtown neighborhood that Charles Marsland once described as the murder capital of Hawaii, "crawling with prostitutes, pimps, thieves, perverts and addicts." These riffraff were Ching's people, and he ruled over them as an independent gangster, separate from those involved in the Syndicate, demanding tribute from Chinatown's gambling operators, whores, and drug dealers. Failure to pay such tribute could bring stiff consequences, as proved by the case of Ruth Bender, an eighteen-year-old prostitute who was found nude in a dump with eight or so bullet wounds in her body. According to prosecutor Keith Kaneshiro, it was upon Ching's orders that Bender was killed. The young woman supposedly owed two hundred dollars.

"People were afraid of him," Kaneshiro said of Ching. "He would not hesitate to kill."

Ching's life of crime supposedly had started in earnest at age sixteen, when Ching claimed to have "made his bones," or killed for the first time. This murder was the beginning of a criminal career that would include turns as a thief, pimp, drug dealer, and professional killer. In short order Ching went from being a high school dropout and Naval malcontent to Hawaii's most notorious hit man, allegedly responsible for a dozen or so deaths. When acquaintances described him, they used words like "cold-blooded," "reptilian," and a "stone killer."

Among Ching's earliest misdeeds was the assassination of State Senator Larry Kuriyama, who was shot with a silenced pistol in 1970 as he arrived home late one evening from a political rally. For this murder Ching claimed only to be a lookout, that another man pulled the trigger as the senator exited his automobile after parking under his carport. Still, Ching was close enough to help finish the job if necessary. Like Kuriyama's family inside the house, he heard the dying senator's screams.

In 1978, freshly released from prison, Ching took a much more hands-on role in the abduction and murder of Arthur Baker. In his final hours Baker had been enjoying the comforts of booze and women, passing a Sunday evening in the Sunday Lounge, a Honolulu hostess bar where he sometimes performed odd jobs. But his weekend, and life, came to a violent conclusion when Ching and a crew of heavyweight men stormed into the lounge and headed his way. They flashed police badges to the startled lounge patrons and then savagely pummeled Baker, destroying any illusions that these men were legitimate police officers. The large men handcuffed Baker and dragged him from the bar. Outside he was forced into a waiting station wagon, which quickly left the scene.

Baker was driven to a beach that night and unloaded from the car, along with shovels. His four abductors continued to beat him, and Baker could put up little fight. Beyond being cuffed, he was outnumbered and undersized. Ching weighed close to three hundred pounds, and yet that was only half the weight of another alleged abductor, Pierre "Fat Perry" Wilson. Wilson was so large that when he was jailed six years later, authorities had to weld two bunks together to make him a bed. He could not walk more than ten feet at a time and was consequently transported around jail on top of a food cart. The 670-pound man's girth was so substantial he could not fit into the jail's medical examination rooms and would ultimately die behind bars of massive heart failure.

But in November 1978 the massive Wilson was alive and allegedly blocking any chance Baker had of escape. Ching, Wilson, and the other abductors allegedly dug a crude grave for their captive at Maili Beach on the rural Leeward Coast of Oahu. Before throwing Baker into the shallow pit, the men beat him again and again. For his part Ching no longer only used his thick fists, but also a claw hammer to smash Baker's skull.

Once Baker was beaten senseless, his inert body was covered with sand. Realizing that he was being buried alive, Baker summoned his remaining strength and began to struggle. His tormentors saw the sand of the recently filled grave start to shift. Some of the men then allegedly stood atop the grave, using their considerable heft to keep Baker underground. They heard mumbling and groaning from Baker below, and then saw a depression open in the sand just above Baker's mouth as their victim inhaled one last time. Then all was quiet.

Ching later expressed regret over the incident.

"If I had anything to do all over again," said Ching. "I would hit him again with the hammer one more time, just for the fun."

A year and a half later, Ching again terrorized bar patrons by murdering rival gangster Bobby Fukumoto in an ambush at one of Fukumoto's favorite watering holes in Honolulu, the Brass Door Lounge. The fifty-one-year-old Fukumoto's criminal record reflected more than a dozen gambling convictions. He also had sold heroin and was convicted by a federal court in 1970 for narcotics offenses. That conviction came after two trials and despite the pretrial murder of a government witness's wife. Fukumoto and Ching had once been close, with Fukumoto acting as a criminal mentor to the young thug. Then they had a disagreement, and Ching, who at this period of his life was often under the discombobulating influence of heroin and other drugs, believed Fukumoto to be a threat. For Ching it was kill or be killed. There was also talk that Fukumoto had become an informant, which would have been another reason to kill him.

Fukumoto's demise began when a bartender at the Brass Door Lounge called Ching to inform him that Fukumoto had arrived at the bar. Then Fukumoto's bodyguard, a man named Fluff, betrayed his boss and also called Ching to give him notice of Fukumoto's location. Leery of being set up, Ching called a waitress at the lounge to confirm Fukumoto was sitting at the bar and vulnerable. She said, yes, Fukumoto was there.

Ching then moved quickly, arriving at the Brass Door just after midnight on May 20, 1980, carrying an automatic rifle, automatic pistol, and two grenades. Two accomplices waited outside as a backup and driver. Ching pulled a hood over his head as he strode into the bar, the automatic rifle in his hands. Putting

Fukumoto in the rifle's sights, he motioned for the bartender to back away from his target. Ching then called out "Bobby" and let loose two bursts of fire, putting ten bullets into the back of the man he referred to as a father figure. As the other patrons scrambled to find safety, Ching disregarded his getaway vehicle and jogged merely a block or so back to his home at the Chateau Blue apartment building in Waikiki. No witnesses would come forward to identify him to police.

For years Ching acted with such impunity. One federal agent claimed Ching routinely "thumbed his nose" at investigators, and Ching was so bold in 1980 as to meet Honolulu policeman Don Carstensen for lunch and discuss, albeit cryptically, several murders in which he was a suspect. Despite Carstensen making it plain that he sought eventually to arrest Ching, the policeman and the hit man enjoyed a unique rapport, with Ching boasting that his criminal lifestyle was giving Carstensen job security. At one point Carstensen confronted Ching over rumors that Ching was going to kill Carstensen. Not true, said Ching. If that was so, Ching continued, Carstensen "would be dead before hearing about it."

At the lunch meeting with Carstensen in a downtown Honolulu restaurant, Ching nibbled at a chef's salad and drank tomato juice. He would not directly address several of Carstensen's inquiries regarding gangland murders and suspected underworld figures, but nonetheless provided a rare view into the life of a professional killer. Ching, who seemed to revel in his coyness, was unaware that Carstensen was secretly recording their ninety-minute conversation, which was occasionally interrupted by a waitress asking if they'd like salad dressing and more to drink.

Carstensen asked about the disappearance of Baker from the Sunday Lounge, to which Ching responded by laughing and saying he knew him to be a "really down to earth guy." Carstensen asked about Fukumoto, whom Ching said was killed for extorting innocent people, and that his death saddened him. Then the hit man laughed again, professing his innocence in the matter.

Though he would not admit to these specific murders, Ching was not shy about discussing generally the ins and outs of killing. He told Carstensen he had killed "plenty" of times and offered a number of insights into how to take a life. By piecing together his statements from this conversation, one can create a hit man's tutorial.

First of all, a killer should take precautions, such as keeping handy a container of urine or WD-40 lubricant. Either of these substances can be splashed onto one's hands following the discharge of a firearm. That way the killer can foil a paraffin test, in which police press wax onto a suspect's hands to collect nitrates, which can be evidence of gunshot residue.

"That's why you gotta carry one canister of piss. Whenever you shoot one gun you gotta acid your hand," said Ching, who also conceded that a killer could take the precaution of wearing long sleeves and gloves, though such attire would be out of place in Hawaii.

Second, a killer should act calmly and deliberately when executing someone. To soothe his nerves, Ching often swallowed quaaludes before killing. It helps, too, for a killer to try to instill reason in his victim, so as to lessen his resistance. Part of Ching's schtick as a hit man was that, seconds before murdering his target, he brandished his gun and informed the victim that he was about to end his life. Call it a killer's courtesy.

> *You see it's not one of those fucking things, you know, like you go down the road you shoot somebody, like somebody was fucking lolo [crazy] and you get off with that. You know what I mean?*
>
> *It's different. You know what I mean? You grab somebody, you take 'em, tell 'um hey brah, sit down, make it easy, you going anyway . . . there ain't no fucking way. No can beg. That kind you gotta block from you mind, yeah.*

Third, remember to have fun. While it's important to stay calm and focused when killing, that doesn't mean a killer can't enjoy himself. Killing can be intoxicating, what with the danger of resistance and arrest.

"That's part of the high. You know what I mean?" said Ching. "You playing the games, the gun powder, the fucking bullets go zinging by. That's part of the high."

Finally, the killer's job is not finished until he takes care of the victim's body. Ching favored burying his victims, and he joked to Carstensen that this was a favor to the victim's family given that no one would have to pay for an interment. He suggested burying people under cover of a camping tent, or to use the beach, specifically Makua Beach on the Leeward Coast of Oahu.

"You know why Makua is good? Best place in all Hawaii," said Ching. "The thing change about three times a year—the beach formation. So you know, if you dig on certain times of the year sometimes the fucking thing going wash out. And then certain times of the year the fucker going to be twenty feet down instead of one, eh. Unreal, eh?"

Ching had a high opinion of his abilities as a killer, boasting that he was always a step ahead of the authorities. The only way he would get caught, he told Carstensen, was if the police used technological advances to arrest him for a crime he had not yet committed, but would in the future. That would be the only way, he said, to prevent him from successfully covering his tracks. It is unclear if Ching said this in jest.

Similarly he once told Honolulu lawyer James Koshiba of his efforts to conceal the method of murder by shooting his victim from above, hiding the bullet wound within the man's thick head of hair. After shooting the man, Ching allegedly wiped clean the blood and stuffed something, such as a rag, inside the wound. Then he tousled the man's hair, covering over the hole in his skull.

Koshiba could not believe the words he was hearing.

"I shoot him right here," said Ching, touching the top of his head. "They cannot find the bullet."

"Ronald, they're gonna find it," said Koshiba, mentioning how thoroughly a coroner performs an autopsy. "They're gonna cut everything out."

"Yeah, but they're gonna have a hard time," said Ching.

Just as silly, and sick to some, was Ching's contention that his unlawful activity had some kind of greater purpose, that he was part of a criminal revolution.

"There are people who had peace movements; he believed in the crime movement," said Peter Carlisle, who interacted with Ching as a deputy prosecutor. "He was going to be a part of it. He was going to be in the vanguard."

As one of Ching's girlfriends explains further: "He had a warped sense of pride that he was doing the right thing," she said. "In his mind . . . it was justifiable, absolutely. He just didn't hurt people to hurt people. He was a teddy bear to people he cared about."

Who exactly was the brutal killer fond of? His girlfriends, apparently, of which he had many. By all accounts they were gorgeous, too, with one having competed in the Miss Universe beauty contest in the 1970s as Miss American Samoa. Another girlfriend, who bore him a son, claimed Ching fathered seven children, with seven women. Or, perhaps it was seven kids with six women; she wasn't quite sure.

"Pretty much he left trophies for all the women he cared about," she said.

Such magnetism perplexed others who encountered Ching, a thick, black-haired man of Chinese, Hawaiian, and Portuguese descent. Ching was fat and missing teeth. He was uneducated. He was addicted to heroin. He killed people for a living. Yet the girls loved him.

"The American people, women especially, and I'm no different, we have this romance going with gangsters," said the former girlfriend. "Women fantasize about gangsters, men fantasize about being gangsters. It was part of the attraction. This bad boy!"

Was Ching's violent behavior not pause for concern?

"I knew he would never hurt me," the girlfriend said. "So the fact of what he did for a living, it had nothing to do with me."

Critical to this woman's romance with Ching, and to the couple's existence in general, was heroin. Both were addicts, though the girlfriend said Ching exaggerated when he claimed to spend one thousand dollars a day on the drug. Heroin was just not that expensive in Hawaii, owing to the state's proximity to opium-producing countries in Asia. To spend that much daily on heroin would mean Ching would be incapacitated day and night, week in and week out.

"He was a busy man. Yes, we were heroin addicts, but we were functioning addicts. We weren't just trying to nod off for the whole day," said the girlfriend. "You can't build a business or a reputation if you're on the nod 24/7."

Neither of the pair was faithful, not that they pretended to be. When this girlfriend informed Ching she was pregnant, the hit man was happy, but also dubious that he was the father. She didn't blame him.

As casual as the romance could be, there were still surprises, like when the girlfriend arrived home to find another woman in her own bed.

"I knew there were other women. I knew there were always going to be other women. That was part of who he was and what he did. Was I jealous of it? Absolutely. Did I live with it? Absolutely," admitted the girlfriend. "At that time I didn't have a lot of self-esteem . . . It was easy for me to accept whatever I could get."

While accepting of humiliation, the girlfriend would not stay under Ching's yoke. Yet attempts at independence became difficult when it came to their heroin supply, which Ching tried to control. Part of his motivation seemed to be his girlfriend's own protection.

Ronnie wanted to be my knight in shining armor. I can remember some people that were heavily into drugs and heroin specifically. Ronnie had gone to them and told them if they wanted to meet their maker sooner than they were supposed to they would continue selling me dope, which made it very difficult for me because he wanted to be my only source, so he could, so he could keep a handle on how much I was using.

Such tactics failed.

"I was a rebellious little bitch and I wasn't having it. I pretty much back then felt like Waikiki was mine," said the girlfriend. "We were gun toting, drug using, just running amok. You do what you gotta do to support your lifestyle."

Ching felt, too, that Waikiki belonged to him. He was such a comfortable criminal, in fact, that he befriended some of the local policemen who patrolled the nightlife district in plainclothes.

"Ronnie was a man about town," said his former girlfriend. "Ronnie didn't hide who he was or what he did. He was very out there in the public."

One of these police officers was Raymond Scanlan, who, despite Ching's well-known reputation, allowed the gangster to ride in his car. Together they cruised the streets of Waikiki, passing a revolver back and forth to shoot out streetlights. Once during their joyrides Ching said something insulting to the cop driving him around. Scanlan became irritated. In retaliation he took out his service revolver and pointed it in the direction of Ching, who was sitting in the passenger seat. Scanlan pulled the trigger, letting loose a deafening boom inside the cab of the car. A bullet flew inches in front of Ching's face and traveled out the passenger window, across the Ala Wai Canal, which runs along the northern edge of Waikiki and separates the entertainment district from other Honolulu neighborhoods. Supposedly after yelling at each other a bit, Ching and Scanlan laughed about the incident and remained friendly.

Years later, following Ching's release from the penitentiary in Lompoc, the hit man and cop became coworkers, though by this time Scanlan had left the police force. Like Ching, Scanlan was now a felon, having pleaded guilty to drug charges stemming from his arrest during a major heroin bust in Punchbowl Crater in September 1976. During that undercover operation police seized a pound of heroin, as well as a .22 caliber pistol and ten-inch silencer found in Scanlan's car. Scanlan admitted to negotiating the drug deal while he was a police officer, though he had resigned from the Honolulu Police Department a week before his arrest.

Ching and Scanlan were employees of the Hawaii Teamster Production Unit, working as drivers for movie and television productions on Oahu, including the television show *Magnum, P.I.* The job paid conspicuously high wages, with Ching earning thirteen hundred dollars a week. Also hired by the Teamster Production Unit was Naone, who by 1981 had finished serving his prison terms for robbery and the illegal purchase of ammunition. Hawaii Teamsters leader Art Rutledge defended the hiring of ex-cons for this work.

"As long as I'm around, I'll give any man a break. If you save one man, make a respectable citizen out of him, St. Peter will say you did a good job," said Rutledge. "If anybody doesn't like it, tough. A man is entitled to not be a menace to the public and the best way to do that is to give the guy a job."

Yet, whether Rutledge knew it or not, men like Ching and Naone intended to remain menaces to the public. The job provided by the Teamsters was essentially Naone's last in life, as he would later scrape by unemployed, sometimes mysteriously arriving home with bundles of cash that he stored in recesses in the bottom of the kitchen stove. Naone maxed out credit cards with no intention of paying his debts, tried for years to collect on a worker's compensation claim for a back injury that occurred on a construction site, and always attempted to collect favors he believed owed to him. Never, though, did Naone seem to contemplate an honest day's work as the way to boost his bank account.

"He felt like it was a sign of his intelligence to not work," said Naone's daughter Erica, explaining her father's thinking. "I'm a smart guy, why would I get a real job?"

Yet he was quite proud of his illegitimate occupation as a gangster. According to his lawyer and his daughter, Naone would often describe himself to others as a criminal, savoring the shock value. He took equal pleasure in the sometimes-sadistic treatment of his so-called friends, almost none of whom were tolerated by Naone for very long. His daughter Erica mentioned how he would have unsuspecting acquaintances walk the family's pet Tosa, or Japanese fighting dog, and watch with glee as the strong hundred-pound beast dragged the hapless leash holder across concrete.

Then there was the time when Naone thanked a handful of friends for helping him with some carpentry by taking them out to lunch. As the men finished the large meals, Naone decided to play a joke and ordered another round of food. Wary of upsetting Naone, the men stuffed themselves to finish the additional grub. One man became so full he began to vomit at the table and had to rush to the bathroom. But getting sick was better than getting Naone angry.

In the same vein, Naone would invite a friend to lift weights with him and then design a training session meant to exhaust his workout partner. As his guest struggled with a grueling routine, Naone would complete the same exercise with relative ease, casually smoking a cigarette between reps as to further establish his superiority.

"[As to] why he behaved in such a crazy way with me and our family and these friends of his and everything, I think some of it was posturing and the sense that it made him safer if he seemed very dangerous to everybody," said Erica Naone. "There was this paranoia that was part of it, because he wanted to establish that he was extremely dangerous and you shouldn't fuck with him."

Erica Naone said that although her father terrified her, she developed an emotional closeness to him and sought continually to please him. Her father had a sensitive side, she said, and engaged in artistic spurts during which he wrote poetry and painted feverishly. The masterpieces did not last for long. Any art he created on canvas, Naone's daughter said, was quickly covered over with white paint.

Yet Naone could not as easily whitewash his darker impulses and experiences. Erica Naone recalled her father being preoccupied with war movies. She later learned of his Army exploits in Vietnam, and how he claimed to have snuck into villages at night to kill people in their beds. Not content to just terrorize the enemy, Naone boasted of how he would humiliate fellow American soldiers he did not like, beating them with poles to emasculate them. Though Naone was always the victor in his stories, it seemed obvious to others that Vietnam had been traumatic for the man.

"He told me once that what he had done is come back [from Vietnam] and took that information and put it in a box in his head, and bur[ied] that box under the tallest, heaviest mountain and just [left] it there," said Erica, whose parents met when her father was a federal inmate in Colorado and her mother taught a class at the prison.

Perhaps just as formative and scarring an experience as Vietnam was federal prison. Though he found a wife while incarcerated, Naone did not want to return behind bars. When it came to the execution of his criminal deeds, he could be quite cautious, said Erica Naone, and never had an answering machine at home for fear that someone would record an incriminating message.

"He was definitely really scared of repercussions," said Erica Naone, who lived alone with her father for a few years following her parents' divorce, sometimes being forced to skip school to accompany her father on criminal errands.

In contrast to Naone, Ching was not quite as discreet. Since the gangster's release from prison in 1979, and during his employment with the Teamsters, the gangster acquired a substantial arsenal. He kept this weaponry in a storage closet outside his twelfth-floor Waikiki apartment, ostensibly so he could deny the guns were his in the event of a police raid. In February 1981 such a raid occurred, with federal agents discovering a trove of deadly devices, including ten handguns, a silencer, and a pen gun, which is a single-shot device meant to be pressed against a victim's head or heart. Inside Ching's apartment authorities discovered a box taped under the kitchen sink. It contained C-4 explosive. Authorities also found Thai stick marijuana and close to twenty-eight thousand dollars in cash.

Though it was a federal raid, Charles Marsland and Honolulu Police Chief Francis Keala were on the scene when Ching was arrested. Marsland was in the courtroom, too, six months later, when Ching was sentenced to twenty-one years in prison for firearms and narcotics offenses. Perhaps Marsland was repaying a favor. Three years earlier Ching had inexplicably appeared as a spectator in court as Marsland tried to convict Wilford "Nappy" Pulawa and other Syndicate members of kidnapping and murder. When asked about his presence at Ching's court hearing, Marsland had no comment.

Ching's lawyer, however, did have something to say. David Bettencourt complained to a federal judge that Marsland was pursuing a "vendetta" against his client because "Marsland believes Ron Ching murdered his son."

"Marsland has been after him for years. Everybody in town knows it," said Bettencourt. "He will stop at nothing to get at my client."

CHAPTER FOUR

Enemies in Common

The woman awoke to the pressure of a pistol being jammed against her neck. This was no dream. That much was clear from the discomfort of having a cold steel gun barrel jabbed into her throat. It was after midnight on February 26, 1979, and the thirty-three-year-old was supposed to be alone in her Honolulu apartment.

She screamed and struggled, briefly grabbing the barrel of the gun, which was unusually smooth and wide, at least an inch in diameter. The gunman overpowered the hundred-pound woman and placed a pillow over her head to muffle her shouts. Soon the terrified woman stopped screaming and started praying. She prayed out loud, through the pillow, not for herself, but for her attacker. She prayed for this man as he sodomized and raped her. He told her to shut up.

The man explained to his victim how he had let himself into the woman's apartment by using a key. Though the man was a stranger, his voice, as well as the distinct way he pronounced her name, was familiar to the woman. He sounded a lot like the man who had called her apartment a few times in the last month asking very personal questions. She had no idea who he was, but his face was now unforgettable. Despite the darkness of her bedroom and the pillow that kept being put over her face, the woman had gained a clear view of her attacker, if only through glimpses. She said as much to him when he removed the pillow, unbelievably suggesting to the intruder that he ought to shoot her because otherwise she would identify him in court.

The gunman agreed—he ought to shoot her. When he finished raping the woman, he flipped her on her stomach. Don't move for ten minutes, he said. Before that time period elapsed, the woman felt heavy blows to her head. She surmised she had been beaten with the butt of the gun. In actuality she had been shot. Her confusion may be attributed to the fact that three bullets now sat in her skull. Or perhaps she was confused because the gun had not made any sound when it was fired, not for the woman to hear, nor her neighbors down the hall. The woman's assailant had attached a silencer to the barrel of his .22 caliber pistol, and this was the smooth, thick cylinder the woman had grasped earlier in the attack. After being shot in the head, the woman's world went black.

Hours later she awoke. She was alone now, but in desperate need of help. Despite the gunshot wounds in her head, which were still not apparent to her, she put on shorts, crawled down the hallway, and roused her neighbors. She was taken to a hospital, where she stabilized. It was only when the doctors took X-rays that the woman learned she had been shot, not pistol-whipped, and that fragmented bullets were lodged in her skull. Miraculously she had survived three shots to the head at point-blank range, including two shots to the base of her skull and a third behind her left ear.

The Honolulu Police Department quickly identified a suspect in the rape and attempted murder, Vernon Reiger Sr. A well-known member of the Hawaiian underworld and alleged hit man for Wilford "Nappy" Pulawa, Reiger was already the prime suspect in a year-old incident that bore many similarities to this recent attack. In the year-old case, a twenty-five-year-old woman who lived in the same apartment building had also been shot in the head with a silenced .22 caliber pistol. Unfortunately she had not survived.

Upon investigation of the latest incident, the police found more clues to Reiger's possible involvement. Neighbors had seen Reiger at the McCully Villa apartment building many times in the last few weeks, including late at night on the seventh floor, where the rape and shooting victim lived. Reiger, who lived elsewhere in Honolulu, was spotted at the McCully Villa as recently as the day before the attack.

Reiger's face was not a difficult one to remember. He had a hard and memorable countenance, with intensity about his eyes. Former deputy prosecutor Peter Carlisle went so far as to describe him as "spooky" and "Satanic-looking." From her hospital bed the attack victim was able to identify Reiger from a photo lineup. Weeks later she identified him in person from a lineup at the police station, which prompted Reiger's arrest on charges of attempted murder, rape, sodomy, and burglary. He denied attacking the woman or entering her apartment, and Reiger's wife and son claimed he was home the night of the attack.

The case fell to Charles Marsland. He had now been a deputy prosecutor in Honolulu for three years, encountering all types of indecency in his job, from petty theft to grisly murders. Marsland successfully prosecuted the first murder-for-hire case in Hawaii, and, in another notable trial, he persuaded a jury to convict a man who, after stabbing his roommate to death, removed the man's heart and deposited it in a trash can. Such experience and success helped earn him a promotion in late 1978 to become the director of the Career Criminal Unit in the Honolulu prosecutor's office. Charged with focusing on repeat criminal offenders in Hawaii, Career Criminal Units across the Hawaiian Islands had a standing policy to push for the revocation of bail, to refuse plea deals, and to insist on maximum punishment when prosecuting cases. In short, they were supposed to get tough on crime.

Marsland dutifully followed such protocol. In this most recent case, Marsland asked during pretrial hearings that Reiger's $130,000 bail be revoked in light of Marsland's discovery of unusual, and potentially fraudulent, property transfers used to satisfy the bond and spring Reiger from jail. To Marsland's chagrin the judge denied the request. This refusal did not endear Judge Edwin Honda to Marsland, and it was only the beginning of their troubles.

While Reiger was out on bail, his alleged victim was temporarily placed within a witness protection program. Honolulu police told her there was talk on the streets of a hundred thousand dollar contract for her murder, as well as threats made against other witnesses. For months she was kept under close guard and regularly moved between hotel rooms. Always, she said, the drapes in these rooms were drawn closed.

"I could not sit close to any window and there were always two or three police officers with me twenty-four hours a day," she later recalled. "It was not a normal life."

Compounding her ordeal was her slow-going physical and mental recovery. Though she had escaped the incident with her life, the woman suffered tremendously from Reiger's alleged attack. Her brain was damaged. Her hearing and peripheral vision were impaired. She experienced vertigo. Her coordination became clumsy, causing her to take twice as long to accomplish basic tasks.

The emotional trauma was just as severe. Not only forced to adapt to a more limited existence, the woman chose to forgo much sympathy, refusing to disclose to strangers the reason for her handicaps.

"I know that there are a lot of things I used to do that I can't do now," she said. "It's something I have to live with and I have to deal with. I will not tell anybody about it."

Nightmares were common. Fear invaded her waking hours, too, even after she left police protection and resumed a seminormal life. The woman could not, for example, enjoy most sports, as she was afraid of an errant tennis ball or poorly thrown Frisbee.

"I have to protect my head," she said. "I will not let any kind of flying object get close to my head."

The woman's stoicism and resilience inspired great affection in Marsland. He admired the petite woman for withstanding such a brutal attack and credited her spirituality for saving her life. Marsland went so far as to suggest that a higher power had intervened to save the rape victim. He noted how unlikely it was that none of the bullets fired by Reiger traveled cleanly through the woman's head—a circumstance that would have certainly resulted in her death.

"When somebody steps up and puts three bullets in the back of your head, unnecessarily, and every one of those bullets fragments! Now there's something there that . . . you know, even one bullet fragmenting is pretty unusual, but when three . . ." said Marsland, trailing off. "She had two of them right at the base of her skull. Two shots were placed there, and the third, the coup de grace, was right behind the left ear. And, hey, she did live, she did identify the man."

For as much affection as Marsland felt for the victim, the crime engendered an equal amount of rage toward the perpetrator.

"I look at the Reiger case and what happened to the kid who was the victim in that, and it still drives me up a wall," said Marsland.

Such passion served the prosecutor well when Reiger's trial began in June 1979. Heavy security was in place at the courthouse on account of Reiger's connections to the local underworld and the threats made against the shooting victim and witnesses. Police swept the courthouse for bombs, frisked anyone who entered the building, and posted patrolmen in plainclothes inside and outside the courtroom. Marsland wasted no time in leveling the state's accusations against the defendant, detailing Reiger's alleged crimes to the jury in his opening statement and casting Reiger as the author of this "gross and ugly" tale. In his own statement Reiger's attorney countered that his client was unfairly targeted as the culprit by biased police investigators.

Next Marsland called the prosecution's witnesses, which included Shannon Scott, Reiger's former girlfriend. Scott had been romantic with Reiger intermittently over the course of five years, even believing they were married. The pair had exchanged vows and rings in November 1973 during an unofficial ceremony at their home, when Scott was eighteen years old. Two years later Scott discovered Reiger was married to another woman.

That duplicity wasn't the only obstacle to their happiness. Scott said Reiger beat her, demanded to have sex, and "wouldn't take no for an answer." As further leverage in their relationship, Reiger paid Scott's rent and car expenses.

Scott's testimony not only painted Reiger as an abusive, albeit financially responsible, boyfriend, but also implicated him in the rape and shooting that occurred in the McCully Villa apartments. Scott testified that she had lived in the victim's seventh-floor apartment for nearly a year, moving out just before the rape and shooting victim replaced her as a tenant. When she lived there, Scott testified, Reiger surprised her one day by suddenly appearing in the apartment, even though they had broken up. Reiger told Scott he could open any lock within the building, likely due to the possession of a master key.

What's more, in February 1979, a month after Scott had moved out of the apartment, Reiger accosted his ex-girlfriend and demanded that they have sex. He suggested they head to her old apartment at the McCully Villa. He still had a key, he explained, and he knew the apartment would be vacant since he had studied the work habits of the new tenant.

When Scott refused to join him, Reiger punched her and threatened to "take care of" her new "punk" boyfriend. He also threatened to kill her if she left him. In response Scott tried to commit suicide. When that didn't work, she fled to the mainland to escape Reiger.

A week after Scott's swift departure, the new apartment tenant was raped and shot three times in the head. The tenant had changed the apartment's locks, but her assailant still was able to gain entrance. The police surmised that the attacker must have had a master key. In further testimony that Reiger's own attorney deemed "devastating," Scott told the jury how Reiger kept an arsenal at Scott's home that included two rifles, two handguns, and a silencer.

Beyond this testimony the jury had physical evidence to consider, namely semen recovered from the attack. This semen was somewhat distinct in that it contained no sperm, leading Reiger's defense attorney to label it the "immaculate ejaculate." And because this semen contained no sperm, said the same attorney, it could not have come from his client. Although Reiger had previously undergone a vasectomy, a urologist called by the defense explained, the surgery had later been reversed, meaning sperm should again be present in his semen.

A different urologist called by the prosecution, however, said Reiger's sperm count was so small—120 times below the lower limit of a normal sperm count—that it seemed evident the corrective surgery had failed. According to this doctor the spermless semen, or immaculate ejaculate, could have indeed come from Reiger.

Such discrepancy made for heated questioning of the expert witnesses. As Marsland cross-examined the urologist called by the defense, his voice kept rising, prompting Judge Honda to repeatedly ask the prosecutor to lower his tone. Even at lower decibels, the questioning was intense, with Marsland unable to conceal his contempt for the witness. At one point Marsland asked the urologist if his testimony was influenced by his friendship with Reiger's defense attorney and the fact that their offices were contained in the same building.

"Are you saying I lie?" asked the urologist.

"No," Marsland shot back, "but I suggest you don't know what you are talking about."

After nearly two weeks the trial concluded with closing statements. Reiger's attorney asked the jury to keep in mind the alibi witnesses of Reiger's son and wife. Marsland gave an impassioned speech, arguing the attack served as a message from Reiger to his ex-girlfriend Scott, who had just fled the state.

"That message was, 'You're dead,'" said Marsland. "'When I find you, you too will be defiled and despoiled in the most contemptuous way, and this victim is the symbol of you.'"

Marsland's argument was convincing. Beyond the witness testimony and physical evidence, the prosecution's case benefited from the gravitas imparted by Marsland's handsome physical attributes and forceful delivery. Marsland's tall stature, blue eyes, mature head of silver hair, neat moustache, and impassioned speech communicated a certain self-assurance to his audience. In behavior and appearance Marsland looked every part the lawman. As one description of him went: "Marsland's a colorful figure. He looks like a riverboat gambler, talks tough like Clint Eastwood, and carries himself like the sheriff of Dodge City, walking down Main Street at high noon. If it's an act, it is one that has been honed over many years."

Finishing his closing statement, Marsland's confidence did not waver. He proclaimed to the jury that Reiger was undoubtedly guilty of "a cold-blooded attempt at execution . . . a gangland execution . . . an assassination." The jury agreed with the prosecutor. Within five hours of receiving the case, they returned a verdict finding Reiger guilty on all counts.

Any elation Marsland felt over the conviction was short-lived. Upon hearing the verdict, the prosecutor immediately asked Honda to revoke or significantly increase Reiger's bail, reminding the judge that beyond Reiger posing a threat to the public as a convicted attempted murderer and rapist, a number of threats had been made to assorted witnesses at the trial. Honda denied Marsland, saying the prosecutor would have to make a change in bail request in writing. Meanwhile Reiger could remain free until his sentencing hearing, scheduled more than forty-five days later.

Marsland fumed over Honda's decision, upset that protocol would prevent a dangerous convict from being jailed until his prison sentence was determined. Other judges did not require written requests for bail revocation, and Marsland found it difficult to understand why Honda would prioritize such protocol over public safety. Honda was a respected judge and, like Marsland, a veteran of World War II, having fought in the 522nd Field Artillery Battalion of the famous 442nd Regimental Combat Team. The infantry regiment, which consisted almost entirely of Americans of Japanese descent, fought with such distinction in Europe, and suffered such heavy casualties, that it became one of the most decorated regiments in the US military, never mind the fact that these soldiers fought for a country that meanwhile placed their families in internment camps. Among other feats, Honda's field artillery battalion helped liberate the Dachau concentration camp in Germany.

Back home in Hawaii after the war, Honda was a stickler, having little tolerance for lawyers who did not abide by the rules. Accordingly, the next day prosecutors formally submitted to Judge Honda a written request to change Reiger's bail. Marsland, however, was not content to let that suffice. Circumventing Honda, Marsland convened with federal prosecutors on Oahu and asked them to seek an order from a federal judge to arrest Reiger for violating his probation for a federal tax evasion conviction he had received two years earlier. The federal order was granted, and, a week later, US marshals arrested Reiger as he arrived at the Honolulu courthouse for the bail hearing that Honda had eventually scheduled at the behest of the prosecutor's office's written request.

The arrest, and a federal judge's subsequent jailing of Reiger, embarrassed Honda, whom Marsland had publicly criticized for "bad judgment" and "ridiculous" legal reasoning. Honda was stunned that federal authorities thwarted the bail hearing he had scheduled, especially since he may have been on the verge of revoking Reiger's bail himself. Marsland, meanwhile, never one to let a perceived slight go unreturned, reveled in the victory, though he was careful not to publicly claim credit for Reiger's jailing.

"I'm just happy with the way it turned out," said Marsland. "As long as they got him off the street, I don't care who does it."

Marsland had more than the public's interest at heart in arranging for the jailing of Reiger; he had concern for his own safety, too. In the middle of the trial he had returned home from a bicycle ride one night and noticed a car parked up the street from his home. The rear of the car bore two conspicuous spots of paint primer, just like the car Marsland had seen Reiger driving near the courthouse. Marsland approached the vehicle, but it quickly sped away, its headlights off and the driver unrecognizable in the darkness.

"I don't even know if it was [Reiger]," said Marsland. "It could have been any part of his family or friends or whatever. Maybe they were trying to leave a message. But I quit riding my bike around late at night."

After this incident the prosecutor received round-the-clock police protection, with officers staying at his home overnight and accompanying him during the day to the extent that Marsland remarked he "couldn't even go to the bathroom without one of them beside me."

In the months to come, as Reiger's sentencing hearing approached, tensions had not eased between Marsland and Honda, partially because the judge began to hold separate court hearings to determine if Marsland should be held in contempt of court for his pretrial investigations into suspicious property transfers used to secure Reiger's bail. Honda's patience grew short during these hearings, and he advised prosecutors and Reiger's defense attorney that they would be fined for causing anything more than a thirty-second delay in his courtroom. Ultimately Honda dismissed the contempt charges against Marsland, though he deemed the prosecutor's tactics "questionable." Marsland countered that the judge was "asinine."

At Reiger's initial sentencing hearing, Honda and Marsland again butted heads. Marsland insisted to Honda that Reiger deserved a life sentence not only for his most recent crime but also for a lifetime of criminality that included robbery and tax evasion convictions, connections to organized crime, and being a suspect in at least three murders. The alternative, a maximum twenty-year sentence, was insufficient, Marsland said.

Honda was not sympathetic to Marsland's plea. Echoing their earlier confrontation over the written request for the change in bail, Honda scolded Marsland for not providing sufficient proof of the claims he made verbally in court.

"You drop something on the court's lap without supporting evidence or law," said Honda.

Annoyed with Marsland, Honda deferred Reiger's sentencing to another date. Next time, he told the prosecutor, "I want you to be totally prepared."

But there would be no next time. A month later Marsland was no longer a prosecutor. He had been fired.

———

In the late 1970s few thought Honolulu could afford to shed its prosecutors. To many residents crime was out of control in Hawaii. Unlike what was filmed in Hawaii for television shows like *Hawaii Five-O*, most island lawbreaking was either too ordinary, or too brutal, to be of much amusement. Instead such crime provoked a range of negative emotions in the populace, especially those who paid attention to the local newspapers or had the misfortune of knowing, or being, a victim. Juvenile crime was disheartening. Theft and robbery were aggravating. Rape and murder were upsetting, even bone-chilling, given the cruelty with which some attacks and killings were committed. Altogether, crime of every variety became exasperating to the point where a number of citizens were motivated to confront the problem.

A journalist in Honolulu described this anticrime feeling as a massive wave rolling across the ocean, slowly "gathering force" and poised to "crash ashore." It was imagery most appropriate for surf-crazy Hawaii, especially for the crowd of two hundred people gathered at the seaside Outrigger Canoe Club on July 23, 1979, watching waves break off the shore of nearby Waikiki Beach while listening to a slate of speakers. The well-heeled crowd had gathered at the private club to voice their shared frustration over crime on Oahu, bemoaning the frequent rapes, beatings, burglaries, and general lawlessness that flew in the face of aloha spirit and seemed to be overtaking the otherwise tranquil island. There's a problem, they said, when residents can't safely walk on Oahu's beaches, take a nighttime stroll down Kalākaua Avenue along Waikiki Beach, or even relax within their own homes.

The residents heard from Honolulu Mayor Frank Fasi, who called for stricter laws and tougher punishment of juvenile offenders. They heard from a police officer who drew applause when he suggested they "lock 'em up and throw away the key." They heard from a rape victim who described how her perpetrator escaped punishment for violating her and then raped another woman. And they heard from Honolulu deputy prosecutor Marsland, who told them compassion for criminals is nothing but "bullshit."

"You're faced with who's going to run this city, punks or people," Marsland told the cheering crowd. "It's your island, your government. I suggest you take it back."

The Hawaiian crime statistics circa 1980 were sobering. On average a violent crime occurred in Hawaii every three and a half hours. A property crime occurred every eight minutes. And perhaps most bothersome, for every hundred persons in Hawaii arrested for a felony, eighty-six were soon released by police and never tried in court. Of the remaining fourteen people, only three received a conviction and prison sentence. In 1980 the state's murder count spiked to eighty-four victims, the highest yearly total on record. Sixty-five of those murders occurred on Oahu, and 1980 was also a banner year for other crimes, such as rape, assault, and robbery. Though Mayor Fasi said many of these crime statistics were comparable to other major American cities, most residents felt there was room for improvement.

As an editorial in the *Honolulu Star-Bulletin* put it a year later: "We are a community very much on edge about crime."

Or, as Marsland said quite plainly, "The criminal justice system is a joke."

Not only was there too much crime, Marsland argued, there was insufficient justice. And the perpetrators of injustice in Hawaii, at least in Marsland's eyes, were manifold. State legislators refused to tighten laws and stiffen punishments. Other local and state government leaders preferred maintaining cozy relationships with supporters than good public policy.

Too often, he felt, justice was forfeited because of incompetence, cronyism, or outright corruption. Crime victims received little sympathy from the public and court system alike. Hawaii was indeed paradise, felt Marsland, but for criminals.

"Everything right now is geared for the protection of the defendant," Marsland later complained. "Screw the victim and screw the general public—that's what it comes down to."

Worst of all, he said, were the local judges. For Marsland's tastes bail was too often set too low. It could be nearly impossible, he said, to obtain prison sentences for convicted burglars and auto thieves. A general sense of leniency permeated the judicial system, to the point that Marsland suggested taking bail and sentencing powers away from judges in order to eliminate "intercession by do-gooders and politicians." It was time, Marsland said, to "turn the spotlight of publicity on the judiciary" and "demand that justice be swift, certain, predictable and tough."

The frustrations Marsland had encountered a few weeks earlier in Judge Honda's courtroom were consistent with those he had experienced throughout the Hawaiian legal system and government. Beyond the courts, even the prosecutor's office in which Marsland worked suffered from a lack of integrity, at least from his perspective. So when his boss, the city prosecutor Togo Nakagawa, asked him for a report in 1979 on the performance of the newly created Career Criminal Unit, which Marsland led, the frustrated veteran prosecutor delivered a polemic that would lead to his termination.

To begin with Marsland complained that the Career Criminal Unit was overworked, overwhelmed with cases, and constantly belittled despite its success. Since its creation nine months earlier, Marsland wrote in his report, the unit had not lost a trial.

Yet "there had been no single word of encouragement to any member of the unit since its inception—not a word of congratulation or compliment for any of the cases tried and won—no acknowledgement (other than sarcasm) of the expenditures of countless hours by (attorneys) with no compensatory time off," wrote Marsland. "Rather there has been a continuing stream of criticism directed against certain members of the unit, suggesting they are 'screwing off' and doing less."

Marsland proposed that the unit's mission be modified. Instead of focusing on repeat criminal offenders, he felt the unit should concentrate on violent criminals alone. He also wanted the unit to have more autonomy from the top brass, which would include the unit controlling its own budgeting and hiring. As it stood, morale among the prosecutors was a "very fragile asset," and the Career Criminal Unit operated "without a shred of independent authority."

"The front office treats the staff like high school kids, making them sign in and sign out of the office, even on coffee breaks," said Marsland. "There are deputies who work incredible hours without a single penny of extra pay, yet if they take an hour off to go to the dentist they are docked."

Later Marsland would say, "The only thing you don't sign out for is to go to the john. And they probably have that by now."

More damning was Marsland's accusation that Nakagawa and other top administrators in the prosecutor's office were overly chummy with defense lawyers. Their relationships were so casual, in fact, that Nakagawa allegedly handed over entire case files to defense lawyers whose clients were being prosecuted by the office. While the legal system requires prosecutors to share evidence and other information with defense counsel prior to a trial, and vice versa, certain materials are exempt and can be withheld. Though Nakagawa denied this, Marsland claimed defense counsel were given memos detailing the prosecution's trial strategy as well as the names and addresses of witnesses who might be subject to intimidation or threats from accused violent criminals.

The office was so porous, said Marsland, that deputy prosecutors took to hiding case files from Nakagawa and other managers for fear they'd be too freely distributed. In one case involving a robbery and murder, a defense lawyer who was particularly friendly with the bosses didn't bother to ask Marsland for any discovery material. The only explanation Marsland could think of was that his superiors had already granted the lawyer full access to the files. Such seeming betrayals rankled the lawyers within the Career Criminal Unit, who Marsland said routinely worked seventy-hour weeks.

"Deputies are used to working long and thankless hours. That's part of the job and you accept it," said Marsland. "But when you feel your efforts are being undermined by your bosses, that's hard to swallow."

Because someone leaked this report to the local newspapers, many, many more people read this criticism than just Nakagawa. Given the widespread attention, the city prosecutor publicly responded to his underling's report. Nakagawa attempted to downplay Marsland's comments as "normal differences that you find in any office," but also made sure to return the criticism.

Marsland, he said, was "trying to be overly selective about the cases the unit handles. He fails to understand that the objectives of a career criminal program are to concentrate on getting as many repeat offenders as possible off the street. Instead, he prefers to go after the glamour cases, the cases that will generate headlines."

Plus, Nakagawa said, "He seems to have lost sight of the fact that I'm still the boss."

It was not long before Nakagawa asked Marsland to resign. When Marsland refused, he was fired. Nakagawa allegedly told Marsland "he couldn't have anybody in the office bucking him." Marsland, who denied leaking the report to the press, called his former boss, who had also fought in World War II as a member of the highly decorated 442nd Regimental Combat Team, a "paranoid little man."

Following Marsland's firing, deputy prosecutor Carlisle took over the Reiger case and eventually attended the sentencing hearing Judge Honda had deferred after scolding Marsland for being unprepared. Just like his former boss Marsland had done, Carlisle argued that Reiger deserved life imprisonment for his extensive criminality and the vicious attack. He thought the facts of the case were ample proof that Reiger was a menace to society.

"The arguments from a prosecutor's standpoint were just overwhelming," said Carlisle. "He's abused his girlfriend, he's got a gun with a silencer which is the trademark of [the] mob . . . this is an attempted execution of a completely innocent woman who's miraculously survived, and if he had succeeded in killing her we would never have solved this case."

Judge Honda, however, was not persuaded, claiming that although Reiger's crimes were "brutal, senseless and cruel," he was "troubled by the quality of evidence" the prosecution cited to link Reiger to the Hawaiian Syndicate. Honda said, too, there were "serious questions" still to be answered about whether Reiger's "criminality is so extensive" that he must spend the rest of his life behind bars.

To Carlisle's dismay Honda gave Reiger a twenty-year sentence.

"When he did that there was a gasp in the courtroom. There was a gasp from the media, there was a gasp from the observers, there was a gasp from everybody. They could not believe this guy was not getting a life sentence," said Carlisle. "It was an exceptionally poor exercise of discretion and judgment."

For Marsland, Reiger's twenty-year sentence affirmed his conviction that Hawaii's criminal justice system had fundamental problems. Though no longer a prosecutor, he attended Reiger's sentencing hearing and became visibly angry when Honda rejected a life term for the criminal. Marsland deemed the punishment "the most gutless ruling by a member of the judiciary that I have ever seen."

Marsland was further dismayed when, two months later, his former colleagues in the prosecutor's office agreed to a plea deal that gave confessed criminal Rodney Kiyota a maximum ten-year sentence for raping a college student and for raping and killing a twelve-year-old girl. This deal, said Marsland, was "the final straw." If assorted judges and city prosecutor Nakagawa, Marsland's former boss, did not share Marsland's low opinion of Hawaii's criminal justice system, so be it. By this point Marsland had pivoted to address a new audience with his appeals to overhaul Hawaii's legal system and to get tough on crime. As evidenced by his speech to the crowd at the Outrigger Canoe Club, Marsland began to take his case directly to the public.

Despite the seemingly spontaneous straight talk and raw anger on display before these crowds, Marsland's actions were not without calculation. He knew that Honolulu had recently changed its laws regarding the appointment of the city prosecutor and that in 1980, for the first time in modern history, the city and county prosecutor of Honolulu would not be appointed by the mayor but elected directly by voters. That Marsland had been fired from a job he loved was of little consequence. He planned to be back in the Honolulu's prosecutor's office soon enough, though not as a deputy, but as the head city prosecutor. Then he could begin his own bare-knuckled fight against crime, everyone else be damned.

⌒

No matter the turmoil Marsland endured, or perhaps created, in the prosecutor's office and courtroom, there was always one refuge available to him: the national cemetery within Punchbowl Crater. Marsland visited almost every day, crossing the crater to visit Chuckers's grave within Section T, at Site 140. Though cemetery rules forbade it, Marsland sometimes brought a few tools to tidy up Chuckers's grave, supplementing the cemetery's landscaping work by snipping back grass encroaching on the stone marker. Marsland had a permanent vase installed beside the marker, too, to accommodate some of the fresh flowers he brought his son. Marsland was observed spending a lot of time arranging flowers for Chuckers. Should cemetery workers remove the flowers to mow the lawn in Section T, Marsland made sure they relaid the flowers carefully, as he had left them. If the workers failed to do so, Marsland would march to the administrator's office and politely lodge a complaint.

Marsland was certainly not the only regular visitor to the cemetery. Some family members of the deceased would bring beach chairs when visiting their loved ones, sitting graveside for hours. Yet it's unlikely there were many other people who visited as regularly as he did.

Looking around the cemetery, it might have seemed to contain a remarkable number of graves given that it was only thirty years old. More than thirteen thousand soldiers who died in World War II were buried within the first year the National Memorial Cemetery of the Pacific was created. Among them was Ernie Pyle, a World War I veteran and famous Pulitzer Prize-winning World War II correspondent for the Scripps-Howard newspaper chain. The forty-five-year-old Pyle was killed by a machine gunner on the small Japanese island of Ie Shima [also known as Iejima], near Okinawa, on April 18, 1945. Revered for reporting from the perspective of the common soldier, Pyle had written two months before his death about his distaste for the subject he covered.

"Anybody who has been in war and wants to go back is a plain damn fool in my book," he wrote. "I'm going simply because I've got to, and I hate it."

Pyle was one of five servicemen buried during the public opening of the cemetery in July 1949. In the six months prior, a massive construction project in Punchbowl Crater had already buried nearly twelve thousand servicemen killed in the war. The bodies of the soldiers had been stored for years since the war ended in mausoleum warehouses in Hawaii and Guam.

In August 1948 the crater began to be graded by earth-moving equipment. By January 1949 burials began, out of public sight, with crews interring as many as 216 soldiers a day. A three-day cycle was established for the mass burials.

After two days of preparation, trucks—carrying eighteen caskets apiece—left a warehouse at six thirty in the morning under military escort, chugging up Puowaina Drive to reach the cemetery. Less than three hours later, all the caskets had been set by crane beside long trenches dug into the crater, their placement noted on a master list. Plastic-bagged flags were placed atop each casket, and then all construction work was called to a halt. One casket, chosen randomly, was then used for a general burial service. A military honor guard held a flag taut above the casket. Protestant, Catholic, and Jewish clergymen then read their respective burial services, three rifle shots were fired, and a bugler played taps. The taut flag was refolded and presented to another officer, and the rest of the flags also were collected for delivery to next of kin. Then a crane began lifting the caskets into the trenches, one at a time, while a bulldozer covered them with soil. The next day the cycle began anew, continuing for months until the stock of dead soldiers in military warehouses was exhausted, the soldiers all given permanent burials.

Standing in the cemetery in Punchbowl Crater in the late 1970s, it would have been hard to imagine such a construction site. The landscape now was peaceful and manicured, filled with flowering trees and bushes and singing birds. It was an exceedingly calm setting, and in 1979 Marsland used the cemetery to meet with at least two men he thought might help advance his agenda.

The first was Raymond Scanlan, the former Honolulu police officer who had been arrested three years earlier in Punchbowl Crater during a heroin bust. He returned to the scene of that crime to meet Marsland and disclose the names of the three men who supposedly killed Marsland's son. Marsland had communicated frequently with Scanlan since Chuckers was killed, speaking on the phone, meeting in Marsland's office, and even enjoying dinner together. Marsland was obviously very interested in the information Scanlan had to share. Whether he wholly believed what the corrupt ex-cop had to say was another matter.

The other man Marsland met by Chuckers's grave could not shed light on the past, but promised instead to better Marsland's political future. To unseat his former boss and win the election to become Honolulu's prosecutor, Marsland needed an effective campaign. That's where he thought Rick Reed could help.

Marsland was familiar with the reports Reed published in his newspaper, the *Valley Isle,* concerning organized crime in Hawaii. One day, Reed says, he received a call from the former prosecutor.

"You don't know me. My name is Chuck Marsland," said the voice on the other end of the line. "We have enemies in common."

Soon enough they arranged for one of their first meetings-beside Chuckers's grave. Face-to-face, Marsland stood an inch or two taller than Reed, who himself was over six feet tall. Reed noticed Marsland was conspicuously trim and fit, especially for an older man. He seemed to have a discipline about him, perhaps owing to his military experience. Marsland also spoke with intensity.

"Obviously a guy with a mission kind of thing. He had a bearing that reminded me a bit of Wyatt Earp," said Reed, referencing the legendary lawman of the Old West. "[He had this], 'Don't fuck with me,' gunslinger kind of vibe about him."

Standing above his son's grave, Marsland told Reed about the murder of Chuckers and how, due to the lack of any arrests for the shooting, he had conducted his own investigation of the crime, which included stalking the streets of Waikiki with a gun beneath his coat. Marsland told Reed he had learned who was responsible for killing his son. He knew who shot Chuckers in the head and chest. He knew who drove the car that carried Chuckers to his death.

Marsland told Reed of his experiences as a prosecutor, of his firing, and of his intention to supplant his former boss through a run for the office of the prosecuting attorney for the City and County of Honolulu. Marsland wanted to restore law and order to the islands, and he said he could use Reed's help.

Reed was puzzled. "Why me?" he asked.

"I'm a fan of yours. I'm a fan of your newspaper. We have enemies in common and you're not afraid," Marsland told Reed. "I need somebody who can write and who can do what you do."

The offer was tempting, especially since Reed no longer published a newspaper. In late 1978, under mounting legal problems, Reed shuttered the *Valley Isle*. In its final months he reported extensively on the underworld, including publishing the research of the Hawaiian Crime Commission. Now Marsland was offering him an opportunity to continue the fight. Finally Reed had an ally in not only wanting to expose the Hawaiian underworld, but eliminate it. Reed accepted Marsland's offer.

"To me it was a really compelling story and mission. I've always been a bit of a crusader. I'm not ambitious in the way that is common. I've never cared about making money. When I was younger I was intent on saving the world and that kind of moved into saving myself, trying to achieve self-enlightenment," said Reed, who has practiced meditation daily since his twenties. "Other things are important to me that aren't to a lot of people. So the idea of helping this guy that I felt a bond with, that I liked . . . a lot, was appealing enough to me that I decided to move to Oahu."

No matter Reed's enthusiasm, the campaign job came with challenges. First of all, when it came to public commentary, it was apparent that Marsland could be a loose cannon. Reed recalls that other campaign workers were leery of a man being sued for libel being put in charge of campaign communications. In truth, Reed said, it was Marsland who was reckless with his words and more likely to broadcast an impolitic message.

> You had to watch him because he'd say whatever he thought. He was completely apolitical and non-diplomatic. Didn't give a shit. Didn't seem to care who he offended. Niceties put him off. And so as incomprehensible as it would have been to my critics, my role and my relationship with him was to control him and try to put into palatable language what he wanted to say.

It didn't help that Marsland was fond of using off-color language better suited to his Navy days. Reed was no prude, and admits to using strong language himself, some of which he no doubt heard in the locker room of Washington State University, where he played football. But even the allegedly libelous Reed said he recognized limits in certain social situations. Marsland did not. Among the expressions that made Reed cringe were Marsland's instructions for people to take a hold of his genitals while he shook about.

"Like, 'Hey, you asshole, grab my cock and I'll jump up and down,'" Reed recalled Marsland saying, more or less, when his boss was angry at someone.

Fortunately Marsland possessed enough self-control to refrain from saying things quite that crude on the campaign trail. But his confrontational style, brash delivery, and strong opinions regarding Hawaii's criminal justice problems could only be tempered so much. There was little to do but embrace Marsland's forceful persona and leverage this distinction to his advantage. Reed was then confronted with the other significant challenge of the campaign: convincing Honolulu residents that not only was there a significant crime problem in Hawaii, but that Charles Marsland was the right man to fix it.

Reed ran advertisements and sent out mailings that contained alarming crime statistics. "Every five days, one of us is murdered. Every day, at least one of us is raped . . .," said one brochure. The campaign literature touted Marsland's extensive experience as a prosecutor in Massachusetts and Hawaii and listed some of his more prominent convictions of notorious Hawaiian criminals. Careful not to portray him as a one-dimensional crime fighter, one brochure showed a picture of Marsland sitting on the beach beside his pet poodle. In the photo, Marsland is relaxed, sporting stylish Adidas sneakers, a Puka shell necklace, and an aloha shirt unbuttoned halfway down his chest. The literature mentioned briefly, too, Marsland's personal loss and how he was familiar with the plight of crime victims. In short, there was no candidate better suited to be Honolulu's prosecutor.

"Once in a great while, a public office and a candidate match perfectly," said the campaign. "Such is the case with the Office of Prosecuting Attorney and Chuck Marsland."

In public appearances Marsland said he was in favor of a "bare-knuckled" approach to fighting crime, favoring the reinstitution of capital punishment and severely reduced plea-bargaining. The reduction of violent crime and organized crime would be his top priorities, though he also said juvenile offenders ought to be treated more severely, too. In one public appearance, he likened some juvenile delinquents to animals who "swing down from a low branch for breakfast."

Too often, said Marsland, the courts are concerned with protecting the rights of killers and rapists. "Perhaps," he said, "our concentration really should be on protecting the general public."

Some residents of Hawaii were offended by these remarks and Marsland's get-tough-on-crime policy suggestions. Others in Hawaii found Marsland's brand of justice sorely needed, and agreed with campaign literature that claimed "what was once the Paradise of the Pacific is now a jungle prowled by thieves, pimps, prostitutes, robbers, rapists and murderers." Though some residents found it easy to characterize the candidate as focused almost entirely on the violent crime generated by Hawaii's underworld, Marsland was expansive in his ideas to transform the prosecutor's office. He proposed establishing a research and legislative bureau within the office, improving services to crime victims, and better accommodating witnesses to crimes, even suggesting that the prosecutor's office help arrange childcare for witnesses due in court. Additionally he suggested making the prosecutor's office a nonpartisan elected position.

Marsland claimed that if it were up to him, he would have run to become prosecutor without a party affiliation. Just before a filing deadline, though, he chose to run as a Republican. It was a strategic decision, as this affiliation decision enabled him to avoid a crowded Democratic primary field that included his former boss, Nakagawa. While advantageous in the short term, this decision was not without potential long-term consequences. Republicans in general were not popular in Hawaii. Since Hawaii became a state in 1959, a vast majority of its elected officials have been and continue to be Democrats.

After winning the Republican primary, Marsland was slated to run against Democrat Lee Spencer, a Honolulu lawyer and onetime deputy prosecutor who had bested Nakagawa and a few other candidates. Marsland and Spencer held many of the same views when it came to battling crime but nonetheless tried to distinguish themselves at the other's expense. Spencer claimed Marsland couldn't get along with people and that some of his ideas, such as restricting those on parole and probation from entering Waikiki, were far-fetched or unconstitutional. Marsland, who had gained the political support of unions of teachers, policemen, and hotel workers, dismissed Spencer, who had moved to Hawaii from California, as inexperienced. Marsland claimed he was the best bet for truly changing the culture of criminal justice in Honolulu, and it was high time to do just that.

"I was born and raised in this city and I'm going to try and change it for the better," he said. "Right now, 90 percent of the people in Honolulu are afraid of its streets after dark. You don't go camping, you don't walk your beaches after dark, you don't walk your parks after dark. When a city is influenced by this kind of fear, something is terribly wrong."

In campaign commercials featuring him walking barefoot on the beach, looking comfortable in blue trousers and an aloha shirt, he emphasized the same message.

"When I was a boy we didn't have to lock our doors. Today crime has cost us one of our basic freedoms—the freedom to live without fear," said Marsland. "Those who have put fear in our lives have stolen our Hawaii of old. For as long as crime makes us live in fear we can't enjoy the beauty that was once Hawaii. I'm running for prosecutor to make our Hawaii safe once again."

Marsland also denied what was being whispered about Honolulu, that his son Chuckers's murder was the overriding reason for his campaign.

"I don't have a personal vendetta going. Understand that now," said Marsland. "I never brought his name into this campaign. Other people have and I bitterly resent it."

The voters liked what Marsland had to say. On Election Day 1980 Charles Marsland trounced his opponent by a two-to-one margin. While Marsland benefited from a national sweep by

Republicans, including Ronald Reagan's victory over President Jimmy Carter, it was believed that the fifty-seven-year-old prosecutor won so resoundingly because of his strong personality and candid commentary on Hawaii's criminal justice system. Clearly people bought into Marsland's swagger and believed in his strategies for making Honolulu safer.

"It's a mandate from the people on crime. The people are saying, 'We're tired of it and we want you to do something about it,'" Marsland said at his victory celebration. "So that's what I'm going to do."

CHAPTER FIVE

If You Looking for Trouble

In January 1981 Charles Marsland assumed office as the prosecuting attorney for the City and County of Honolulu, taking charge of a staff of more than seventy people in downtown offices on Bishop Street. About half of the staff was made of deputy prosecutors, but Marsland judged this number insufficient. He made an immediate request to the city council to hire ten more as part of a strike force dedicated to pursuing repeat offenders and organized crime. Marsland was adamant that his office needed more manpower to effectively combat crime.

Marsland wasted little time, too, in addressing what he perceived to be weaknesses in Hawaii's criminal justice system. The prosecutor suggested a number of new laws and policies, including a general toughening of laws regarding drugs and prostitution. Some of these ideas were controversial, including a proposal for criminal juries to operate like civil juries in Hawaii, able to reach verdicts without a unanimous vote. To Marsland's liking, only ten of twelve jurors would need to agree to convict a defendant. That way any minority opinions would not impede his brand of justice.

"There are so many cases where you have a ding-a-ling or two on the jury," said Marsland. "As a consequence of holding it up, you end up with a mistrial and you have to go through it again."

The prosecutor-elect also saw flaws in the application of insanity defenses in Hawaiian courts. Insanity, Marsland argued, should

not be a factor in a judge or jury determining whether or not someone is guilty of a crime—the defendant either committed the act or
didn't. Instead, he said, insanity should be considered strictly during sentencing. This was no minor issue, as the insanity defense was
raised by a number of defendants in Hawaii for several exceedingly
violent and high-profile crimes in the late 1970s and early 1980s.

But never mind the policy discussions, what really agitated
Marsland were Hawaii's criminals. Just two months into his term,
his office lost a trial that sent the prosecutor into fits of rage.
The case involved the alleged rape of a twenty-six-year-old Finnish tourist by at least nine teenagers on Nanakuli Beach, about
thirty miles outside Honolulu. The Finn had gone to sunbathe
on the beach in 1979 and was waiting for a bus to return to the
city. As she waited, the teenagers invited her inside a tent they
had erected beside the beach. The Finn accepted the invitation
and smoked marijuana with the teenagers. Then they allegedly
attacked her and ripped her clothes off before forcing her to have
sex. After eight long hours she was released from the tent.

A year or two later, the five youngest teenagers, all less than
sixteen years old at the time of the incident, were convicted as
juveniles for the rape of the woman. The four older teenagers,
however, were tried as adults and acquitted by a jury in March
1981. People were stupefied over the acquittal. Thousands
marched on the grounds of the state capitol in protest of the decision. The outrage stemmed in part from the contention of defense
lawyers that the victim, whose skirt was torn in the incident, did
not resist sufficiently to signal a lack of sexual consent.

To the protesters the case was typical of the lax manner in
which sexual assaults were handled in the Hawaiian criminal justice system. A year earlier, in 1980, there were fifteen hundred
charges of sexual assault, yet only thirteen cases went to court,
and only four ended in convictions. Following the trial, the Finnish tourist expressed regret for having returned to Hawaii to testify against her alleged attackers and rapists.

"I feel very sorry for anyone who comes in touch with the legal system," she said. "I'm very glad to get out of here and leave this society with its criminals. I think it's much too violent here."

Marsland's office took some criticism, too, for the trial, with observers complaining that defense attorneys overwhelmed the sole prosecutor in the case. Marsland said that the case was weakened by the Finnish woman's "stilted language" on the witness stand. Nonetheless he was appalled by the jury's verdict.

"I doubt very much if they would have nailed John Wilkes Booth for the shooting of Lincoln," said Marsland.

Soon enough they were not juries but more familiar foes that rankled Marsland: judges. A handful of decisions provoked the prosecutor so much that his first year in office was consumed by his animus of the Hawaiian judiciary. In particular he took repeated aim at three judges he could not stand, their actions fueling a sustained public airing of grievances by Marsland regarding perceived corruption and incompetence in Hawaii's courts and government. He ridiculed the men, insulted their intelligence, and belittled their competence, all from a very public stage. Marsland went to war with the men in robes.

These three judges were not the only ones to earn his ire. Marsland kept a "judicial atrocity book" on his desk at the prosecutor's office. Within this manila folder were pages of documentation from his deputy prosecutors about disagreements and alleged mistreatment by Hawaiian judges. The documentation was substantial, the folder stuffed thick. Without even glancing inside, Marsland could summarize the folder's contents, rattling off a litany of alleged abuses of judicial power:

When you have cases that are being mishandled, cases that are being thrown out of court for spurious reasons, indictments that are being dumped, judges that are so defense-oriented it's

sickening, when my deputies come back and ask to be trans-
ferred out of certain courts because of rulings of the judges and
because of the way they are treated, when I see witnesses mis-
treated by judges and I see police officers mistreated by judges
. . . when I keep hearing about members of the judiciary
reputedly having lines of credit at Nevada casinos, when I
see my deputies file motion for disqualification and absolutely
nothing happens, as far as I'm concerned, something is wrong.

Few lawyers dared to criticize judges so viciously, if at all. Such attacks were considered foolish. Publicly complaining about a ruling would not change it. What's more, chances were that a lawyer would again appear before the judge. What was the advantage of annoying him?

That's not to say lawyers didn't have their gripes about the judiciary. They just usually kept their complaints to themselves, sympathizing privately with Marsland.

"You've got a real mixed bag of judges out here," said Honolulu lawyer David Bettencourt. "I have seen outright corruption in court but I can't really say I see it in criminal cases more than civil cases. There's certain cases where somebody is just not going to win. There's certain cases that prosecutors just don't want to push. They'll dump it on the least excuse they can find."

Historically, said Bettencourt, when Honolulu still seemed like a small town, some judges would overlook gambling and prostitution. Other judges were honest, but ineffective.

"Some of these judges we were dealing with had gone to night school for five years to become a lawyer. They had families, they had children at the time. I just can't conceive going to law school under those conditions," said Bettencourt.

"I would see these people. They weren't the sharpest judges. They came from all walks of life . . . and they had a lot of experience," said the defense lawyer. "But there were some that I always would wonder. You'd see DUIs [driving under the influence charges]. They'd be hard on DUIs, and they'd cut two loose in a day with private counsel. We were public defenders, so you'd wonder, hmmm, friends of the judge?"

Of the three judges who particularly exasperated Marsland during his first year in office, the one to perhaps receive the mildest rebukes was James Wakatsuki, a former speaker of the house in Hawaii. Judge Wakatsuki denied Marsland's office its attempts to stop illegal cockfighters and marijuana growers through obtaining civil injunctions, which one could argue was either an innovative, or inappropriate, way to combat these criminals. The appropriate thing, Wakatsuki ruled, was to pursue alleged transgressors through police work and criminal prosecutions. It was not proper, he decided, for the prosecutor to take shortcuts using civil law and ask a judge to curb suspected criminal behavior by issuing an injunction. Marsland was enraged at the lack of cooperation, deeming Wakatsuki a "jackass" in front of a large luncheon crowd.

More caustic commentary was reserved for Judge Simeon Acoba. An early fight between Acoba and Marsland occurred during the case of Warren Miller, a man asking to be released from the mental health unit of the state hospital. In 1977 Miller was accused of the kidnapping, attempted rape, and attempted murder of a female tourist from Seattle on a ridge just east of Honolulu. Miller had driven the twenty-year-old victim to the top of the ridge and then, unprovoked, broke a beer bottle atop her head. While she bled, he removed her clothes, using the sash of her skirt to gag her mouth. He pushed the woman down a slope and attempted to rape her while she was on her hands and knees. Unable to become aroused, Miller substituted his fingers, violating the woman's vagina and anus.

When Miller finished the assault, the victim tried to flee. She was caught and pushed to the ground again. This time Miller used a beer bottle to penetrate the woman, occasionally pulling it out of her body to pour out beer. He then threw the woman off a cliff. The fall was only ten feet, so Miller followed her down and threw her off another cliff, this time fifteen feet high. Still the woman would not die. As Miller approached her yet again, the woman herself jumped off a remaining cliff. Upon landing, she played dead. Miller left the ridge.

When Miller was tried in court for the attack, witnesses testified he was a misogynist and under the effects of drugs and alcohol during the attack. A judge acquitted him of all charges in 1978 by reason of insanity and committed Miller to the state hospital for supervision and treatment. Three years later he was petitioning to return to society. But his case first caught the attention of Marsland when it was discovered that the state hospital had already been allowing Miller, under the supervision of a chaperone, to attend classes at a local college and enjoy overnight stays away from the hospital at his brother's home. Marsland was incredulous that someone so violent would be allowed to leave the hospital and mingle with college students.

Marsland's office appealed to the hospital administrator to terminate Miller's visits to the college. The hospital administrator refused, citing the visits' importance in Miller's rehabilitation. Next Marsland's office appealed to the courts to stop Miller's attendance in college classes. After deliberate consideration, Judge Acoba said he would be overstepping his bounds if he forbade Miller from leaving the hospital on a temporary basis. Such decisions regarding Miller's rehabilitation, ruled Acoba, should be made by the hospital, not a judge. Marsland derided Acoba's ruling as "positively absurd and a travesty of the criminal process."

Marsland had little sympathy for judges who went by the book at the expense of what he perceived to be justice. Acoba could reason away his decision all he liked; to Marsland it seemed plain that the judge was permitting an extremely sadistic offender to return to society just four years after sexually violating a young woman in an egregious manner and then twice throwing her body off a cliff. That, Marsland was convinced, was simply unacceptable.

"This one really bothered me," said Marsland. "What [Miller] did was unprintable and unspeakable."

Marsland was further inflamed by the fact that another hospital patient with a violent past had recently been released into the community with less than desirable results. This man had originally been committed to the state hospital's mental health unit after being found not guilty by reason of insanity for shooting a woman in 1974. Soon after his release from the state hospital, he shot two more people. And he was again acquitted of the shootings by reason of insanity.

On top of this Marsland fumed that furloughs were regularly granted to prison inmates on Oahu. One of these prisoners, a convicted murderer, escaped for two hours between sets of playing tennis at Honolulu's seaside Ala Moana Beach Park. Marsland was incredulous.

These are people who are supposed to be doing time but they've let them out. They let them out for job furloughs, education furloughs, extended furloughs, resocialization furloughs, recreation furloughs, Christmas shopping furloughs. I'm not being facetious, they have that. And some of the bums they let out would scare the hell out of you.

Here we have a major, deadly problem on our hands, and we have a group of slapstick comedy incompetents and bleeding hearts running the operations.

When it came to Miller, Judge Acoba said he could not interfere with the hospital's granting of temporary leave for its patients. The permanent discharge Miller was requesting, however, was another matter and subject to Acoba's authority. During subsequent hearings regarding Miller's discharge request,

Marsland's office asked Acoba that the violent mental health patient be kept within the hospital and under supervision.

Acoba was not entirely accommodating to this request. The judge denied prosecutors their last-minute attempt to have Miller's victim testify during a hearing regarding his release. Prosecutors protested that they had just learned the victim, now living in California, would be willing to testify again. The judge dismissed the prosecutor's office's efforts as not only belated, but theatrical. Acoba said the victim, who had flown in from the mainland and was sitting in the courtroom in anticipation of testifying, could offer nothing new beyond her original testimony.

Acoba's decision upset veteran deputy prosecutor Kenneth Nam so much that he left the courtroom in a rage and began to rant about the judge, calling him a "fucking shithead" and "the worst appointment ever made in the state of Hawaii." The decision, sixty-three-year-old Nam said, was "utterly stupid . . . goddamn, I should live so long to see anything like this."

Not to be thwarted, Marsland invited reporters to his office, where the victim was free to share details of the brutality of the crime. Her leg was broken during the attack, she said, and when Miller assaulted her with the beer bottle, he tried to break it inside of her. In the end it did not matter that the victim's statements were not shared in court. Acoba denied Miller's release from the hospital.

Any satisfaction felt by Marsland over this ruling was short-lived. Just three days later, Acoba's decision to deny Miller's release was eclipsed by the action of another judge, Harold Shintaku. In September 1981 Shintaku overturned a jury's conviction of organized-crime figure Charlie Stevens for the 1978 murder of two people whose bodies were found dismembered in garbage bags buried in Oahu's Waianae Valley. Given the inconsistency of witnesses' statements and incredible evidence, Shintaku said, the jury could not have responsibly convicted Stevens. So he reversed their decision.

Marsland was dumbfounded. Responding to the judge's reasoning, the prosecutor claimed there's "inconsistency in any case that you try—that's why you have a jury."

"The people of the state have been ripped off," said Marsland. "What about justice? Consider the victims' families and the victims themselves."

As shocking as the overturned verdict was to the public, Shintaku's action did not take Marsland's office by surprise. The prosecutor had previously complained about Shintaku's behavior at Stevens's murder trial. The judge was observed in court nodding his head in agreement with defense lawyers and shaking it in disagreement with prosecutors. After the trial he was seen to put his arm around, or at least upon, Stevens, the murder defendant. The judge said the contact was incidental. Marsland claimed to have met with the chief justice of the Supreme Court of Hawaii three times to share these concerns, but to no avail.

Beyond Marsland's perception of Shintaku's bias in the Stevens case, other factors contributed to the prosecutor's low opinion of the judge. Earlier in the year, Shintaku acquitted by reason of insanity a necrophiliac who shot a woman in the head with a pellet gun in the Ala Moana Center shopping mall parking lot and then stabbed her to death when she did not respond to his petting of her. Shintaku reached this decision despite a court-appointed panel of psychologists testifying that the defendant was indeed sane and could control his actions.

Shintaku was also known to be fond of having a good time. He was a regular at Nevada casinos and known to enjoy the nightlife in Honolulu, as well. Deputy prosecutor Peter Carlisle recalled trying his first murder case in front of Shintaku as a young man. Following closing arguments Carlisle began waiting for the verdict, which the jury indicated it would likely deliver soon. Shintaku, however, didn't intend to pass the time in the courtroom while the jury deliberated.

"You know what? They're not going to come back for a while," Shintaku said to Carlisle and the defense lawyer. "Let's go out and have a drink."

Carlisle was uneasy about the proposition, but thought it unwise to decline an invitation from the judge. Besides, the verdict was expected any minute. At about nine o'clock that evening, the men went to a bar and had a round of drinks. And then another. As the fate of the murder defendants hung in the balance, Judge Shintaku was imbibing merrily.

"First off, he's getting sloshed. Second off, he's talking about all the mama-sans and, you know, which one do I want," said Carlisle. "I'm going, 'What the hell is going on?' I'm just flabbergasted by it."

At about two o'clock in the morning, a phone call came through to the judge at the bar: The jury had reached a verdict. Shintaku, Carlisle, and the defense lawyer hustled back to the courtroom.

"So we go back there, I'm sure we're all smelling like a brewery," said Carlisle. "The jury comes in, down the line they're found guilty. Then Harold wants to go back out again. I'm going, 'No, no, no, I gotta go home.'"

Following the overturning of the murder verdict for Stevens, about three hundred people marched on the state capitol to protest Shintaku's action. Then Marsland called a press conference to reveal that a majority of the twenty-page decision released by Shintaku was copied verbatim from a memo submitted by the defendant's lawyers, David Schutter and Judith Pavey, that urged for Stevens's guilty verdict to be overturned. The judge's decision even reproduced nine erroneous references to transcript pages that were part of the defense lawyers' memo, said Marsland, leading one to believe that Shintaku put little thought into the writing of the decision. In fact, Marsland said, as much as 85 percent of the decision was lifted directly from the memo.

Wrong, said an unabashed Judge Shintaku. It was more like 90 percent.

Too bad it wasn't 100 percent, said defense lawyer Schutter.

In contrast to Marsland, Shintaku and the defense lawyers said there was nothing improper in a judge using language provided by the prevailing side of a case. Such practice is actually common, they said, accusing Marsland of manipulating the public's unfamiliarity with the norms of the legal world.

Schutter's memo "wasn't that dissimilar from what I would have written," said Shintaku, "but his language is way better than mine."

Firing back at Marsland, Shintaku said, "I hate to be vicious about it, but I thought this guy graduated law school."

Marsland responded just as tartly to the judge.

"I'm sure he didn't graduate from law school. I'd be surprised if he got a degree from Waimano Home," said Marsland, referencing a Hawaiian facility for the mentally disabled.

Just after releasing his written decision explaining the overturned verdict, Shintaku headed to a downtown bar called, appropriately enough, the Jury Box. The judge, as he was known to do, enjoyed himself. Afterward, he was arrested for drunk driving. Upon being released by police that same night, the judge somehow made his way to a family cottage on Mokuleia Beach on the North Shore. Then, according to Shintaku, he took a swim in the ocean to clear his head and then went to sleep.

The next day family members walked into the cottage to discover Shintaku dazed and bleeding. His collarbone was broken and his skull fractured. Doctors and Shintaku surmised that he was attacked in the middle of the night and struck with a blunt object. Police, however, were of the opinion that Shintaku's injuries came from a fall during a failed attempt at suicide. Shintaku denied this, and, as time went on, the cause of his injuries remained a mystery despite much public speculation. Some wondered if Shintaku was beaten for failing to pay gambling debts. Others pointed their fingers at Marsland, accusing him of riling the public against Shintaku after the judge reversed the jury.

Among those accusing the prosecutor of being responsible for Shintaku's injuries, however they occurred, was defense attorney Schutter, who accused Marsland's office of conducting "a calculated campaign aimed at inspiring distrust and hatred of judges.

"There is no doubt in my mind that Judge Shintaku, if it was an attempted suicide, was driven to it by the vicious nature of the demagoguery engaged in by the prosecutor's office," said Schutter. "And if it was an assault, it was clearly an assault that was caused and fomented by the vehemence of the rhetoric engaged in the prosecutor's office."

Schutter was among the most prominent, if not the most prominent, defense attorneys in Hawaii, and therefore popular with some of the state's most notorious criminals. He represented Syndicate members Wilford "Nappy" Pulawa and Alvin Kaohu during their original double kidnapping and murder trial in 1974, which ended in a mistrial. He negotiated the controversial ten-year sentence for manslaughter for Rodney Kiyota, who stabbed a twelve-year-old girl to death in the 1970s. Schutter was also famous for his so-called "white wine defense." When a man shot three people in a Waikiki yacht club after an argument, Schutter successfully argued for his acquittal by claiming an ingredient in the white wine consumed by his client caused an "organic brain dysfunction" and "pathological intoxication" that freed his client of culpability.

Years before he was elected prosecutor, Marsland had hired Schutter's associate Frank O'Brien to handle the civil lawsuit filed against John Does 1 to 10 that sought to compel information regarding Chuckers Marsland's murder. O'Brien described his former colleague Schutter as one of the best trial lawyers he had ever encountered, superior even to legal luminaries like F. Lee Bailey, whom O'Brien had personally seen argue during the Great Plymouth Mail Truck Robbery trial in Massachusetts in 1967, when Bailey helped win the acquittal of two men accused of stealing more than a million and a half dollars from a mail truck.

Bailey and Schutter later worked together on a case, and Bailey allegedly once asked Schutter to carry his briefcase.

"Carry your own fucking briefcase," Schutter told the great lawyer.

Not necessarily always so profane, Schutter's sharp tongue, theatrics, and bluster made him a legendary trial lawyer in Hawaii who fearlessly attacked witnesses, rival lawyers, and, like his nemesis Marsland, even judges.

"He had an almost photographic memory and was a nasty sonofabitch in the courtroom," said O'Brien. "If he was cross examining someone he would eat them for lunch."

Schutter was born in Wisconsin and adopted six days after his birth. He attended college and law school at the University of Wisconsin, graduating at the top of his class. On campus his cleverness extended beyond the classroom.

"God, he was brilliant. He told me . . . the way to get laid in college is to go to Laundromats because everybody is bored," recalled Honolulu lawyer David Bettencourt, who counted Schutter as a friend. "They want to talk about or do anything other than being at a Laundromat."

After college Schutter began work in 1965 for the Phoenix law firm Lewis and Roca, whose lawyers successfully argued *Miranda v. Arizona* before the US Supreme Court, establishing the routine disclosure of Miranda rights to people arrested for a crime, including the right to remain silent and the right to legal counsel. Schutter came to Hawaii in 1968 when his National Guard unit was stationed at the Schofield Barracks. He organized a petition and lawsuit to prevent his unit from being sent to Vietnam, but, in a rare instance, did not prevail. Upon returning from war in 1969, Schutter stayed in Honolulu and opened his own law practice. He would become so rich from this practice that he later owned a seventeen-bedroom house in the fashionable beachside neighborhood of Kahala that was listed for forty-five million dollars. His auto fleet included a Rolls-Royce with the personalized license plate reading SUE EM and a red Ferrari with a license plate reading LITIGR.

Though admired for his intellect, his fellow lawyers also described Schutter as obnoxious. His friend Bettencourt remembered once correcting Schutter as they tried a case together. Schutter threatened to wallop Bettencourt if he didn't shut his mouth.

Few people could stand to work with Schutter for long. Bettencourt estimates fifteen lawyers went through Schutter's office serving three-month stints. As former Schutter associate O'Brien puts it, "David would overpay you for the fact that you had to put up with him." On the other hand Ben Cayetano, who would become governor of Hawaii, once worked with Schutter and remained on good terms with him.

Beyond legal partners, Schutter had trouble keeping romantic partners, too. He was married at least three times, twice to the same woman. Bettencourt recalls that Schutter's "version of how he got married was coming back and saying 'I did something to reduce the income taxes.' That was how he announced his wedding."

As Schutter grew older, his health deteriorated and he became increasingly petulant, according to legal colleagues.

"Towards the end I'd see him stand, stand in front of a judge and say the most contemptuous thing you can think of to a judge in a tone that just would make you cringe," said Mike McGuigan, who worked as a deputy prosecutor in Marsland's office. "Turn his back on the judge and walk out the door with the judge just sitting up there."

Schutter's discourse was no better with Marsland. The men despised each other and often traded barbs. When the defense attorney donated money to create the nonprofit Schutter Foundation, which urged a reduction in crime and a ban of handguns, Marsland laughed the effort off as a *shibai*, or ruse.

"[Schutter] is going to tell us how to improve the criminal justice system?" Marsland asked incredulously. "Brother that has

CHARLES MARSLAND

Swimming 11; Track 10, 11; Junior Football 11; K. P. 10, 11; Junior Carnival Booth 11; Today and Tomorrow 11.

This handsome exponent of what the well-dressed student should wear attached himself to us in the seventh grade, and since then has made quite a reputation for himself as a dancer de luxe and a number one good sport. Charlie's amiable grin has been a contributing factor in making him quite a popular fellow.

Portrait of Punahou School senior Charles F. Marsland Jr. from the 1940 Oahuan yearbook. COURTESY OF PUNAHOU SCHOOL ARCHIVES

Charles Marsland, prosecuting attorney for the City and County of Honolulu. COURTESY OF ANYAA VOHIRI (FKA MIGNONETTE DIGGS PELLEGRIN)

Charles Marsland (r) leaves the prosecutor's office in downtown Honolulu in June 1984 with his spokesman and assistant, Rick Reed. Five months later Marsland was overwhelmingly reelected as prosecutor of the City and County of Honolulu. COURTESY OF THE *HONOLULU STAR-ADVERTISER*

Charles F. "Chuckers" Marsland III, shortly before his murder in 1975 at age nineteen. COURTESY OF CATHY (CLISBY) GALKA

Chuckers Marsland with girlfriend Cathy Clisby. COURTESY OF CATHY (CLISBY) GALKA

Alema Leota, one of Hawaii's original crime bosses and alleged leader of the Syndicate, was an unsuccessful candidate for governor of Hawaii in 1978. COURTESY OF THE *HONOLULU STAR-ADVERTISER*

Alleged Syndicate gangsters Alvin Kaohu, Henry Huihui, and Bobby Wilson (l to r) speak to reporters in 1974 in front of Ali'iolani Hale and a statue of Hawaiian ruler Kamehameha the Great following a mistrial on conspiracy, kidnapping, and murder charges. COURTESY OF THE *HONOLULU STAR-ADVERTISER*

Ronald K. Ching, Hawaii's most notorious hit man. COURTESY OF *HONOLULU* MAGAZINE

Confessed killer Ronnie Ching sits in a Honolulu courtroom, the tail of a shark tattoo visible on his left forearm. COURTESY OF THE *HONOLULU STAR-ADVERTISER*

Witness Clarence "Rags" Scanlan stuns the courtroom by producing a police revolver missing for more than ten years during the final days of the Chuckers Marsland murder trial. Prosecutors and hit man turned government witness Ronnie Ching had alleged such a revolver, one of two guns used to kill young Marsland, had been dumped in a yacht basin. COURTESY OF THE *HONOLULU STAR-ADVERTISER*

Former policeman, strongman, cattle rancher, businessman, and alleged Hawaiian godfather Larry Mehau, as seen at a political event in 2006. Mehau has never been charged or convicted of any major crime.
COURTESY OF WWW.HAWAIIFREEPRESS.COM

to be the joke of the year. It's tantamount to appointing a prostitute to run a church social."

In 1979, when Marsland spoke to a crowd of people at the Outrigger Canoe Club who were agitating for reductions in Hawaii's crime rate, telling them that compassion for criminals was nonsense, Schutter crashed the party. He castigated the anticrime crowd for being racists and hypocrites, saying if it was their own children who were accused for crimes, "you'd applaud your fool heads off for leniency."

Schutter went on, blaming the criminal justice system for not only failing to correct the misbehavior of juvenile delinquents, but for hardening the youths further, essentially guaranteeing that the delinquents continue to break the law as they mature into adults.

"They hate you, they hate your goddamned guts," said Schutter. "You locked 'em up and you didn't do a thing. I'm talking about rehabilitating an eight-year-old."

The crowd was hostile to these comments, and it was not the only time Schutter inspired controversy. No matter the crowd's reaction, Schutter remained a popular lawyer. Among his clients was Larry Mehau, Hawaii's alleged godfather, for whom Schutter filed libel lawsuits against assorted media entities and persons that included Rick Reed, Marsland's assistant and spokesman and the former publisher of the *Valley Isle* newspaper.

Larry Mehau had legal issues much larger than libel accusations. Reed, it turned out, was not the only one with suspicions about the former police officer.

In the 1970s the US government twice investigated Mehau for being the alleged leader of Hawaiian organized crime.

⌐⌐

Since retiring from the police force at the age of about thirty-four, Mehau had fashioned a cattle ranch on Hawaiian homestead land he had been awarded on the Big Island of Hawaii. Such land was available due to the Hawaiian Homes Commission Act of 1920, which set aside nearly two hundred thousand acres for native Hawaiians to use for housing or agriculture. The act, which provided long-term lease of property for a nominal amount, was meant to remedy the massive displacement of Hawaiians from their land following the arrival of foreign settlers and changes to Hawaiian kingdom laws regarding land ownership. For Mehau it meant that nearly three hundred acres of rolling pasture outside of Waimea on the long, broad slopes of Mauna Kea volcano were his to ranch.

A large, nearly cost-free estate in Hawaii might sound like paradise, but ranch life was no vacation. After working hard to develop the ranch each day, the hulking Mehau, his wife Beverly, and their five young children would retire to a tiny two-bedroom shack already built on the property. No electricity. No telephone. They made do, said Mehau, with a kerosene stove and lots of conversation. Not that anyone was complaining. Since childhood Mehau longed to be a cowboy. He spent weekends and holidays visiting ranches on the Big Island, often skipping family events.

"To watch them on a horse, wow! You never saw cowboys like this, nowhere in the world. They're running through rocks and cactus plants and they're not afraid of anything," said Mehau. "All my life, I thought about this. Bev and I used to draw up plans, how we would paddock off the fields."

Eight years after obtaining the ranch lease, the family moved into a new home they had slowly built with much help from visiting friends. Mehau's buddies warned each other not to visit unless you were willing to lend a hand. The result was impressive.

"The large home befits the master of the house," wrote Eddie Sherman, a columnist for the *Honolulu Advertiser* and Mehau's friend. "It's big, and strong-looking like the two-hundred-and-fifty-pound human rock that is Larry."

The Mehau home sat atop a small hill. Its fireplace was constructed from boulders collected from the property, and the lanai, or porch, featured large columns of twisted ohia tree trunks that Mehau had dragged from a forest. Mehau was once offered five hundred dollars for one of the trunks. He declined.

"These ohia logs are for the rest of my life," said Mehau. "The money I'd spend quickly."

The interior of the home featured lots of koa wood, which, like ohia, grows only in Hawaii. The home's massive front door, too, was made of koa, and was conspicuously missing a lock. Few, it seems, would be foolish enough to intrude upon the strong-man's castle. And if they did, reasoned Mehau, "no sense they ruin my door."

Following a visit to see Mehau, Hawaiian comedian Andy Bumatai offered another explanation for why the security expert would forgo a lock on his own home. "No wonder Larry never locks up his house," said Bumatai. "He's the only one strong enough to open it."

And yet another explanation for the absence of a door lock was the bull terrier and German shepherds that lived on the ranch. One of the shepherds, Bruno, was noted to bite tires in half and to rip chrome auto parts off vehicles with his jaws.

Other, less ferocious animals roamed the property, too, including 18 horses, 24 pigs, and 225 heads of cattle. Their care was not for the fainthearted. Once Mehau delivered a calf stuck in the breech position during a torrential rainstorm, though the calf and its mother died. Another time newspaper columnist Sherman's ten-year-old son Shawn was visiting the ranch and riding a mare in heat. Suddenly a stallion chased the mare, resulting in the boy being thrown to the ground and slightly trampled. Shawn complained to Mehau and exhibited a bruise. Mehau then stomped off toward the stallion with a rope in hand.

"What are you gonna do, Uncle Larry, hit the horse?" asked Shawn, running after Mehau.

"Worse than that," said Mehau.

"You gonna kill the horse?" asked Shawn.

"Worse than that," said Mehau, who promptly put the stallion on the ground, produced a knife, and bloodily castrated the animal on the spot, horrifying the boy. Mehau had planned to castrate the animal anyway, but seized the opportunity to shock his young friend and impress upon him the visceral existence of a rancher.

"It's a good life . . . it's a healthy life," said Mehau. " I wouldn't change it."

Clean living, though, does not necessarily make for good living. Recognizing that a small-scale rancher could only make a very modest income, Mehau sought other business opportunities. In the early 1960s he invested in a private security company, Hawaii Protective Association, which had been founded by a pair of policemen. At first Mehau was a passive investor, but within a few years he had taken control of the company and bought out his partners. Under Mehau's leadership Hawaii Protective Association prospered, its staff doubling in less than ten years as it obtained more and more clients across Hawaii. By 1980, Hawaii Protective Association employed more than nine hundred people through contracts that included a number of hotels, the University of Hawaii, the Aloha Bowl football stadium, as well as Hawaii's seaports and airports.

Controversy accompanied the increased revenues. Mehau, who counted Governor George Ariyoshi and a number of other prominent Hawaiian politicians as friends, was suspected of benefiting from cronyism, as his firm obtained a number of state contracts for security services. In 1974, after having provided security for a year at several Hawaiian airports, Hawaii Protective Association was underbid by a rival company, Burns International Security Forces. But just as Burns International was set to take over the $2.7 million contract in 1975, Burns's general manager began complaining that a labor union to which many Hawaii Protective Association employees belonged urged the guards to refuse to work for Burns International in the hopes that the contract would then possibly revert to Hawaii Protective Association. At the same time, Hawaii's state transportation department was subjecting Burns International to scrutiny and bureaucratic obstacles that a *Honolulu Advertiser* investigation described as unprecedented. Burns International was made subject to rules that were not enforced against Hawaii Protective Association, the newspaper reported.

In the end, thanks to intervention of the Federal Aviation Administration, who vouched for Burns International's competence, Burns International kept the contract. But a year later Hawaii Protective Association won back the contract, and then, too, successfully bid for the contract in ensuing years. In 1978 they were the only bidder on the contract, and critics complained that the bidding requirements were written in a way that no other firm could compete with Mehau's company.

Five years later Burns International again underbid Hawaii Protective Association for the airports contract, as well as for providing security at a foreign trade zone. But Burns International's new contracts were soon voided due to a licensing snafu related to their corporate restructuring, and security for the airports and foreign trade zone was again awarded to Hawaii Protective Association. Burns International complained that the state was being unfairly strict with its enforcement of the licensing requirements, but the Supreme Court of Hawaii ruled the government was within its rights to cancel the airport contract. Despite the high court's blessing, some people still viewed the awards to Mehau's firm with suspicion, with several residents also grumbling about the extra $180,000 that would be incurred by taxpayers because of Hawaii's decision to forgo the low bid because of a licensing technicality. Throughout the controversies, Ariyoshi hotly denied accusations of favoritism by his administration.

"Larry Mehau is my friend, no if, ands, or buts about it," said the governor. "However, I don't operate on a friendship basis. So far as I am concerned, what is best for the state prevails."

Mehau, too, denied that politics played a role in his firm's success, explaining that he knew the governor since the 1950s.

"[I] was his friend. Glad to be his friend. Then he was just a lawyer," said Mehau. "Now he's governor. Am I supposed to cut all my ties with people who become powerful—if that's the term they would like to use? I don't think I'm powerful. But I do have friends like you do, and we all do."

Mehau was a policeman when he met Ariyoshi, and already well-known to almost every local lawyer, thug, and judge in Honolulu. Ariyoshi and his law colleagues sometimes defended the men Mehau arrested, meaning their paths crossed often in court. The lawyer and policeman became friendly enough through these interactions that in 1970, when Ariyoshi ran to become lieutenant governor of Hawaii, Mehau offered to assist him in his campaign. It was not Mehau's first taste of politics, as he had previously helped another Democrat, John Burns, in his successful campaign to become governor. Mehau and Burns had become friend years earlier, establishing an easy rapport, because Burns was also a former policeman. It was Burns who appointed Mehau to the State Board of Land and Natural Resources in 1970, where for eight years Mehau voted on matters that ran the gamut from coastal and rural development to policy regarding scientific research atop Mauna Kea, the snow-capped volcano on the Big Island that is prized by astronomers and home to several high-powered telescopes.

By 1970 the rumors concerning Mehau and the underworld had been repeated enough that the policeman turned cattle rancher asked to be kept in the background of Ariyoshi's political campaign.

"I know I'm controversial," said Mehau, "so don't put me out front."

Ariyoshi refused the plea.

"I've known you for a long time and know you to be a good and honest person," Ariyoshi told Mehau. "What kind of friend would I be if I said, 'I want your help but I don't want anyone to know you're helping me?' I'm not afraid to have people know of our friendship."

Mehau soon helped provide security for the Ariyoshi family. He was also named the campaign's Neighbor Islands coordinator, responsible for all of the vote gathering beyond Oahu. To drum up support for Ariyoshi, Mehau arranged rallies featuring prominent Hawaiian performers. The shows were immensely popular, especially since many residents of the Neighbor Islands could not easily travel to Honolulu to see these musicians perform in Waikiki. For one of the first rallies on the Big Island, organizers hoped to attract three hundred people. Actual attendance was about seventy-five hundred. Events like these helped cement Ariyoshi's victory. As Hawaii's First Lady Jean Ariyoshi recalled in a memoir: "[Mehau] knew all the entertainers and got Don Ho, Al Harrington, Frank DeLima, Zulu, and the Surfers to fly around the islands to perform at campaign rallies. Thousands flocked to see them, hear good music, eat the stew and rice cooked by volunteers, and listen to what George Ariyoshi had to say."

Four years later, in 1974, it was much of the same, as Mehau helped secure Ariyoshi's election as governor of Hawaii. Again the First Lady wrote of her family's gratitude to Mehau as they campaigned feverishly in the final month before Hawaii's residents cast their votes: "We started at nine o'clock every morning, going where potential voters gathered. We attended all the rallies, and they were phenomenal, thanks largely to Larry Mehau, who rounded up entertainers to donate their talents, singing, dancing and playing music, all to help George."

Not everyone was so appreciative. According to a government informant, several musicians complained about being made to play the political rallies without compensation. According to FBI files: "Source stated these two former members of the Surfers terminated their relationship with that organization sometime in mid to late 1978 after numerous entertainers had been forced or pressured into performing on behalf of the Governor of the State of Hawaii for no pay . . ."

This same informant alleged that a female saxophonist lost a gig in Waikiki as a result of her own protests regarding pressure to play for no pay. But crooner and heartthrob Don Ho denies there was any strong-arming by Mehau.

"That's a bunch of malarkey," said Ho. "Everybody was calling us, wanting to be on the show."

Yet even Mehau conceded that some entertainers declined to participate, and that he took offense:

I was the one [who] called the entertainers and some said no, said they had Republican customers, not just Democratic ones. I said, "Okay, I understand that." And I told the ones who said no that I wouldn't let 'em on stage even if they changed their minds. I stood by the stairs and wouldn't let 'em up. I said, "You didn't want to stand by us in the campaign."

The entertainers' complaints were collected as part of Operation Firebird, an investigation begun in 1978 by the Drug Enforcement Administration and Honolulu Police Department that explored Mehau's rumored role in the underworld, including allegations that he was a major heroin trafficker. It was the second major investigation of Mehau, following an FBI investigation started in 1973 that inspected Mehau's alleged interactions with gangsters in Honolulu and prominent gamblers in California. That case was closed two years later without any criminal charges being filed against Mehau.

Operation Firebird was a more robust examination of Mehau's activities and associations. Beyond the lead agencies, the investigation also counted the help of the FBI, IRS, US Customs, and the Bureau of Alcohol, Tobacco, and Firearms. For two years police and government agents delved into Mehau's professional and personal life. The government learned Mehau's travel habits, including which hotels he stayed in and who he met during trips among the Hawaiian Islands and to Los Angeles and Las Vegas. The government tracked down the phone numbers he called, learned his business dealings, and, according to Mehau, even infiltrated his security company. When Mehau traveled internationally, he complained of being given extra scrutiny while going through customs to the point that he was pulled out of line by officials and searched.

Among the men the government knew Mehau met with during his travels was Marcus Lipsky, an older California businessman and reputed gangster. As a young man in Chicago, Lipsky, who had been born in Kiev in 1905, allegedly stole a liquor truck belonging to Al Capone and then sold it back to the mobster. Years later he had not shaken his reputation for criminality. During a 1958 hearing on organized crime in the US Senate, Lipsky was referred to as a "well-known hoodlum" and was said to have tried to take over gambling in Dallas on behalf of a Chicago mobster.

Lipsky was also a very successful businessman, owning companies that distributed liquor, distributed movies, and sold surplus war provisions. He was also said to associate with mobsters who ran Chicago-area dairy businesses. Perhaps owing to this experience, one of Lipsky's best investments was in instant whipped cream maker Reddi-Wip, Inc. where he served as president and board chairman from 1947 to 1969. As detailed in court filings, Lipsky oversaw a number of cutthroat business acquisitions to grow the company and arrange for its eventual sale to a food conglomerate. After this sale, FBI files indicate, Lipsky was paid $800,000 a year from the conglomerate.

By 1970 Lipsky had retired to Beverly Hills, where he bought a country club, engaged in philanthropy, and dabbled in the entertainment industry. He also began a business relationship with singer Don Ho that was not very lucrative for the singer.

Mehau was said to have intervened on behalf of his friend Ho and amicably end, or amend, the venture. In the process, Mehau and Lipsky became chummy, with Mehau claiming he enjoyed listening to the "old man" tell stories about a bygone era of organized crime. The two were so close that Lipsky allowed one of Mehau's daughters to live at his home in Los Angeles when she was a young adult. Mehau said Lipsky was a stern guardian.

"He was more strict with her than I was," said Mehau. "I can remember her complaining to my wife about she had to bring all of the guys who wanted to date her in the house, and he had to meet them and give them the third degree . . . He was more protective of her and thought of her as his daughter."

After Mehau's intervention everything was copacetic. Lipsky seemed happy, as did Ho. It was not the first time the celebrity singer had asked his former high school classmate for help.

"Along the way, some members of the local underworld tried to shake me down. I called Larry," said Ho. "In the beginning, my association with him was for security. But then I found out he's a pretty smart businessman. He helps me in making deals. He's like a big brother to me."

Years later Mehau talked about helping Ho extricate himself from problems with mainland gangsters. An envoy had arrived to Ho's dressing room, Mehau recalled, threatening to call the mob bosses back home if Ho or anyone else was uncooperative. Mehau handed the visitor a phone.

"OK, you better start calling, pally, because you're in trouble here. If you looking for trouble, I'm gonna help you find it," Mehau told the man. "Go call whoever told you to come over here. And if your orders are to continue, I hope you can swim good. There's no place for you to hide, and you're going to have to swim a long way."

Reflecting on that episode, Mehau stated that gangsters "don't like that kind of talk. But if they talk to you like that, what are you supposed to do? Eat it? Bullshit."

That Mehau could resolve quarrels between Ho and members of the underworld was a testament to his power. Suspicious minds, however, believed such influence came about dishonestly. Investigators with Operation Firebird wondered how Mehau could have so many criminal associations and not be a criminal himself.

The list of suspect associations extended far beyond Marcus Lipsky. Federal investigators believed Mehau once tried to broker a peace settlement between gangsters Earl K. H. Kim and Wilford "Nappy" Pulawa. Another time, Mehau admitted, he negotiated a truce between underworld thugs Penrod Fanene and Eric Naone. It felt good, he said, to prevent violence.

"There's tensions and headaches for me, and I don't get anything for my time," Mehau said of these interventions. "But I've saved some lives, so I guess it was worth it."

Mehau's defenders said the strongman and rancher should be praised for this kind of underworld mediation, not condemned.

"If it weren't for Larry there would be a lot of bloodshed in this town. A lot of bad people would have gotten away with things. He took a lot of bad boys and made them good boys and these guys are loyal to him to this day," said Ho. "Larry has the capacity to go to these guys because he's as tough or tougher than all of them . . . And he knows them all and has done innumerable favors for a lot of these guys. They consider him someone they don't want to cross."

Oftentimes a favor came by way of a second chance. Mehau's security firm, Hawaii Protective Association, employed a number of men with criminal records. One example was the head of the Kauai office, an ex-cop who pleaded guilty to smuggling marijuana. Another was Arthur Baker, the man who Ronnie Ching later abducted from the Sunday Lounge in 1978 and buried alive on a beach. Mehau had previously fired Baker because he didn't listen to directions.

That same year, Hawaii Protective Association deputized sixteen men for a day's worth of security work at Hilo International

Airport on the Big Island, where there was a protest over the expansion of the airport. These temporary hires were a large, tough bunch and included two former professional football players, three men with felony convictions, and a former police officer who had been fired for using excessive force. Mehau did not shy away from the controversy inspired by his company's hiring practices.

"[I] told them whatever they did in the past, that's done with," said Mehau. "My feeling was if they deserved to not be helped, they should be left in jail. When they came out, they served their time; and I would give them a chance, and most of them proved out to be fantastic workers."

Mehau was said to socialize, too, with men involved in organized crime in Las Vegas and Japan. This included Ash Resnick, a man the government characterized as a debt collector for Las Vegas casinos. According to investigators, Resnick was very effective at his job, in large part because of his association with Mehau. Investigators also noted Mehau's interactions with Japanese businessmen associated with the Yakuza, or Japanese organized crime. Among them were racketeer Kaoru Ogawa and billionaire hotel magnate Kenji Osano, who owned the Sheraton Hotels in Hawaii, as well as a number of other hotels in Waikiki. Osano, who was once a confidant to a Japanese prime minister, was often seen in the company of Yakuza members. He was convicted of perjury in relation to testimony he gave in Japan's parliament regarding the 1976 Lockheed bribery scandal, in which Lockheed Corporation paid Japanese officials to spur the purchase of Lockheed aircraft.

But these men were hardly Mehau's only buddies. Mehau was an extremely popular, albeit private, man. He and his family counted many upstanding and prominent Hawaiian residents as friends. When one of Mehau's sons got married in Waimānalo on Oahu, the family sent out 500 invitations. Three thousand friends showed up. When daughter Dana was married in 1980, the family sent out 750 invitations. Again, more than 3,000 guests showed up.

But forget friendship, the crowds might have come to the wedding party for the food alone. The wedding party for Tony Vericella and Dana Mehau featured piles of lobster, giant platters of sashimi, two hundred pounds of Korean short ribs, a sushi booth, huli-huli chicken, hamburger, hot dogs, and eleven gallons of opihi, a shellfish found in Hawaiian waters. That was just a portion of the Mehau smorgasbord. There was also lots of chilled papaya and watermelon and seven barbecue pits.

"I don't know how many pigs we've got," Mehau said at the wedding reception. "Some are in imus, some on spits, and some in the Chinese oven. My friends bring 'em. Each one of them is sure he knows how to cook his pig better than the others."

Mehau's friends included the governor, state legislators, a US congressman, bank and airline executives, labor leaders, hoteliers, entertainers, and at least one judge. To celebrate the nuptials, these guests and more packed into the former beachside estate of heiress Kamokila Campell, in Ewa on the Leeward Coast of Oahu. As one attendee noted, "There were people strolling on the beach, people leaning against palm trees, people piled three-deep around the food booths and four-deep around the beer stand. There were people of every race and size and shape."

The actor Jim Nabors, famous for playing Gomer Pyle on the *Andy Griffith Show,* was flabbergasted at the crowd.

"I had six hundred guests at my housewarming in Hana a few weeks ago," said Nabors. "I thought that was quite a wingding but it can't compare to this. I've never seen anything like it."

Given all the people, food, and alcohol at the Mehau weddings, some questioned if the parties might get rowdy. Not a worry, said guest Tommy Trask, a local union leader.

"That's the last thing you have to worry about at one of Larry Mehau's parties," said Trask. "There's enough security here to police Aloha Stadium."

For Mehau, arranging such star-studded events was nothing new. For many years the well-connected businessman and intimate of the governor had organized opening-day festivities for the Hawaiian Senate, which included inviting beloved Hawaiian entertainers to sing, dance, and tell jokes to a chamber packed full of jovial politicians and local bigwigs. The most popular Hawaiian entertainers showed up each year, and that might be because an invitation from Mehau was one that could not be refused. As Moku, the wooden dummy of ventriloquist Freddie Morris, joked one year to the crowded Senate chamber, he'd rather do what Mehau says than end up as part of the governor's desk.

During the opening festivities for the Hawaiian Senate in 1980, Mehau, per usual, stayed just out of the spotlight. Yet people still caught sight of the almost-mythical giant, including a newspaper reporter who captured the aura that surrounded "Hawaii's official man of mystery and power:"

> *One is left with two images of Mehau. In the first, this huge, powerful man's hands reach out to gently support a tiny, very old haole lady who seems just able to maneuver up the steps leading to the gallery of the Senate. He bends near, smiles very warmly at her and truly it is a touching moment. In the other, he stands at the wings of the chamber as the senators and assembled VIPs file out past him, and hardly a man or woman passes who does not embrace him, or at a minimum, acknowledge his presence.*

CHAPTER SIX

No Rock Da Boat

In his first year on the job, Charles Marsland took aim at a handful of judges in his fight to reduce crime, verbally assaulting them after each unfavorable decision. In year two the pugnacious prosecutor set his sights on another bunch that he thought stood in the way of law and order—the state legislature.

Marsland's displeasure with Hawaiian lawmakers stemmed from their refusal the previous year to enact his office's suggestions on how to improve Hawaii's criminal code and justice system. To be fair, a few changes were made. Out of the sixty-nine crime-fighting bills Marsland's office suggested to lawmakers, including calls for tougher trespassing statutes and allowing for crime victims to sue the parents of juvenile offenders, three bills were passed into law. This fell far short of Marsland's expectations.

"I keep hearing about what a great job the legislature did in getting tough on crime," said Marsland. "Bull!"

In 1982, as the Hawaiian legislature prepared to convene, the tireless Marsland again presented a comprehensive package of crime bills for the lawmakers' consideration. Part of Marsland's wish list were bills that would allow crime victims to testify during sentencing hearings and for judges to be able to revoke a criminal's probation when the criminal was arrested for another crime. As it stood, a judge could only revoke a criminal's probation when he or she was convicted of a more recent crime, not simply upon the arrest for the alleged crime. In other words judges could only revoke probation and send a criminal to prison when the criminal had already been put in prison for the more recent conviction. Prosecutors called it Hawaii's Catch-22, and Marsland believed these kind of rules typified Hawaii's justice system, with the laws so overwhelmingly in favor of the accused that at times it seemed ludicrous. Over and over again he asked, why did Hawaii's laws more often protect the defendant than the victim?

Others were more sensitive to the rights of the accused, including Hawaiian lawmakers. These legislators did not look favorably on the scores of crime-fighting bills Marsland's office suggested, including more controversial bills calling for reinstating the death penalty, loosening wiretap restrictions, and allowing voters to retain or dismiss judges a few years after they are appointed to the bench. Representative Yoshiro Nakamura complained that to pass Marsland's list of bills was to create a "police state."

"Anyone on the outside can scream, scream, and scream that the legislature should do that or do this," said Nakamura. "But when you're sitting over here, you have a big responsibility. Making a safe community is our No. 1 mission, but when I say a safe community, I also mean preserving the rights of all the citizens. We have to be deliberative."

Marsland thought Nakamura's rationale laughable.

"If a police state means concern for victims and witnesses," replied Marsland, "[then] yeah, we are asking for a 'police state.'"

As head of the House Judiciary Committee in the Hawaiian legislature, Nakamura saw to it that Marsland would not receive his police state, complaining that, "Chuck Marsland has taken it upon himself to be the entire criminal justice system." The legislator also criticized inadequately trained prosecutors for bungling criminal cases, and he declared that the issue of crime in Hawaii was overblown and "manufactured" for use in political campaigns.

Again Marsland disagreed, stating Nakamura was "blowing smoke out of his ears and he doesn't have the slightest idea of what the hell he's talking about."

Nakamura wasn't the only one inclined to stymie Marsland's efforts, given the fact that Marsland did not exactly endear himself to the legislature, especially when he learned how poorly his legislative agenda was again being received. In public speeches he noted how there was not a single prosecutor who was a legislator, but plenty of lawmakers who are defense attorneys "who don't want to pass any laws that will offend their pocketbooks."

Of the legislative body in general, Marsland characterized the elected officials as "a bunch of half-assed politicians who subscribe to the first conclusion, and who tiptoe around the state capitol saying, 'Eh, no rock da boat, eh brah.'"

Marsland, on the other hand, was proud not to tiptoe.

"I rock the boat. If anybody doesn't like it, it's too damn bad," said the prosecutor. "There are representatives of the Yakuza here, and there have been for a long time. The Mafia is here also, from the United States mainland. We have our own local homegrown Syndicate, which is very heavy."

Of the leadership in the state capitol, Marsland told a luncheon crowd that it was composed of "a few arrogant, imperious and ambitious egotists who don't give a damn what you want."

Perhaps it is no wonder that Speaker of the House Henry Peters openly spoke of Marsland's bill suggestions as having slim chances of becoming law, especially ones aimed at restricting judges.

"If we do," said Peters, "that will look like a slight aimed at the judiciary and a pat on the back for Marsland."

At the end of the 1982 legislative session, just a few of Marsland's forty-six bill suggestions became law. One victory for prosecutors was a new law giving prosecutors the ability to appeal a judge's decision to overturn a jury's verdict. This law was inspired by Judge Harold Shintaku's controversial decision the year before to reverse a murder conviction for underworld figure Charlie Stevens. The legislature also agreed to fund a statewide witness protection program and increase the penalties for drunk driving and shoplifting.

Marsland was not alone in achieving a low yield on his legislative wish list. Governor George Ariyoshi also failed to get a majority of his crime-fighting suggestions passed into law. It was the same with the state attorney general's office, the state crime commission, and the Honolulu Police Department. Getting laws passed was not easy. But Marsland took this lack of success personally and complained loudly about the legislature's inaction. The criticism rankled the lawmakers.

"Every man has a role to play in the war against crime, and no man alone is going to do it," said Nakamura, the House judiciary chairman. "[Marsland] looks to have his way in the legislature by intimidating us to hear all his bills. Despite his crude, sledgehammer tactics, we still gave him due consideration. But he can't expect to get everything he submits."

Marsland said it was Nakamura who came to his office a year earlier and told him to "cool it" for trying to increase punishments for drunk driving and prostitution.

"Hey, Chuck, the boys like get some fun, too, you know," Marsland recalled Nakamura telling him. "When you learn how to play ball, you going get couple bills through."

Nakamura denied making those statements. He urged Marsland to work better with lawmakers and judges if he was sincere about fighting crime.

Marsland did not heed Nakamura's advice, especially in regard to State Senator Ben Cayetano. Marsland disparaged the man's haircut, of all things. Cayetano replied that Marsland was not qualified to carry the jockstrap of a judge running the Honolulu Marathon. Then, on the Senate floor, Cayetano offered for his Filipino barber to give Marsland a "Waipahu special," which Cayetano explained was a free shave. The only thing, said

Cayetano was that "unlike the typical shave where the strokes are up, Filipino style the strokes are horizontal." Cayetano then drew his hand across his throat and produced a special razor to be used for the shave—a machete.

Marsland's war of words quickly expanded beyond the legislature. He accused recently elected Honolulu Mayor Eileen Anderson of denying him funds for the creation of an organized crime unit in his office. He castigated the newspapers for employing uninformed editors and reporters, and for giving prominent, front-page coverage to acquittals in criminal cases, but little coverage of convictions. Then Marsland and some of his deputies revived their criticism of the judiciary, particularly of Judge Simeon Acoba. During a court appearance deputy prosecutor Kenneth Nam, who had previously labeled Acoba an obscenity, turned his back on the judge and said he was "just trying to hide my contempt, your Honor."

An astonished Acoba said Nam was being childish and ordered him jailed for twenty-four hours for contempt of court. Nam and Marsland were outraged, especially since they considered Acoba routinely rude to prosecutors. Marsland characterized the jailing as "Acoba's indirect and gutless retaliation for our candid public description of his incompetence."

When the Supreme Court of Hawaii upheld the jailing of Nam, Marsland attacked the high court for their tolerance of inept and corrupt judges.

"If they were truly interested in justice," he said, "they would clean their own house."

With Marsland insulting so many targets at once—he was delivering an average of two speeches a week to civic groups and other audiences—he was bound to strike a nerve and trigger something more than a verbal counterattack. It finally happened in April 1982, when Marsland referred to Alema Leota, the alleged former Syndicate leader, as "total scum." The next morning, as Marsland stepped off an elevator on the way to his office, he was confronted by an angry man.

"My uncle is Alema Leota, and if you don't stop talking about him, we're going to shut you up," shouted Penrod Fanene, who then punched Marsland twice. "We going off you."

Upon seeing their boss attacked, the office secretaries began screaming. Several investigators and Marsland's spokesman and assistant, Rick Reed, rushed to Marsland's aid. The skirmish continued, however, with Fanene yelling at Marsland before charging the prosecutor again. This time Marsland struck Fanene back, putting one fist, by his own account, "right down his throat." Marsland was sorry, he said, "that I didn't get to whack him a few more times.

"When he gets out of jail, I hope he comes back," said Marsland. "I'd like to deal with him when I can see him coming."

Marsland suffered a broken rib, a loosened tooth, cuts, and facial bruises during the attack. Fanene was eventually convicted of assaulting and threatening Marsland and sentenced to a year in prison. Fanene said he attacked Marsland in part because his mother fell ill after reading the prosecutor's comment about Leota, her notorious brother.

"My mom always gets sick when my uncle's name or my name gets in the paper," said Fanene, a known underworld figure in his own right, whose extensive criminal record included convictions for burglary, assault, and battery against a police officer, weapons violations, and more.

Following the ambush against Honolulu's prosecutor, there was little public outrage. Perhaps people thought the tough-talking prosecutor could handle a few jabs to the face, especially since he was able to fight back. No doubt some of Marsland's detractors thought that the loudmouth got what was coming to him and were grateful that someone tried to shut him up. In any case, Marsland's office saw the lack of sympathy and the absence of fellow politicians' inquiries into Marsland's recovery as further confirmation of everyone else's complicity in Hawaii's crime problem.

As spokesman Reed wrote in a letter to the *Honolulu Adver-tiser:* "The silence that has followed the attack on Chuck Marsland frightens me. The implications of that silence should frighten all of us, for it means that Chuck Marsland truly is alone in the fight to make Hawaii safer."

Accusing nearly every other elected official in Hawaii of con-tributing to Hawaii's crime problem did indeed isolate Marsland, though he could always count on a loyal group of supporters within his office to share his passion and convictions. Among those he trusted most were his right-hand man, Reed, as well as investigator Don Carstensen and a pair of deputy prosecutors: Peter Carlisle and Mike McGuigan.

Within this inner circle of advisors, the pair of deputy pros-ecutors had the more formal, though still friendly, relationship with Marsland. Hired in the 1970s by Marsland's predecessor, Togo Nakagawa, both Carlisle and McGuigan had experi-ence handling high-profile cases involving violent crime. One of the first major trials Carlisle worked on was the murder and kidnapping retrial of Wilford "Nappy" Pulawa, during which he assisted Marsland, then a deputy prosecutor, too. When McGuigan arrived to Hawaii from Washington State in 1979, he was assigned a sensitive case involving a policeman who shot a Korean youth in the head. McGuigan suspects Nakagawa assigned him the case to spare the local veteran prosecutors a headache.

With Marsland in charge, however, there was no shying away from controversy. For each case he demanded a best effort at obtaining justice.

"He was just passionate about what he did. He assembled a completely different office," said McGuigan. "The culture was much more aggressive in doing the right thing.

"You didn't back down from anything. And you had the lati-tude to do what you thought was right. You never compromised your values," McGuigan continued. "There were plea bargains;

there always will be. But I can tell you I turned down more plea bargains than I accepted."

Though Marsland's passion for justice seemed boundless—he was known to cite case after criminal case to journalists visiting his office as examples of what was wrong in Hawaii—he was careful not to meddle with his deputies' work. Outside the office he was happy to overstep the traditional role of the prosecutor, casting blame on so many people for the alleged failings of the criminal justice system and Hawaiian government to the point that he had few long-standing allies. But within his fourth-floor office on Bishop Street in downtown Honolulu, a different, more deferential Marsland presided.

"He had really come in and allowed people to do their job and do it well. He wasn't a micromanager," said Carlisle. "Where I ended up having ideas of how to put career criminals in jail, he was 100 percent, gung ho, 'Go do it!' He did the same thing with the people in the misdemeanors and the other divisions as well."

McGuigan made a similar assessment of Marsland's management style and credited Marsland for drastically reducing the high turnover rate traditionally associated with the prosecutor's office.

"He surrounded himself with good people and he respected them for what they did," said McGuigan. "It was mutually beneficial, both to [Marsland and] everyone in the office, that they could appreciate they weren't being thumbed down on. That they could do their work."

More personal was Marsland's relationship with Reed. Though Reed was twenty-four years Marsland's junior, the men enjoyed a deep friendship, as well as the trust and understanding necessary for Reed to speak, without hesitation, on Marsland's behalf. Reed's office was beside Marsland's, and he likely spoke to the prosecutor more than any other employee. Oftentimes, said Reed, their conversations involved Reed refining Marsland's comments so they could become palatable to the public, and profanity free.

Sometimes he really wanted to say something that I knew was really dumb, [something he] really should not say. I remember one specific time we were sitting in his office and he really wanted to say something, and I kept trying to explain to him why that was a mistake.

He finally said, "Okay, what do you think we should say?" So I told him what I think we should say. He said, "Alright, go say that." I got up and as I was walking out he said, behind my back, so I could hear, he said, "Chicken."

Reed could understand why Marsland disliked having his comments tempered. He, too, sometimes had difficulty expressing the messages he wanted to deliver on behalf of Marsland.

One of the frustrations of working at the prosecutor's office was it was 125 lawyers. If you want to have something to dampen your good time, or keep you from having fun, or being creative, or really all, you know, balls out and getting something done, ask a group of attorneys for advice. They think their job is to discourage you from doing anything that might get you in trouble.

Upon Marsland first entering the prosecutor's office, Reed recalled his boss asking him to write his public commentary. Upon each request Reed would dutifully research and write a draft of a speech. That draft would then be reviewed by not only Marsland, but also by a handful of prosecutors. Not surprisingly the speeches underwent major revisions, and, in Reed's opinion, were more or less neutered.

"Early on it would drive me nuts . . . I spend a few days writing this speech and Marsland would read it and say, 'I love it, I just love it,'" said Reed. "Then, the next thing I know he has five or six attorneys in there, all with a copy of the speech. It was just awful, and he'd called me in to hear all their complaints and stuff."

Apparently Marsland found the extra consultation as counterproductive as Reed.

"Finally he quit calling them in, " said Reed. "Pretty soon it was just me and him."

Reed had originally come to Hawaii in 1976 to attend a meditation seminar on Maui. The seminar ended up being canceled, but Reed came anyway, intent on exploring some of the larger questions in life. He had been reading philosophy books and exploring Eastern religions. On Maui he began to consider Chris Butler, a yogi who goes by the title Jagad Guru, or teacher of the world, as his spiritual mentor. Reed's own spiritual philosophy was straightforward.

"Do that which will help you remember God and avoid doing that which causes you to forget," said Reed.

Reed had grown up in Snohomish, Washington, and earned an education degree from Washington State University. After graduating he wrote for a public relations firm, spent a year penning part of a novel, and also worked as a bricklayer. By the time he was thirty years old, he had been married, and divorced, twice. His first marriage, to his high school sweetheart Sandra, broke up three months after the couple had a baby boy. Years later Sandra complained that Reed abandoned his son and neglected child support obligations.

"[He] forgot us," said Sandra. "He erased us from his life."

Reed's second marriage followed a similar pattern. After having two daughters with his wife Linda, Reed left Linda and the toddlers in Seattle to meditate in Maui. When meditation gave way to publishing the *Valley Isle,* divorce followed. Within a few years Linda would sue Reed for missed child support payments, too. In both cases Reed claimed to have sent some money to his ex-wives and made private arrangements for child support payments that each of the women reneged upon.

In Hawaii Reed found love again. His new wife, Carter, became Marsland's secretary. The Reeds, though, would eventually divorce, necessitating that Reed move his office a floor below Marsland's. But in happier days the couple, both vegetarians, would bring extra food to the office for Marsland to eat at lunch. Like he did a decade earlier when working at the bank, Marsland favored using his lunch hour to exercise at the Armed Services YMCA, frequently working the speed bag. If he ate a midday meal, it was a no-frills sandwich he consumed at his desk in a few seconds flat.

Noticing that Marsland was losing weight on account of his hectic schedule and poor diet, Reed and his wife intervened, regularly bringing him lunch.

"We were happy to keep Chuck healthy," Reed said. "Vegetarians are always happy to share their food, try to turn somebody else on to it."

There were other thoughtful gestures. For Marsland's birthday Reed presented his boss with a .38 caliber handgun. The gun Marsland had been carrying, said Reed, was not practical.

The two men were so close and so often in each other's company that people occasionally confused Reed as Marsland's son. Some colleagues begrudged Reed for his closeness to Marsland. On one occasion, Reed said, a deputy prosecutor walked into Marsland's office to discover Marsland and Reed engrossed in conversation, each sitting back in their chairs with their feet propped up on Marsland's desk. The deputy prosecutor quickly reversed course. Later a colleague warned Reed: "You gotta be careful showing that kind of familiarity with Chuck," the coworker said. "Some of the deputies are really envious and becoming resentful."

Others were frustrated by the favoritism Marsland allegedly gave to deputy prosecutors Carlisle and McGuigan. Keith Kaneshiro, a deputy prosecutor whom Marsland placed in charge of the office's newly created organized crime task force, characterized McGuigan and Carlisle as Marsland's "two pets." It could be difficult for Kaneshiro to work with the two men.

"It's hard to trust them," said Kaneshiro. "You can't tell them too much because they're there to tell the boss what I'm doing."

According to Kaneshiro, he and Marsland became estranged when Kaneshiro refused to prosecute potential voter fraud, considering the case a waste of resources and outside the scope of organized crime. It would be better, Kaneshiro said he argued to Marsland, to go after street criminals. Marsland disagreed and removed Kaneshiro as head of the task force. Kaneshiro says he was not particularly upset about the change. He was still the sole prosecutor on the organized crime task force and had a long list of murder cases to try.

"Basically he wanted somebody who fell into his line of philosophy [about] how to run the strike force. Apparently I didn't," said Kaneshiro. "He had the right to bring in his own people to do that. I didn't hold it against him."

Kaneshiro's replacement was Carstensen, a former Honolulu police officer and martial arts expert previously hired as an investigator for the task force. Carstensen had endeared himself to Marsland a few years earlier during the trial of Vernon Reiger Sr., when death threats against Marsland required that the prosecutor receive around-the-clock protection. While Marsland slept at night, Carstensen would stay awake in the prosecutor's living room, ensuring his safety.

Carstensen, whom Marsland referred to as a bulldog, was an energetic and diligent crime fighter. As evidence of his fastidiousness, when he joined the Honolulu Police Department in 1974, he was recognized for being the recruit with the best police notebook. Within three years the Honolulu policeman was detailed to federal investigations dedicated to organized crime. As part of this work, he routinely kept suspected underworld members, including the Yakuza, under surveillance. He ended up becoming more familiar with Hawaii's criminal underworld than others in Marsland's office.

"Don fit a role that Chuck needed. He was a very proactive investigator. He had a lot of informants on the streets," said Kaneshiro. "Chuck liked that type."

Among the gangsters Carstensen knew well was suspected hit man Ronnie Ching. It was Carstensen who persuaded Ching to join him for lunch in 1980 and discuss his life as a gangster. Little did Ching know that Carstensen was tape-recording their meeting and that the transcript of their conversation would later show up in court. When federal agents raided Ching's Waikiki apartment and adjoining storage closet in 1981, discovering his illegal arsenal, the absentee Ching supposedly phoned the apartment midraid and spoke to Carstensen.

Ching told the cop that he'd be willing to turn himself in. But first, he said, he wanted to get high and get laid. Just don't tell my girlfriend, Ching pleaded with the cop. Hours later Ching was arrested in downtown Honolulu.

❧

History repeated itself for Ronnie Ching. In 1977 he was incarcerated at the federal penitentiary in Lompoc, California, as punishment for the illegal possession of bombs and firearms. Four years later he was sent back to Lompoc, again for illegally possessing bombs and firearms. No matter the additional exposure, living behind bars did not grow on the heavyweight hit man.

During his first stay in prison, Ching's chief grievance was how frequently inmates stabbed one another. During his second trip Ching had another complaint relating to sharp pains: kidney stones. This ailment caused Ching considerable suffering, to the point that he was transported numerous times between Lompoc and the US Medical Center for Federal Prisoners in Springfield, Missouri. Doctors at both facilities quickly lost sympathy for their patient. After removing stones from Ching, they accused him of faking his symptoms and attempting to manipulate the medical staff. Ching was offended by this treatment, especially when the doctors labeled Ching obese. The prisoner sued the doctors and prison officials for allegedly refusing him medical treatment and inflicting cruel and unusual punishment.

Ching's discomfort and antagonistic relationship with prison doctors did not bode well for the remainder of his twenty-one-year prison sentence. What's more, Ching faced the prospect of additional time in prison since authorities in Hawaii were ramping up investigations of unsolved gangland murders in which he was the prime suspect. Soon enough Ching was in contact with the prosecutor's office in Honolulu, eager to explore the possibility of a plea deal in exchange for information regarding unsolved crimes, including the murders of Arthur Baker and Bobby Fukumoto, both of whom Ching was believed to have killed. Though Marsland harbored suspicions that Ching killed his son, too, he was eager to possibly use the hit man to target more organized crime members, including Hawaii's supposed godfather.

When Ching was brought back to Hawaii and spoke with members of the organized crime task force, he shared details about assorted killings but would not name names, said Kaneshiro. Ching might say how many people comprised a killing crew, but he would not identify those people until he had a deal. Despite this hiccup, the negotiations were pleasant.

"Ronnie is a smooth guy. He is very personable. He and I got along really well," said Kaneshiro, who accompanied Ching on some flights between Hawaii and California, where Ching remained imprisoned.

"The fact that he is pleasant to talk to is kind of deceiving because it hides the viciousness of his character," he added.

Congeniality aside, the discussions left Kaneshiro uneasy. It was clear that Ching had been the killer in the majority of the murders they discussed, and the deputy prosecutor knew "it's not going to look good to use a triggerman as a witness to testify against accomplices."

Marsland, however, was still hopeful that Ching could be of value. This inclination may have been supported by the fact, said Kaneshiro, that Ching denied killing Marsland's son. In any event, Marsland and Kaneshiro visited Honolulu Police Chief Francis Keala to discuss the possible plea deal. Keala objected to it entirely, recalled Kaneshiro.

"You cannot give this guy a deal because the information I have is that he is the murderer of your son," Kaneshiro recalled Keala saying to Marsland.

Not true, replied the prosecutor, affirming his belief in Ching's denial of culpability.

"You're making a mistake," said Keala. "Don't give him a deal."

In the end Marsland agreed with the assessments made by Kaneshiro and Keala. No plea deal was granted. Ching was sent back to Lompoc.

The decision was difficult for Marsland. Ching had extensive knowledge of the underworld, and his cooperation promised the chance to convict a number of killers who so far had eluded police and prosecutors. His cooperation, too, promised insights into the death of Marsland's own son. For seven years Marsland had collected as much information as he could about Chuckers's death, even coming up with a shortlist of suspects that included Ching. Yet no matter how hard he sleuthed, and how often the same few names were whispered to him, Marsland could not be absolutely certain who shot his beloved Chuckers. There always remained at least a sliver of doubt.

The subject of Chuckers's murder was not one Marsland often gave voice to, publicly or privately, much like the topic of his ex-wife and daughter in Boston. When he did publicly discuss his experience as the father of a murdered son, he was often vague and reluctant to portray himself as unique in his suffering. As Marsland said in a campaign commercial: "I've watched the anguish, shame and loathing play across the face of a rape victim. And I've known the unbearable agony of being a member of the victim's family. I will do absolutely everything within my power to see that not one of you, nor anyone else, suffers through a similar experience."

Despite the limited mention of Chuckers's death, Marsland's acquaintances knew it weighed heavily on the father's heart.

"With all that he had endured, I think he kind of held himself with grace, let's put it that way," said McGuigan. "It was never something that he publicly displayed, [but] you knew it was there."

While Chuckers's death may have helped spur Marsland to run for public office, Marsland seemed to revel in his broader attack on lawbreakers, especially violent perpetrators and members of organized crime.

"It was very interesting. Here was this guy who's gone through this really horrific thing. Obviously someone who has gone through that type of trauma is bitter," said Carlisle. "But I remember we were walking across the street, heading off to some new, new big trial . . . he was there to watch [and] he was saying, 'You know this is getting to be fun.'"

Carlisle, McGuigan, and other staff were among the select group of people who saw both sides of Marsland: the abrasive, aggressive, tough-talking, fed up prosecutor determined to clean up Hawaii, and the soft-spoken, kindly gentleman content to live a comfortable but modest life outside the office.

"When it came to doing his job he had a persona," said McGuigan. "But if you were to meet him in Safeway [supermarket] or Longs [pharmacy], he would be like your, you know, your uncle, always asking about how you were, family and that sort of thing."

Phil and Joan Hester, Marsland's longtime friends in Hawaii, said they would often field questions from other friends asking why Marsland always seemed so angry, or why he was so quick to cast blame on assorted judges and elected officials. The Hesters would respond that in private they knew Marsland to be unassuming and polite. He was not one to rant and rave or cause controversy.

"He was just a wonderful man who hated to see so [many] terrible, terrible things that were going on in Hawaii," said Joan Hester.

Yet even they expressed some wonder over the confident public image Marsland projected.

According to Phil Hester:

As long as I knew him, I didn't see him as a public figure per se. But when he'd make his speeches and get the write-ups in the paper afterward and whatnot, you'd hear people talking about his speech last night and so on. It was a little surprising to me. I didn't realize he had the power that he had with the public. But he surely did, he really did.

At home Marsland enjoyed gardening, tending carefully to orchids and tropical fruit trees that bore avocados, papayas, and mangoes. He also loved babying his dogs, including two he owned when he was elected prosecutor: Missy and Stinky. Both had been adopted from the pound, and Stinky's true name was actually something along the lines of Henri, as given by Marsland's longtime partner, Polly Grigg. Marsland couldn't stand the prissy name, however, so he called the French poodle Stinky.

Such a name was a term of endearment from the gruff prosecutor. He loved the dog so much that in the morning, though he would forgo making himself any lunch, Marsland would cook Stinky a meal of chicken, vegetables, and steamed brown rice. Stinky was too refined to eat a meal of plain white rice. Marsland and Grigg were also known to bring the dogs to an ice cream parlor and buy them frozen treats, and Marsland, the tough-talking prosecutor, had been heard speaking to his pets in baby talk.

Marsland doted just as much on his tough-as-nails mother Sadie. For many years Sadie Marsland had a bigger and tougher reputation among Oahu residents than her son, having been a longtime schoolteacher known for her strict classroom admin- istration. She seems to have been similarly stern with her own son, though he loved her for it. Even when Marsland was in his sixties, his mother would call the office and ask to speak to "Boy," the name she used to refer to him his entire life. The secretaries had orders from Marsland to always patch his mother through, no matter what he was doing.

"This time I remember, we were in there with members of the organized crime strike force, a really important closed-door meeting, and the secretary knew not to put the calls through, no matter who it was. The governor could have called, he wouldn't have gotten through," said Reed. "But it was Sadie. She got through."

During this meeting, Reed recalled, Marsland had adopted a tough tone, trying to inspire his deputy prosecutors and inves- tigators to be fearless in their pursuit of gangsters. When Sadie called, said Reed, Marsland at once turned submissive, asking how he could help.

As Grigg said of her quasi-mother-in-law: "Whatever Sadie says, goes."

Marsland was not so accommodating of his lover. Despite ultimately having a romantic relationship for approximately forty years, Marsland and Grigg never married. This may have been attributable to the unpleasant, yet dissimilar ways in which their respective marriages had ended: Marsland had divorced, and Grigg was widowed. Marsland and Grigg each had a son from their first marriages, too, which could have complicated the dynamics of their relationship. Though Chuckers's friends said that Grigg was well regarded by Chuckers, she confessed she sometimes found it hard to stomach the teenager, believing him to be "so conceited you could hardly listen to him."

Marriage also may have been avoided due to the couple's acknowledgment of their frequent tiffs. Grigg herself said that if she and Marsland had married, she "probably would have divorced him at least fifteen times." The fights between Marsland and Grigg could become so heated that Grigg would leave Marsland.

"She was one to fly off the handle pretty easily," said Phil Hester. "[But] she wasn't about to give up on Chuck, I'll tell you that. She went back to California a couple of times, but not for very long. She was locked into him like a cable and never thought about anybody else from the time she met him, I'm sure."

At times Marsland was seen to be stunningly rude to his companion. Reed recalled once attending an election-campaign committee meeting held at Marsland's home. During the discussion Grigg spoke up and shared her opinion with the gathered supporters. Marsland was irked, evidently placing little value on Grigg's thoughts about the matter.

"I thought I told you to wait in the truck," he snarled at Grigg, dismissing her.

Grigg went outside. Reed followed. The two friends talked. At that point in time, Grigg and Reed were those who knew Marsland best.

"It was really bad. I just couldn't believe it . . . It was just embarrassing," said Reed. "Maybe he wasn't really in love with her, I dunno. He didn't treat her with respect, as much care as she took of him, redesigning his home, just pretty much organized his life for him."

In Reed's opinion Grigg was intelligent, attractive, and interesting. He didn't see what his boss's hang-up was.

"If he had treated Polly the way he treated his dog," said Reed, "they'd have been very happy."

In 1983, beginning his third year in office, Marsland resumed his warring ways, renewing feuds with two familiar foes, the state legislature and the judiciary. Sometimes the prosecutor was able to annoy both groups at the same time. During a confirmation hearing in the Hawaiian Senate for Judge James Wakatsuki, whom Governor George Ariyoshi had appointed to the Supreme Court of Hawaii, Marsland was among a small minority who felt the circuit court judge was unqualified for the post. When he testified as much to the Senate, his commentary was so barbed that several senators flinched.

The prosecutor derided the judge, who had previously been a Democratic lawmaker and speaker of the house, as a "party hack" who lacked an adequate legal background. Marsland said the appointment reeked of cronyism and personally disgusted him. Of course the prosecutor had not forgotten how Wakatsuki had ruled against his office and thwarted Marsland's attempts to curb cockfighting and marijuana growing on Oahu through the use of civil lawsuits in place of criminal indictments.

"Wakatsuki is neither an accomplished attorney nor an experienced judge," said Marsland. "You don't need to even practice law—all you need to do is get elected to the legislature and then kiss the right okoles."

Despite Marsland's bluster, the Senate confirmed Wakatsuki to the Supreme Court of Hawaii.

The judicial confirmation was not Marsland's only disappointment with lawmakers during this legislative session. As in the previous two years, Marsland urged the legislature to pass a number of bills relating to crime, including a comprehensive package of bills regarding the rights of victims of crime. For the third year in a row, few of these bill proposals became law, at least as proposed by Marsland.

It did not help the prosecutor's cause that on the second day of the session, Marsland publicly accused lawmakers of palling around with gamblers from the Neighbor Islands, allegedly promising to legalize a state lottery and greyhound racing. Or that Marsland engaged in a heated and accusatory exchange in a judiciary hearing with his nemesis Senator Ben Cayetano, each man calling the other a gutless liar. Or that Marsland cynically predicted at the beginning of the legislative session that few of his fifty-eight bill proposals would merit serious consideration. When this prediction proved true by the end of the session, Marsland was nonetheless dismayed.

"I don't know whether today if this legislature is crooked, stupid or achieved new heights of asininity," said Marsland.

At the same time, Marsland began a fresh line of attacks on judges, including old favorites like Judge Simeon Acoba, and new targets, such as Judge Wendell Huddy. Marsland became enraged at Huddy when the judge, presiding over what he deemed to be a difficult murder case, suggested to deputy prosecutors that they consider plea-bargaining with the suspect and reducing the murder charge to manslaughter.

The deputy prosecutors rejected that suggestion, proceeded to trial, and won the case. The jury deliberated for little more than an hour before deciding that the defendant was indeed guilty of strangling his girlfriend. Afterward, upon hearing from his deputies that Huddy had suggested the lesser charge, Marsland castigated the judge, declaring it totally inappropriate for Huddy to inject himself into plea bargaining.

"The jury had no problems with a murder charge," Marsland said tartly. "Only the court did."

In response Huddy decreed that Marsland and two of his deputies would no longer be permitted to address him in a courtroom. Marsland said such an order was groundless.

By this time, more than halfway through his first term as Honolulu's prosecutor, Marsland had well established his penchant for conflict. The squabbles with judges, lawmakers, and anyone else he deemed an obstacle to law and order had become so routine that many of his critics who previously had stood silent felt they could no longer in good conscience keep their mouths shut.

"That's what gripes me more than anything else about Chuck," said state public defender Barry Rubin. "Everything becomes a personal vendetta between him and the judge who doesn't give him the result he seeks. That's not what an attorney is supposed to do."

Others pleaded for the media and general public to wise up to Marsland's antics and not succumb to the appeal of his verbal firebombing.

"Our prosecutor is running amok," said Cayetano, "carrying on his political hit-and-run driving again and again, leaving a path strewn with victims, with the media in hot pursuit to find out the identity of the victims rather than stopping him from doing further harm."

No matter Cayetano's appeal, the press could not afford to ignore Marsland. For a journalist, Marsland was a gift that kept on giving.

"Reporters can't resist a Marsland speech. The quotes are simply good copy," wrote Dan Boylan in *Honolulu* magazine. "The lengths to which Marsland will go in creating quotes to garner free publicity are only limited by the mood of the prosecutor himself, who sometimes launches attacks in the bluest of language— thereby rendering them useless for TV or the daily papers."

Marsland's mouth opened so often to spew vitriol and venom that even Acoba, the circumspect judge oft abused by Marsland, finally offered a caution that many interpreted to be directed toward the prosecutor, though his sober statement lacked the inflammatory touch that Marsland had perfected.

"We must guard against mistaking intemperance for toughness, fanaticism for dedication, bombast for wisdom," said Acoba, who later became a member of the state Supreme Court.

These voices echoed earlier complaints. During Marsland's first year in office, he encountered opposition from the American Civil Liberties Union, who deemed his comments "reckless and intemperate" and contributing to public "hysteria."

"Enough is enough—we expect more from our elected officials than what amounts to temper tantrums," said the organization's local office.

A young lawyers' group within Hawaii's state bar association also chimed in, calling Marsland a "poor loser" who offers "implausible excuses" when cases aren't decided in his office's favor.

But for every complaint about Marsland's heavy-handed and rabid criticism, there were also cheers for the prosecutor and his performance. His supporters were happy to see someone confront crime so aggressively. Even some of his courtroom adversaries could pay him a compliment. As one defense lawyer admitted:

> *Many lawyers see Marsland as a loose cannon on the deck. But I think he plays a valuable role. He may wield a meat cleaver when he should use a scalpel, and he certainly goes too far sometimes. But I'd rather have him in the prosecutor's office than a bleeding heart liberal with a probationary officer's mentality. Then we'd really be in trouble.*

For all the hard words, the insistence on minimal plea bargaining, and the characterizations of the prosecutor from his political opponents as someone desiring a police state, Marsland demonstrated that he was not a merciless man. He judged proposed new drug laws as too harsh, objecting to the government's being able to seize the property of suspects caught growing less than three pounds of marijuana. He regularly visited schools to present his "Crime Is for Losers" program in which the prosecutor, a judge, and a prison inmate gave more than ten thousand students firsthand accounts of the consequences of breaking the law.

"If we just keep one of you from committing a crime," Marsland once told his audience of students, "than all the time we spent here has been more than worth it."

In September 1983 Marsland refused to prosecute eighteen people after they were arrested for trespassing during a protest of the demolition of a former treatment center for leprosy, or Hansen's disease. Considering the demonstration peaceful and hardly disruptive, Marsland expressed sympathy for two lepers who refused to leave their condemned residences at the Oahu facility.

Because Marsland refused to prosecute, the state attorney general's office pressed charges against the protesters. In a letter to Marsland, Hawaii Attorney General Tany Hong reminded the Honolulu prosecutor that it was his "sworn duty to prosecute all violations of criminal laws." Marsland dodged the order, parrying that it was his duty to "seek justice, not merely convict." The protesters were grateful for Marsland's stand. To express their thanks, they painted the prosecutor a placard.

"To Mr. Marsland," it read. "MAHALO for CARING. From ALL of US."

They weren't the only folks on Oahu who were appreciative of the prosecutor. In 1980, the year before Marsland took office, murders and violent crime had been at an all-time high in Hawaii. Since Marsland became prosecutor, those statistics dropped. Marsland, it was perceived, was doing well on his campaign promise to combat lawlessness and free people from fear. And, deducing from his public comments, Marsland was just getting started. At the state convention for the Republican Party in May 1983, just six months after the GOP's poor local showing in midterm elections, Marsland told his fellow party members that they needed to pick a fight with the state legislature. Republicans, he said, "are going to have to get louder, tougher and a lot more personal with the clowns running that circus. In other words, you're going to have to stand up, spit on your hands and start a brawl."

During that same spring, Marsland began speaking publicly about Hawaii's godfather, alleging that he had seized control of the underworld in the early 1970s and had cultivated strong ties with Hawaiian politicians, the mainland mafia, and the Japanese Yakuza, becoming the chief power broker among Hawaii's richest and most powerful residents. Marsland said he knew the man's identity and wanted to indict him, but he didn't yet have enough evidence to prove his allegations.

"One does not refuse to discuss a virus, even though its name and treatment are not identified," said Marsland. "You acknowledge its existence, and fight it, and the general public deserves to have been warned."

Marsland's confidence in the existence of a godfather stood in contrast to the opinions of other law enforcement officials, who dismissed such talk as unsubstantiated rumor. Yet no one could convincingly rebut Marsland's claims. The prosecutor commanded too much respect. It was also hard to battle someone so insistent about the depth of Hawaii's crime problem. As he told a crowd attending a symposium on crime: "The only thing that bothers me about our discussion today is its title: 'Organized Crime: Myth or Reality?' Organized crime—particularly here in Hawaii—is such an all-pervasive reality that such a question is absurd. It's like asking, 'Old age: myth or reality?' All you have to do is look around."

Despite some prominent detractors, Marsland's popularity was such that few thought he could be beaten if he ran for reelection in 1984. As the state's most visible Republican, if not the state's most recognizable politician altogether, some of his supporters hoped he would run for higher office, perhaps for governor. He was quick to dash those hopes, stating that he wanted no position but that of Honolulu's prosecutor.

Though he might have appeared angry in public, Marsland found satisfaction in his work. If he often grew frustrated, it was to be expected; he did not campaign to become prosecutor to leave things unchanged. The resistance he encountered validated his mission and confirmed to him that subversive forces still shaped Hawaiian society.

When asked if he was running for reelection, Marsland answered breezily: "I wouldn't miss it for the world."

Later he said, "I kind of like what I'm doing. I have some things I have to finish."

CHAPTER SEVEN

My Bare Hands

They came to the state capitol to sing. As a reward they received subpoenas.

Per usual, the opening day of the Hawaiian legislative session in 1984 featured the song and dance of Waikiki entertainers. But just before six of these performers began their acts in the Senate chamber, an investigator from the Honolulu prosecutor's office intercepted them, putting subpoenas in their hands. In less than a month, they would be expected to appear before a grand jury investigating the reelection activities of Governor George Ariyoshi, on behalf of whose campaign the singers had previously performed.

Despite the surprise of the subpoenas, the show went on. The performers laughed about being called to the grand jury and then sang for the assembled crowd of politicians and dignitaries. Singer Bernard Kalua even tried to profit from the episode, waving his subpoena around on the Senate floor, asking, "Hey, brah, can I cash this in?"

In the audience was Charles Marsland. A few rows behind the slender Honolulu prosecutor, looming over his shoulder, was the hulking Larry Mehau. Just like years past, Mehau had arranged the day's entertainment, and, just like years past, the Big Island rancher and businessman was duly thanked by Senate President Richard "Dickie" Wong.

Wong possessed considerably less gratitude for the party-crashing Marsland.

"Gee . . . they're all my friends," Wong said of the singers who received subpoenas. "I wish maybe he'd chosen another day."

These subpoenas came weeks after Mehau himself was called to testify before the grand jury, which was considering possible impropriety concerning Ariyoshi's most recent gubernatorial campaign and the entertainment expenses associated with it. Mehau refused to testify, invoking his Fifth Amendment rights. His lawyer, the irrepressible David Schutter, accused Marsland of pursuing a vendetta against his client. Mehau himself advised the public that "you better not sue anyone who works for the prosecutor," referencing his still-ongoing libel lawsuit against Rick Reed over the godfather allegations printed almost seven years earlier in the *Valley Isle*.

Since being publicly accused of being the leader of Hawaiian organized crime, Mehau had endured three years of scrutiny and surveillance by local and federal investigators conducting Operation Firebird, which included a probe of alleged heroin trafficking. The investigation was closed in late 1980 without any charges being brought against Mehau or anyone else. Despite this outcome, Mehau and his family still suffered from the stigma of being investigated. Beverly Mehau said her husband instructed their children to hold their heads high no matter what was said about their father.

"He can take care of himself, but he was very worried about the children and myself," said Beverly Mehau. "He wanted us to be strong and not let all of this, the rumors that were going around or the allegations that were going around, to get us down because if we showed it, it would be like a defeat. We had nothing to be ashamed of."

Even absent any criminal charges, Mehau was not vindicated by the termination of Operation Firebird. The top federal prosecutor in Hawaii, US Attorney Daniel Bent, later testified that "the conclusion among the people that I know to be principally involved in Operation Firebird was that Mr. Mehau was a principal organized crime figure in the state of Hawaii, a person of considerable influence in criminal activity among people involved in organized crime and also within people in state government."

Nonetheless, Bent said investigators could not locate sufficient evidence to convict Mehau of any crimes. The government also faced challenges getting witnesses to testify. A letter to the director of the FBI from the bureau's Honolulu SAC, or special agent in charge, summed up that agency's conclusion regarding Mehau: "It was alleged that subject used strong-arm extortion tactics in the entertainment industry in Hawaii. Due to the reluctance of victims to talk about these matters, they do not lend themselves to prosecution. In addition, allegations regarding political corruption were implied; again, these lack prosecutive merit."

Others felt these conclusions overstated what was discovered through Operation Firebird. Keith Kaneshiro, who briefly headed the organized crime task force within Marsland's office as a deputy prosecutor, was privy to the Operation Firebird reports. Kaneshiro says Operation Firebird amounted to nothing more than a number of confidential informants claiming Mehau was the head of organized crime and a cataloguing of Mehau's acquaintances both inside and outside of the underworld.

"It was a guilt by association type of investigation," said Kaneshiro. "[Mehau] was a very popular person. He knew a lot of people, both criminals and not criminals . . . They were all lumped in as associates of Larry Mehau, which sort of gave the implication that this guy's all dirty."

Mehau's reputation remained tarnished, too, because claims of his criminal associations were so often renewed. In 1984 former Syndicate thug Henry Huihui, under suspicion for a number of murders and other crimes, agreed to plead guilty and become a cooperating witness for the federal government. Among the things he told investigators was that when he, Bobby Wilson, and Wilford "Nappy" Pulawa were retried in 1978 for kidnapping and murder charges, Pulawa had discussed killing two men. The first target was to be Marsland, who was leading the prosecution of the Syndicate members. The other target was Mehau, who they knew to be a frequent visitor to the governor's office in the state capitol. The idea, which was apparently never attempted, was to shoot Mehau as he drove his car into, or out of, the state capitol's underground parking complex. Was this a plan by Pulawa to eliminate a rival? Huihui never explained a motive for the possible killing.

Huihui claimed, too, that Mehau had given tacit approval to the murder of labor leader Josiah Lii a year earlier. Huihui said he was sitting outside the Naniloa Surf Hotel on the Big Island in 1977 when a car pulled up to a stop at the hotel. There was a commotion, said Huihui, as Mehau emerged from the vehicle. Mehau greeted a number of the men milling about the hotel entrance, eventually making his way to Huihui, who he greeted with a soft handshake. According to Huihui, Mehau then placed his other hand over the men's shaking hands, giving soft pats as he looked at Huihui and spoke.

"Are you going to take care of Joe?" he asked the gangster.

"You got it," said Huihui.

"Are you going to do it soon?" asked Mehau.

"Yeah," said Huihui.

The next day Huihui ordered the murder of Lii, who was perceived as a rival to Huihui and his criminal associates. One of Huihui's underlings, Michael Ward, walked into the offices of the Inlandboatmen's Union at noontime in downtown Honolulu and shot Lii to death. Huihui claimed that he sped up the execution because of Mehau's inquiry, and expressed surprise that Mehau had already been aware of the plans to kill Lii.

"It was more important now than I ever thought it was," Huihui said of Lii's execution. "Because of that meeting with Larry."

Mehau denied having such a conversation with Huihui. He did briefly see Huihui at the Big Island hotel, said Mehau, but it was months earlier than Huihui claimed, and their greeting consisted of nods of acknowledgement, not handshakes and conversation. Huihui, said Mehau, was telling lies to ingratiate himself with government investigators and lessen his time in prison.

Federal prosecutors were indeed reluctant to believe Huihui's story regarding Mehau.

"I had serious reservations that conversation ever took place," said federal prosecutor Frank Marine. "Here's Henry Huihui giving you a little morsel mentioning Larry Mehau. But it's so vague and ambiguous that you know it's not useful."

The Lii murder was one of two murders to which Huihui pleaded guilty in Honolulu on a busy and momentous day in 1984. After a decade of investigation, the government was finally convicting the Syndicate thug, though for only a fraction of his suspected crimes and killings. Even with the limited charges, the legal proceedings were extensive on account of all the jurisdictions involved in Huihui's prosecution.

The morning of May 8, 1984, began with the notorious gangster sitting in a courtroom on the Big Island, where he pleaded guilty to extortion, conspiracy, and gambling charges. Huihui was then flown to Oahu and taken by police motorcade to a Honolulu courthouse, where police patrolled the building with machine guns and high-powered rifles. Huihui, dressed in jeans, an aloha shirt, sunglasses, and a faded camouflage jacket, noticed Marsland sitting behind him in the courtroom as he waited to plead guilty to the pair of murders.

"How's it, Chuck?" said Huihui.

"Pretty good, man," said Marsland.

"I can't say the same," said Huihui, flashing a smile.

After the murder pleas, Huihui was transported across the street to the federal courthouse in Honolulu, where he pleaded guilty to racketeering and filing false tax returns. It was all cause for celebration. Huihui's long and murderous criminal career was now over.

Yet less than a month later, there was reason for anger and disbelief. Huihui's former Syndicate cohort, Alvin Kaohu, was paroled early from prison. Kaohu had been convicted of ordering the slaying of a Big Island gambler merely three years prior. Police and prosecutors, including Marsland, were outraged at his short stay behind bars.

Just as incredible, they complained, was the job arranged for the paroled Kaohu: He had been given work at an Oahu dairy run by a woman recently accused of murder.

"The people of the state of Hawaii have been ripped off again," said Marsland. "It appears to be an effort to give organized crime a break."

Marsland was already in a sour mood. He had been reluctant to offer Huihui a plea deal, refusing to extend the offer even while his prosecutor colleagues on the Big Island and within the federal government were eager to cut a deal and convict the gangster. Marsland's obstinacy was a sore point among federal prosecutors and investigators, including newly arrived federal prosecutor Marine, who was assigned to Honolulu as a strike force attorney dedicated to combating organized crime. Marsland and Marine did not get along. Part of the problem was that their turfs overlapped. Some of the same gangsters Marine was targeting through federal courts were being accused of local crimes prosecuted by Marsland's office, as was the case with Huihui. It could be difficult to agree how to divvy up the casework. What's more, even after reaching an agreement, say federal officials, Marsland would turn around and change course without notice.

Marine had come to Hawaii from Washington, D.C., where he had worked the last four years as a lawyer handling appeals within the criminal division of the US Department of Justice. Initially he tried to befriend Marsland, arranging a meeting with the Honolulu prosecutor to discuss the racketeering case he had developed against gangsters associated with Huihui. Marine hoped to give Marsland information that would enable the Honolulu prosecutor's office to pursue murder cases against some of Huihui's criminal cohorts, ensuring the chances of incarceration and making it more likely that witnesses would cut plea deals and avoid trials. Marine did so despite being warned by his federal prosecutor colleague, US Attorney Daniel Bent, not to meet with Marsland.

"Dan Bent advised me not to do that. He said look, 'Marsland is a loose cannon, he's untrustworthy, he's a nut case, he's out of control, you shouldn't do this,'" said Marine.

Despite having respect for Bent, who previously served as the federal organized crime strike force attorney in Hawaii, Marine disregarded his counsel and followed his own instinct.

"Look, I don't know the guy from Adam. I've got no hostility toward him. I'm gonna give the guy the case on a silver platter," Marine recalled thinking. "I would think he would be appreciative of it.

"I was wrong. Big time," said Marine. "I should have listened to Dan Bent."

Marsland was at first grateful for the information provided by Marine. Then, Marine says, Marsland began to dictate how their offices' cooperation should proceed, which grated on Marine, but was not entirely unexpected. Communication between the men nearly broke down completely, however, when Huihui himself indicated he was willing to plead guilty and cooperate with the government. As federal and local prosecutors negotiated an acceptable plea deal, someone leaked information about Huihui's potential cooperation with the government to the press.

When this information appeared in the newspapers, Marine was livid. Not only was Huihui's life now in danger on account of the public notice that he might testify against fellow gangsters,

Marine felt the media coverage portrayed federal prosecutors as overly accommodating to the former member of the Syndicate. Marsland, on the other hand, was portrayed as sufficiently tough on crime, supposedly on the fence about whether to grant Huihui a plea deal until the gangster promised to disclose information about the leaders of Hawaiian organized crime.

Marine could not believe what he was reading, deeming Marsland's position "pure bullshit." The agreement with Huihui already called for the gangster to reveal his knowledge about other members of organized crime—that was "standard operating procedure," said Marine. On account of the noble depiction of Marsland and other information, Marine was certain the leak came from Marsland's office.

Within a day or so, Marine and Marsland met with other law enforcement officials to discuss the impasse. Gathering around a conference table within the FBI's office in downtown Honolulu, Marsland immediately berated Marine for accusing his staff of leaking information. Marine responded that the leaks were damaging, and that they must stop. Marsland would hear none of it and began swearing at Marine.

"You fucking cock lawyer," Marine recalled Marsland telling him. "You fucking whorefucker."

Marine remained calm and tried to inject logic into his argument.

"Chuck, if I was going to leak something do you think I'd leak something that makes me sound like a stupid, weak asshole?" Marine asked Marsland. "Of course it doesn't come from us and I know it's from you."

Marsland grew angrier. He then launched into a startlingly profane tirade, labeling Marine a "whorefucker" again, as well as many other derogatory names.

Marine began gripping the table in front of him in an effort to restrain himself. Marsland, however, would not stop. Again and again he called Marine a "whorefucker."

Finally Marine, his temper triggered, could no longer stay silent.

"Whorefucker? The only whore I ever fucked was your mother and she gave me the clap," said Marine, who then proceeded to launch his own profane tirade.

At this, Marsland was apoplectic. "I WILL FUCKING KILL YOU," he screamed, jumping up and slinging his chair against the wall behind him.

At the same time, said Marine, Marsland seemed to make a motion like he was reaching for his handgun. Instantly two FBI agents enveloped Marsland in a bear hug, lifted the tall prosecutor off the ground, and carried him to a chair on the other side of the room. Following the commotion there was dead silence for what felt like an eternity.

Finally the local FBI chief said, "Gee, maybe we can find some common ground here."

The room exploded in laughter. Marsland, however, was not amused. Nonetheless, within a few days the federal and local prosecutors agreed on a plea deal with Huihui, resulting in his guilty pleas in three courthouses across the Hawaiian Islands. Despite this cooperation there was ongoing strife between federal law enforcement and Marsland's office.

Ray Hamilton, a longtime FBI agent in Hawaii, recalled being frustrated with the mercurial and hardheaded Marsland, especially when the Honolulu prosecutor would tell Hamilton and his federal colleagues one thing, and then tell the newspapers something different. He can recall the dismay of Marine upon reading Marsland's comments in the morning paper.

"Frank would shake his head, scratch his head, pound the heel of his hand against his forehead and say 'Wha-, wha-, what is this? Do you know anything about this?'" said Hamilton.

Late one evening Hamilton went to Marsland's home to try to coax the prosecutor into cooperation with federal authorities and to accommodate their strategy for prosecuting local gangsters. Marsland was resistant to falling in line and sacrificing his autonomy, even when Hamilton and others tried to sell him on the political benefits of such cooperation.

According to Hamilton:

> *He always thought that we were out there to screw him, and that was the farthest thing from our mind.*
>
> *If Charlie Marsland had just followed the federal lead and taken the cases that would have come his way, with Henry [Huihui] in his back pocket as a cooperating witness, he would have been governor. He would have been governor of the state of Hawaii.*
>
> *It didn't happen. It was a constant battle about who's in control and who was running the show. And Frank Marine, of course, was running the show. I think Frank was quantum leaps ahead of Charlie Marsland.*

Such admiration and deference to Marine was absent in Marsland's office. There, of course, Marsland ran the show. He and his deputy prosecutors did not like to yield to federal authorities, especially when they were asked to forfeit a case or plea-bargain with a suspect to accommodate a federal prosecutor's strategy.

"We just had different approaches to how we wanted to go about it," said Honolulu deputy prosecutor Mike McGuigan. "Who they wanted to turn, who we didn't think should turn . . . Same goal but you know there's different approaches to it. When you deal with any US attorney's office, you're actually dealing with the Department of Justice in Washington, D.C. We weren't answerable to anybody. Our orders came from Chuck."

Marsland and Marine also had very different prosecutorial styles. Whereas Marsland was emotional and confrontational, Marine was cool and calculating. Whereas Marsland often railed on at great length about perceived injustices, Marine was circumspect and wary of the consequences of a big mouth or loose lips.

"The wrong word or explanation could destroy months and thousands of dollars worth of investigations," said Marine, whom journalists in Hawaii nicknamed "Mr. No Comment."

Marine, a native of upstate New York, enjoyed the challenges of dismantling organized crime in Hawaii and was particularly proud of convicting Huihui and a number of his gang members. He called his post in Honolulu a "honey of an opportunity." Deputy prosecutor Peter Carlisle, however, got the impression that Marine felt Hawaii too provincial. Carlisle was raised in New Jersey, and to his recollection Marine seemed incredulous that someone from the East Coast could find the legal work in Hawaii stimulating.

"For him, it wasn't the big city, and he was used to the big city where all the action was," said Carlisle. "He was a bright guy, and he was a capable guy, but he was a poor fit for Hawaii. It was sort of like he came to Hawaii and he was one of those people who either completely cements over their yard or they kill everything green on it and put pebbles down."

For his part, Marine was not complimentary of the performance of the Honolulu prosecutor's office. Speaking of Carlisle and other Honolulu deputy prosecutors who tried some of the same defendants as federal authorities did, Marine said, "I would not have done some of the things they did."

The record, Marine believes, speaks for itself as to whose approach was more effective.

"They tried two murder cases, couldn't get a conviction," said Marine. "We tried 'em, we got a conviction."

To those on the sidelines, the constant fighting between the offices was tiring and counterproductive. This feuding was nothing short of a "monumental pissing match," said David Bettencourt, the Honolulu lawyer who happened to represent both of the criminals who prompted so many of the prosecutors' disagreements: Ronnie Ching and Huihui.

The chair throwing and screaming at least occurred behind closed doors. But much of the spat also played out publicly, with the Honolulu press giving day-by-day accounts of the squabble between Marsland and Marine. It was one of a number of feuds maintained by the Honolulu prosecutor. Marsland, in fact, was beginning to alienate almost everyone in a position of power in Hawaii. He grew irritated with Honolulu Mayor Eileen Anderson when she didn't agree to a drastic budget increase for the prosecutor's office and then attacked her for not helping combat crime. Despite his Republican credentials, Marsland was not an advocate for small government when it came to the prosecutor's office. He regularly asked the Honolulu City Council for additional staff and salary increases. Marsland usually got his way, too, more or less doubling the office's budget and workforce.

By 1984 there was a new police chief in Honolulu. Doug Gibb began his tenure on good terms with Marsland, but their relationship would soon fracture, just as Marsland's relationship with Gibb's predecessor, Chief Francis Keala, had.

Marsland exasperated Governor George Ariyoshi through his office's investigation of the governor's campaign expenses, especially those relating to entertainment rallies coordinated by Mehau. The governor said he had nothing to hide and would gladly testify before a grand jury.

Marsland did compliment a number of Ariyoshi's judiciary appointments, however. He expanded this praise to the new chief justice of the Supreme Court of Hawaii, commending him for tackling a backlog of felony cases. Marsland realized this harmony between him and at least a few of Hawaii's judges was noteworthy.

"We have entered a new era of exchange and understanding between the judiciary and the prosecutor's office," said Marsland. "It may be dull as hell but it is productive."

The prosecutor's relationship with the legislature, however, remained abysmal. Halfway through the 1984 legislative session, many of Marsland's bill proposals did not receive a hearing. Law-makers also declined to stiffen Hawaii's drug laws, which disappointed the prosecutor.

"Those who run our legislature exhibited the same backbone usually associated with a soggy piece of spaghetti," Marsland complained.

Even for some of Marsland's allies, the acrimony grew tiresome. The constant criticism of judges, defense lawyers, policemen, and politicians complicated his deputy prosecutors' professional relationships. Deputy prosecutor Carlisle, for example, had immense respect for Chief Gibb, whom Marsland would come to excoriate as viciously as any other foe. Carlisle said:

> *If Chuck didn't get his way, everybody else was wrong. The feds were wrong with Frank Marine. Doug Gibb was wrong for not doing something. Ultimately if he's the only person who's right and everybody else [wasn't], and a lot of these people were respected . . . you've got to think that something else is wrong here.*
>
> *We were always trying to rein Chuck in. If you take the sheriff's analogy, he was on a wild horse . . . he was holding onto the mane and charging down the street at a million miles an hour.*

While Carlisle said he yanked on the reins, he blamed his colleague Rick Reed for cracking the whip.

"Rick Reed would take the kerosene and stoke the fire every chance he could. He'd light it up and create all sorts of problems in terms of Chuck being now angrier and more likely to go on a rant that might not have been in his interest or necessarily in the interest of the office," said Carlisle.

Carlisle wasn't the only one who thought Reed irresponsible. During Marsland's reelection bid in 1984, he faced tough questions from newspaper editors over his spokesman's influence on

the office. Reed could not shake the reckless and libelous reputation he had earned upon publishing stories in the *Valley Isle*
about Mehau and organized crime, no matter the fact that the
libel lawsuit had yet to be decided in either Mehau's or Reed's
favor. Marsland, however, could not have cared less what others
thought of his right-hand man.

"I respect what he stands for and what he's done, and I think
he does a fantastic job," Marsland said of Reed.

Marsland was just as firm in his support of organized crime
strike force investigator Don Carstensen, who attracted a similar
amount of controversy. There were hard feelings when Carstensen
resigned from the Honolulu Police Department to join the prosecutor's office as an investigator.

"There was a real rift between him and the department. Any-
time you have a police department, like HPD, and you have an
in-house investigative team in the prosecutor's office, there's a
great tendency to think you've got your own little police force out
here," says deputy prosecutor McGuigan. "There may be times
when they work together, but more often than not they're going
in different directions."

Carstensen's reputation for relentless and hard-nosed police
work may have pleased Marsland, but others dismissed him as
zealous and sometimes misguided.

"A lot of people just didn't care for Don," said McGuigan. "I
never socialized with him, but I just knew people either liked him
or didn't like him."

To the delight of some police officers, Carstensen was arrested
in 1983 for trespassing. The investigator was driving home late at
night when he decided to make a detour and play a joke on a
female friend. Arriving at her house when the friend was already
asleep, Carstensen quietly crawled through a window and then
prepared to leave a note on the table, which would have hinted
at his secret visit. When Carstensen went to exit the house,
however, he realized he was locked inside. At the same time, his

friend woke up, heard the noise of an intruder, and called the police while she hid in a bedroom with her son. When the police arrived, the terrified woman could not believe the intruder was her friend Carstensen.

"It was supposed to be a prank but I lost control of it," said Carstensen, who admitted to drinking alcohol before the incident, though he claimed not to be drunk.

"I was angry and upset with myself. I thought she would explain to the police force that she knew me," said Carstensen. "I didn't argue with them. I ended up typing my own booking. It turned out not to be very funny."

In accord with the female friend's wishes, the prosecutor's office soon dropped the trespassing charges against its own investigator. It was not Carstensen's last brush with the law, however. In the years ahead the investigator was twice involved in scuffles at a Honolulu bar, the Butterfly Lounge. Each time, Carstensen claimed to have subdued unruly customers. Yet in the first incident, a judge found Carstensen guilty of two counts of third-degree misdemeanor assault. Following the conviction Carstensen submitted a letter of resignation to Marsland. The prosecutor refused to accept it.

"He's probably the most truthful person that I have ever met," said Marsland, testifying on Carstensen's behalf. "I don't think he could tell a lie if he wanted to."

When it came to Reed and Carstensen, Marsland was willing to endure the occasional, or frequent, headache. Both men had displayed incredible loyalty to Marsland, which he valued. Just as important, perhaps, was each man's personal conviction that Larry Mehau was the godfather of Hawaiian organized crime. Reed had stated that plainly in his former newspaper, and the dogged investigations conducted by Carstensen affirmed that he felt the same. Both men infuriated Mehau.

"If they didn't have laws against what I would like to do, there would be a lot of problems for Reed and [Carstensen]," Mehau once said, making a fist with one of his massive hands and slowly throwing a punch into his other—THWAP!

"I look at Reed and I honestly see his jaw just going," said Mehau.

Mehau stated that he had refrained from such violence because it would only seem to confirm the criminal suspicions that surrounded him. Additionally, Reed and Carstensen would eventually recover from an assault.

"The pain goes away," said Mehau. "But when someone calls you a name like this man [Reed] did, it's forever."

Beyond his aides' beliefs that Mehau was at the top of Hawaii's underworld, Marsland had other reasons to be interested in the Big Island rancher and businessman. According to a police report, during the final hours Chuckers Marsland was alive, Mehau had been in the company of Ching, Eric Naone, and others in Don Ho's dressing room. Mehau and another friend were apparently waiting for passport photos so they could accompany the singer on a trip to Japan.

The men were not just passing acquaintances. Mehau previously intervened in a feud Naone had began with another tough. As to Ching, Mehau said he first met Ronnie when he was a young boy. Mehau, then a policeman in charge of the canine squad, would obtain dogs to train from Ching's father, who worked at an animal quarantine station.

Years later, when Ching had began a life of crime, the men's paths occasionally crossed. Mehau was aware of the killer's reputation.

"I don't know how many times I've seen Ronnie Ching; but once I knew that he was involved in, you know, action, I always advised him to be careful," said Mehau. "I always informed him that I had heard some bad vibes, and he would always say that he's clean, he's all right. Never once did I allow him to talk to me about anything."

Indeed, before ever visiting Ho's dressing room, Mehau was said to call ahead and make sure characters like Ching were not present. Still, there were other connections and circumstances that made investigators uneasy. When Arthur Baker was abducted by Ching in 1978 and buried alive on a beach, it was known that Baker had once worked as a driver for Hawaii Protective Association. More interesting to government investigators was the fact that Baker had also become an informant for the Drug Enforcement Administration, which had just initiated Operation Firebird to probe the alleged underworld activities of Mehau. According to US Attorney Dan Bent, there was an "operating thesis" among Operation Firebird investigators that Mehau was responsible for Baker's death, though Bent admitted this thesis was never proven.

What illegal activity could be proven about Mehau, if anything? In 1984, following a grand jury investigation that included the subpoena of entertainers performing at the state capitol, Honolulu prosecutors believed they could convict the Big Island businessman on two misdemeanor charges related to donations made to the reelection campaign of Governor Ariyoshi. Prosecutors claimed illegality regarding the accounting of more than a thousand dollars worth of airfare bought for entertainers performing at an Ariyoshi reelection rally on Kauai. Mehau's lawyer countered that the mix-up was nothing more than an honest bookkeeping error. Before the discrepancy could be explored in court, a judge tossed the charges on account of the statute of limitations having expired.

Predictably Marsland was not pleased with this decision, complaining that the judge was either clueless or corrupt. Yet even had Marsland's office prevailed, two misdemeanor convictions of Mehau would hardly have proven his supposed role as an underworld boss or godfather. When it came to Mehau, the government kept coming up short. Some thought this was because Mehau was unfairly accused; some thought this was because Mehau was slick and well insulated.

Despite this setback, Marsland was riding high. Less than a week after the charges against Mehau were dismissed, Marsland was overwhelmingly reelected as Honolulu's prosecutor. Facing political newcomer and former public defender Erick Moon in November 1984, Marsland captured a whopping 73 percent of the vote. Few had believed Moon would unseat the popular prosecutor, yet when the votes were tallied, political observers were still impressed by Marsland's dominance. The prosecutor earned nearly as many votes on Oahu as President Ronald Reagan did in the entire state, prompting many to chatter about the possibility of Marsland becoming the Republican candidate for governor in 1986.

As one political analysis noted, Marsland's oversight of an office that saw crime go down and the prison population go up rendered Moon's chances very slim. Indeed the prison on Oahu was severely overcrowded, in part because of the work of the prosecutor's office. Even without statistics to prove the incumbent's effectiveness, there was broad consensus that Marsland was delivering on his original campaign promises to free Hawaii residents from a fear of crime. Even the *Honolulu Star-Bulletin*, never shy about criticizing the prosecutor, acknowledged Marsland's success and gave him a strong endorsement just before the 1984 election.

> *Marsland has also helped turn the community around on the question of law and order. For all his rhetorical excesses, Marsland has generated a spirit of success in law enforcement. Crime, extortion and thugism seem locally less acceptable than they once were. Our hoodlum elite has lost much of the social standing that once allowed its members to flaunt their criminal chic lifestyles as role models for the young. People are standing up to be counted, as jurors, witnesses, Good Samaritans, voices against crime in the community . . .*

More important to Marsland, a grand jury on Oahu was about to issue indictments for those believed to have participated in the murder of his son. Nearly ten years had passed since Chuckers was gunned down on a lonely rural stretch of road. In that time his father had prosecuted, or overseen prosecutions, of hundreds of men and women, including many of Oahu's most vicious criminals. He had twice been elected Honolulu's top prosecutor. He had initiated war with every branch of Hawaiian state government. He decried the influence of organized crime on Hawaiian society so often that a gangster responded by punching him in the face. He visited the cemetery in Punchbowl Crater hundreds if not thousands of times, reaffirming a promise he made his son when the dirt above his grave was still fresh: to find the criminals who murdered his boy.

As this epic quest for justice neared its conclusion, Marsland had one person to thank for being able to convince a grand jury to bring charges against three men. Of all people, it was Ronnie Ching, who himself confessed to twice blasting Chuckers with a shotgun.

After a lifetime of crime followed by three years of languishing in federal prison, Ronnie Ching was in desperate need of some aloha. On this day, though, he'd settle for a hug.

Rick Reed walked into the killer's jail cell, expecting Ching to be cuffed. Instead he discovered the prisoner was unrestrained. Reed soon found himself within the arms of Hawaii's most renowned hit man, unwillingly forced to reciprocate, or at least simulate, an embrace. Reed's mind raced as he was pressed against the hit man, imagining that the muscular, barrel-chested Ching might pluck his head right off his body, should the admitted killer so desire. Instead Ching just wrapped Reed tight before releasing him. Reed was grateful to escape. He sensed little warmth during the length of their embrace.

"Ching felt like a cold serpent, like a huge anaconda," said Reed. "He was cold and he was dead and he was vicious."

At least the killer was cordial. Ching had returned to Hawaii again from federal prison on the mainland, this time to face charges of abducting and murdering Arthur Baker, the DEA informant who had been snatched from a bar and then allegedly buried alive. Ching pleaded not guilty, but it was not long before the hit man, facing the possibility of life in prison, cut a deal with prosecutors by confessing to the murder and testifying about crimes committed by others. He was generally in good spirits, happy to help shed a light on the Hawaiian underworld.

Or so he claimed.

To the dismay of both local and federal authorities, Ching started lying, even falsely implicating others for murder. He failed a lie detector test administered by the FBI, destroying any faith federal authorities might have had in his statements. Ching was useless to them.

Within Marsland's office, however, there remained hope that Ching would come clean, even after the hit man falsely claimed that Chuckers Marsland was killed by two gangsters who, ten years later, were now dead. It was a ruse tried one too many times before, blaming crimes on the deceased, and the Honolulu prosecutor's office wasn't biting. So the hit man amended his story, finally claiming that he himself shot Chuckers and was assisted in the crime by at least three other people. He also confessed to participating in three other murders: the machine-gunning of gambler Bobby Fukumoto, the kidnapping and beach burial of Baker, and the assassination of State Senator Larry Kuriyama, though Ching denied being the triggerman in that shooting.

Was Ching telling the truth now? Marsland's office thought so. In exchange for Ching pleading guilty to these crimes and testifying in court about others' involvement in Hawaiian organized crime, Marsland agreed to recommend a maximum prison sentence of twenty years for the hit man. This punishment would occur while Ching continued to serve his existing twenty-one-year federal prison sentence for weapons and drug charges, meaning he faced little, if any, additional time in prison for the murders.

The plea deal was a huge surprise. Ching and Marsland had previously sworn off making such agreements. Years earlier Ching had told investigator Don Carstensen that he would kill his own brother should he become a government informant or witness. And Ching said if he should be the one to start talking, he expected his brother to kill him.

"We talk face to face like that," Ching said of he and his brother. "If I one rat, nail me, you know what I mean?"

But years in prison had humbled the hit man and weakened his allegiance to the Hawaiian underworld. He rationalized his cooperation by claiming that it was he who had been betrayed, not the other way around.

"I could see that the whole organized crime movement had been very greedy. [It] had been selfish and dishonest with me. There's been no loyalty toward me. I don't feel I owe none of these people anything," said Ching.

Personal remorse also played a part in Ching's decision to tell all. He felt badly for the family members of his murder victims, though not necessarily for the victims themselves. As Ching told Reed during their meeting in the jail cell, he would beg people's forgiveness in his dreams. Yet not a single person would grant him this wish.

"I realize what I've done," said Ching. "It's terrible. And I'm having a time dealing with that."

Marsland was one of those people who refused to forgive. The prosecutor, in fact, refused to even meet with Ching, the man he had long suspected of killing his boy. One imagines this distance was partly a professional maneuver to keep himself isolated from the witness and avoid a conflict of interest that could jeopardize murder trials. Mostly, though, Marsland didn't speak to Ching because he loathed the man. Having already agreed to the plea deal concerning his son's murder, Marsland would concede nothing more.

"I don't want to say anything to him," said Marsland. "We don't have anything to exchange. This is a guy who murdered my son, okay? And I am not going to exchange pleasantries with him."

Some of Marsland's critics found it incredible that the prosecutor's office was handling the case. Previously Marsland had said he would ask for a special prosecutor to be appointed should his son's alleged killers be found. Reneging upon that promise, he claimed to have put the case squarely in the hands of his deputy prosecutors and investigators, free of his interference. For some this still fell short of the proper course of action.

"There isn't a prosecutor in the country who would not recognize that you cannot prosecute and be personally involved [with] someone who killed your kid. Can you think of a greater conflict?" said Marine. "If I were [a defense attorney] I would have made a motion to recuse the entire office and said it should have gone to the state [attorney general] . . . This is a no brainer!"

Even Hawaii's preeminent defense lawyer, no stranger to seeking leniency or acquittals for violent criminals, was baffled by the deal Marsland gave the notorious hit man.

"Why in God's name would the prosecutor's office enter into a plea bargain with a man who confessed to twenty murders, including the murder of the prosecutor's own son?" asked David Schutter, Marsland's longtime nemesis, exaggerating Ching's confessed body count.

Marsland conceded that the plea bargain with Ching was "the worst personal sacrifice of my life."

He said, "I'll be honest with you, I'd love to see the son of a bitch hanged. This is the man who took away the most beautiful thing in my life."

Despite the anger, on this point Marsland was also sanguine.

"It was hard to swallow," said the prosecutor, "but I had to set aside feelings of personal vengeance to get at the heart of organized crime in this community."

Ching is "the only entrée we have into organized crime and I'm not going to lose any of it," said the prosecutor.

He refuted the charges by Schutter and others that his office's dealings with Ching were motivated by anything but the pursuit of justice:

> *This vendetta BS had been put forth for years by political opponents and defense attorneys who have created it for their own purposes. It doesn't make sense. If I had a vendetta, it would be against the person who killed my only son. The fact that I am willing to set aside a natural and strong desire for revenge—in return for evidence that will allow us to get to beyond the hitman and get the people who actually run organized crime in Hawaii—should put an end to this personal or political vendetta nonsense.*

Marsland and his staff believed Ching to be the key to obtaining convictions of the most elusive members of Hawaiian organized crime. Deputy prosecutors and investigators debriefed him extensively, eager to convict his murder accomplices and his superiors in the Hawaiian underworld—the men who supposedly ordered the hits.

"We spent a lot of time together, sitting down, talking, discussing cases, going through statements he previously made," said deputy prosecutor Carlisle. "At that point he could be very affable . . . He would routinely tell me that, you know, the two of us should go out, either smoke some pot or have a good night drinking together. I was positive that was never going to happen."

As part of these interviews, the prosecutor's office drove Ching around Oahu. Along the way, from his perch in the passenger's seat, he pointed out the places he had murdered people. Baker on Maili Beach, on the Leeward Coast. Fukumoto down in Waikiki. Kuriyama in Aiea, near Pearl Harbor. Chuckers down in Waimānalo, on the windward side. For Ching, it was a greatest hits tour. "An indelible moment," as deputy prosecutor McGuigan put it.

To many minds Ching was also giving information with regard to Hawaii's suspected godfather, Larry Mehau. A day before Ching pleaded guilty to the four murders and stated to a judge that he killed informant Baker after being "instructed by another," defense lawyer Schutter called an unexpected news conference to announce the imminent indictment of his client Mehau. According to Schutter, Ching would testify that some of his murders involved Mehau.

"There's a whole cabal of people over there in Marsland's office who somehow got carried away in their own comic strip beliefs," said Schutter, charging Marsland with carrying out a political vendetta against Mehau and Governor Ariyoshi.

Mehau, who sat beside his lawyer during the press conference, his arms folded across his chest, said he believed the prosecutor's office was targeting him because he had sued Marsland's assistant and spokesman, Reed, over the Hawaiian godfather allegations.

"I have been feeling something like this was coming for a while," said Mehau. "I'd like to say a lot more. I'd love to say a lot more. I really have nothing to be afraid of."

Marsland responded only to Schutter, calling him a "liar."

"I have told this right to his teeth and put it on the record in open court," said the prosecutor.

Also at the press conference was the large and imposing Cyril Kahale, a former aide to Don Ho, whom the singer would introduce to his audiences as his "complaint department." Kahale had been arrested on murder charges a month or so earlier for allegedly helping Ching abduct Baker. Yet just weeks later the prosecutor's office dropped all charges, saying new information, provided by Ching, cleared Kahale of wrongdoing. Schutter announced that Kahale was now suing the city of Honolulu for false arrest. In time Kahale would win a jury verdict that directed the city to pay him more than $470,000 for malicious prosecution by Marsland's office. Marsland called the mix-up regrettable, yet refused to apologize to Kahale.

The mistake served as a reminder that not all information and testimony provided by witnesses was reliable. For all the cooperation Ching offered, there remained the chance that he was duping prosecutors, at least partially. Such duplicity seemed especially plausible since Ching had at least once changed his story about the murder of Chuckers Marsland and wrongly accused at least one other man of murder.

There were more reasons to be skeptical of the claims and charges made by the prosecutor's office. A taped interview with Ching was marred by poor sound quality, leaving some of his statements difficult to verify. Then there were all the aspersions cast on investigator Carstensen, whether from someone like Schutter or former deputy prosecutor Kaneshiro, who worked alongside Carstensen on the organized crime task force until Kaneshiro resigned his position in 1983.

According to Kaneshiro, Carstensen had previously taken a "fill in the blanks" approach to murder investigations. When Ching wouldn't identify an accomplice, for example, Kaneshiro says Carstensen used deductive reasoning to insert a specific suspect into Ching's nameless narrative. Such an approach, said Kaneshiro, fell short of the standards of justice.

Marsland's office rejected such criticisms. As 1984 came to a close, with an indictment of Mehau—Hawaii's alleged godfather—supposedly imminent, Marsland celebrated his overwhelming reelection as Honolulu's prosecutor and prepared to try three men Ching had fingered in the killing of his son. Each man was familiar to the prosecutor, having long been on the anguished father's own shortlist of suspects. Beyond Ching, the men believed to have killed Chuckers Marsland included the following:

- Eric Naone, the local strongman and ex-con who had befriended Chuckers and seen the murder victim just a few hours before his death. Naone, who had been repeatedly invited by Chuckers to dinner at the Marsland home, attended Chuckers's funeral and paid his respects to Marsland just hours after allegedly shooting Chuckers with a pistol five times in the head.

- Gregory Nee, a former doorman at the Polynesian Palace nightclub, who allegedly drove the car that transported Chuckers to his execution. Nee also attended Chuckers's funeral upon the request of Naone and Ching.

- Raymond Scanlan, the corrupt, heroin-peddling ex-cop who dined with Marsland and met him beside Chuckers's grave to allegedly disclose the names of murder suspects Ching, Naone, and Nee. Scanlan, who went on pistol-popping joyrides through Waikiki with Ching in an unmarked police car, was accused of providing the weapons used to murder Chuckers.

As the prosecutor's office prepared for trial, Marsland's spokesman, Reed, sat down with the prosecutor and reflected on Marsland's personal journey since Chuckers's death. A decade earlier Marsland had been a low-profile attorney and single father adjusting to his only son becoming an adult and leaving home. Then, overnight, Marsland became a would-be vigilante, stalking the streets of Waikiki with a pistol under his coat, looking to uncover his son's killers. In the years to come, as he became a deputy prosecutor and then elected city prosecutor, Marsland's instincts for vengeance gave way to the pursuit of justice, through a court of law. Reed wondered, though, just how much of that original primal fury remained in the man.

"If you hadn't had this opportunity to be prosecuting attorney and go after the killers of Chuckers through the legal system," Reed asked his boss, "do you think you actually would have shot Ching [dead]?"

The prosecutor considered the question.

"No," replied Marsland. "I would have used my bare hands."

CHAPTER EIGHT

Love Never Fails

He should have headed straight home. If he had just gone to bed, or to a friend's house, or to his father's place, or onto the beach, he might still be alive today, perhaps with grown children of his own. Instead, after finishing his nightclub shift, Chuckers Marsland hopped in the car that pulled beside him about five o'clock in the morning on Waikiki's Kalākaua Avenue. It was a fatal mistake.

Inside were Ronnie Ching and Eric Naone—two men that Chuckers counted as friends, but also understood to be killers. At the wheel was Gregory Nee, an acquaintance who, like Chuckers, worked as a doorman at a Waikiki nightclub. It was dark as the car left Waikiki and drove across Oahu, but daybreak would be coming soon.

The men made small talk as they drove out of Waikiki, past Diamond Head, and through the Hawaii Kai neighborhood where Chuckers had grown up, and where his father was no doubt sleeping. The car then headed out of town, past snorkelers' paradise Hanauma Bay, past Koko Crater, past the blowhole and Sandy Beach and Makapuu Lighthouse. Chuckers, perhaps a little tipsy from a shot of tequila and the pau drinks he had begged off his coworkers, may not have realized this was the last time he would pass by these sights, some of which were staples of his childhood.

A half hour later the men were on the other side of the Koolau Mountains, stopped along a back road that ran through farmland in Waimānalo. Ching got out of the car and headed to the back trunk. He was high, having smoked a pair of marijuana joints to calm his nerves, but not nearly so stoned that he couldn't complete the job at hand. Opening the trunk he found the shotgun he had previously placed there after obtaining it on loan from a policeman. Picking it up, he checked to see that a round was still chambered. It was.

Inside the car Chuckers was told that Ching had something to show him. He exited the car and walked to the rear of the vehicle. Rounding the bumper Chuckers came face-to-face with the heavyweight hit man. To his alarm he saw Ching was holding a shotgun. The hit man pointed the weapon at Chuckers, but did not immediately fire.

"You going," Ching said. "This is it."

Chuckers seemed surprised, if not in outright shock. He did not move. It did not matter. Ching quickly squeezed the trigger, blasting a hole in Chuckers's left breast and causing the young man to stagger backward. Ching fired again. This time Chuckers went down. He moaned as he lay dying.

Naone got out of the car and helped Ching move Chuckers's body to the edge of the road. After wiping a spot of blood off the car with the inside of his shirtsleeve, Ching returned to the car, settling into the backseat. More gunshots rang out. Ching turned to look out the car's rear window and witnessed Naone, a .38 caliber pistol in his hands, standing over Chuckers's inert body and pumping a half dozen or so bullets into his head. If Chuckers had not already died from the shotgun wounds, he was surely dead now.

The three men soon headed back to Honolulu, leaving Chuckers beside the road, his head, heart, and lungs leaking blood. As the sun began to climb over the horizon, illuminating the Waimānalo farmland that abuts the green Koolau mountainsides, a motorist spied Chuckers's body lying facedown along the edge of Hihimanu Street. Seeing that Chuckers was dressed in a neat blue leisure suit and unsoiled white shoes, the motorist surmised the man must be drunk and hadn't quite made it home. Loath to wake the drunk, no matter how dangerously close he was lying to the street, the motorist asked the manager of a nearby service station to phone the police. When the cops arrived in Waimānalo to rouse Chuckers, they discovered he was dead. The corner of Hihimanu and Nonokio Streets was now a murder scene.

At least that's how Ronnie Ching recalled it all happening, nevermind others' doubts that Chuckers would have willingly entered the car if he suspected trouble.

In June 1985 Ching related these details of Chuckers's death to a jury considering murder charges against three men: Naone, Nee, and Raymond Scanlan, the former Honolulu policeman from whom Ching claimed to have received the weapons used to kill Chuckers. The defendants felt differently than Ching. Each of them had pleaded not guilty to the charges of murdering Chuckers.

This case was the first trial featuring the testimony of Ching following his plea deal with Honolulu's prosecutor's office—a plea deal that saw him confess to four murders in exchange for a twenty-year prison term. Given Ching's long criminal record, prosecutors expected defense attorneys to try to discredit the notorious hit man during the trial. To their dismay Ching's trustworthiness had been questioned long before the defense lawyers began their cross-examinations. And, to Honolulu prosecutor Charles Marsland's chagrin, those doubting Ching's claims were not any of his predictable foes, but fellow law enforcement colleagues who otherwise normally might be considered allies.

The trouble for Marsland's office began in April, more than a month before the start of Chuckers's murder trial. If the prosecutor's antagonism in years past had been reserved for judges, legislators, the governor, the Honolulu mayor, the next Honolulu mayor, and Larry Mehau, among others, lately a considerable amount of Marsland's criticism and rage had been directed toward the Honolulu Police Department and federal prosecutors also investigating organized crime in Hawaii. Rather than embrace a cooperative approach with these authorities as his deputy prosecutors prepared the case against his son's alleged killers, Marsland felt the need to be combative.

In the case of the police department, Marsland was annoyed that a policeman declared during a press conference that Ching had failed several FBI lie detector tests. This statement came in response to Ching's claim during interviews with Marsland's investigators that a twenty-one-year veteran of the Honolulu Police Department, Lieutenant Manny Rezentes, had helped arrange the murder of Chuckers with Naone.

To the police department's frustration, Marsland would not allow detectives to interview Ching about his accusation against Rezentes, or even let them review transcripts of Ching's statements. Bewilderingly, despite the prosecutor's office publicly echoing Ching's accusations of Rezentes's role in planning the murder, Rezentes was not charged with any wrongdoing. A frustrated Rezentes claimed he was innocent and that Ching was falsely accusing him to revenge a slight that occurred years earlier. That slight involved Rezentes allegedly falsely implicating Ching by putting the hit man's name down on a police report without justification.

Speaking about the exclusion of the police, Marsland's spokesman Rick Reed said that based on past experience, the police department could not be trusted to conduct an honest investigation of one of their own, or to make any progress in a number of cold cases involving organized crime, including the murder of Chuckers.

"The police department has had the opportunity for ten years to break these cases and has failed to do so," said Reed. "Their reaction today is symptomatic of HPD's envy and chronic tendency to protect team members."

Then, just weeks before the trial, a memorandum filed by federal prosecutors was unsealed, or made available to the public, by a judge. It revealed that Ching had not only shown deception in lie detector tests, but admitted confusion to the FBI over his allegation concerning Rezentes to the point that he could no longer continue an interview. What's more, Ching admitted to federal authorities that he had wrongfully accused another man of murder "out of revenge."

In short, the police and federal authorities did not believe Ching. And if they didn't believe him, would the eight women and four men serving on the jury for the murder trial of Chuckers Marsland?

Marsland felt betrayed by these disclosures. He thought the attempts to undermine Ching's credibility were nothing short of sabotage. What's more, the attacks against Ching seemed disingenuous. In the case of the police department's press conference, they dodged a question regarding Rezentes's own poor performance on a lie detector test. In the case of federal prosecutors, their star witness, confessed Syndicate killer Henry Huihui, had also admitted failing a lie detector test and had changed his own story regarding his accomplices to certain murders. Arguably, he was no more reliable than Ching.

Federal prosecutor Marine, however, said it was ludicrous for Marsland to accuse him and others of sabotage. Regarding the disclosure in the previously sealed memorandum concerning Ching's unreliability, he had no reservations about putting it on record.

"That information is truthful, it's relevant, and it would have come out anyway at trial because the defense attorneys had it," said Marine. "But [Marsland] of course in his knight in shining armor image, accuses everybody of trying to ... undercut his prosecution."

It was no surprise to learn that people thought Ching deceitful. Years earlier the hit man had lied to Marsland's staff, pinning

Chuckers's murder on two dead men, one of whom supposedly dealt drugs to Chuckers. But Ching had since amended his story, owning up to murdering the young man himself with a shotgun. Should he have confessed everything immediately, said Ching, he would have forfeited all his bargaining power and the ability to negotiate reduced punishment.

"I gave them bits of truth and some lies," said Ching. "That gave them an indication I was interested in reaching an agreement but I was not going to give them all the facts which would give me an inevitable life without parole. I had committed a lot of crimes and I was not going to turn myself in."

So, while the police and federal authorities expressed doubt, the prosecutor's office believed Ching's story. For one thing his information matched what Marsland himself believed based on his own investigation of his son's death. Just two weeks after Chuckers was killed in 1975, Marsland had come to believe Ching responsible, though he could not prove it. In the ten years to follow, Marsland received information that only confirmed this suspicion. Additionally, Ching's version of the murder was compatible with a statement one of his alleged accomplices, Naone, had given to police the day after Chuckers's death.

Naone had told a police detective that he had spent some of the evening before Chuckers's death hanging out in Don Ho's dressing room at the Polynesian Palace with Ching and Larry Mehau, among others. At about three in the morning, Naone said, he walked with Ching and a man named Gregory to the Infinity, where he spoke with Chuckers, before returning to the Polynesian Palace. Then, at about five o' clock, Gregory drove Naone and Ching across the island to Naone's mother's house in the town of Kaneohe, where he picked up a change of clothes. They returned to Honolulu just after sunrise, about seven o' clock. It was not until Chuckers's girlfriend called him hours later, Naone said, that he knew Chuckers had been killed. Upon hearing the bad news, Naone went to visit the Marsland home, encountering an upset Marsland, who told him in the garage, "They took everything away from me."

Ten years later prosecutors were claiming Naone's story contained one major omission: that he, Ching, and Nee picked up Chuckers on their drive across the island and murdered him in Waimānalo. It was hard to know whom to believe. The accusations traded between defendants, witnesses, prosecutors, and defense lawyers made for a very murky mess.

Consider that Ching was accusing Naone, his former friend and the best man at his wedding, of shooting Chuckers five times in the head. Consider that when Naone was arrested four months after Chuckers's murder for his role in an unusual Beverly Hills kidnapping and robbery of a former Vegas showgirl and Playboy playmate, he later testified that Nee was his gorilla mask–wearing accomplice who escaped police. Consider that defendant Scanlan, the heroin-dealing ex-cop who worked with Ching and Naone as a driver for the Teamsters film and television unit and was accused of providing the weapons used to kill Chuckers, had met with Charles Marsland repeatedly to discuss his son's murder, allegedly telling him at Chuckers's grave that Ching, Naone, and Nee were responsible. Consider that as a policeman, Scanlan helped investigate Chuckers's murder, as did Rezentes, the policeman Ching accused of conspiring with Naone to arrange Chuckers's death on account of the young man's loose lips. Consider that Ching, Naone, and Nee all attended Chuckers's funeral just days after allegedly killing him. Consider that one of the defendants, Marsland would never say whom exactly, had allegedly offered to "take care of" Chuckers's supposed killers and deposit their fingers in Marsland's mailbox as proof of a job well done.

To some it might have seemed hopelessly tangled, any truth indistinguishable from many lies. Yet deputy prosecutors Mike McGuigan and Peter Carlisle thought Ching a witness capable of setting the record straight, once and for all.

"Whenever you're dealing with someone that's been turned, you have to be very cautious with accepting what they say," said McGuigan. "They may have some warts, but you've got to convince them that they've got to tell the truth, and you've got to believe they're telling the truth before you go in. If you have any doubts, you don't do it because they're not going to withstand cross-examination.

"I thought our case was good," he continued. "I don't try cases that I expect to lose. Never did."

Following jury selection, the trial began on May 24, 1985, under the direction of Judge Robert Klein, who later would serve on the Supreme Court of Hawaii. By all accounts Klein was fair-minded and impartial in his administration of the trial. Unlike some of his colleagues in the Hawaiian judiciary, Klein had not previously been a target of Marsland's criticism. In fact the prosecutor once asked Klein to join him on a panel of speakers who were discussing criminal justice and sentencing policies. Klein declined the invitation for two reasons. First of all, he said, judicial ethics restricted how candidly he could speak about such matters. Second, Marsland had just tried to block pay increases for local judges, and Klein believed it out of line for the prosecutor to now seek a favor.

"I remember thinking, 'You just testified in the legislature against my pay raise and now you want me to go out there and be a prop in your little talk to the community?'" said Klein. "Sorry, not doing it."

Apart from that, the two had little interaction. Klein was, of course, familiar with Marsland's prominent and outspoken reputation, which in large part was built on derogatory comments he made toward many other judges, including accusations of corruption. Generally speaking Klein did not agree with these assessments.

"I was a judge for a long time. Corrupt judges, ha ha, I don't think they're plentiful in Hawaii," said Klein. "I felt it was kind of overblown."

Nonetheless Klein said this kind of rhetoric was predictable given the friction that will always exist in a courtroom.

"Judges, you know, have to be fair. Prosecutors have to fight crime. We're natural enemies," he said. "Prosecutors like to think in terms of protecting the victim whereas judges always think in terms of protecting the process to give a fair trial.

"Fair doesn't mean perfect, by the way," Klein added. "It means fair."

The trial began with an opening statement by McGuigan. Standing next to a handsome portrait of Chuckers propped on an easel, the prosecutor spoke about the promising life that had waited the young man taking college courses in Honolulu while anticipating the offer of a volleyball scholarship from a university in California. McGuigan said Chuckers was "fiercely loyal and close to his father," but also conceded that Chuckers's job at a Waikiki nightclub brought him into regular contact with members of Hawaii's underworld. Chuckers, said McGuigan, lived in two worlds, until his "life in one became incompatible with his life in the other." At that point, the prosecutor said, "This boy was executed."

The prosecution then began its case, calling witnesses. They included the motorists who discovered Chuckers's body in Waimānalo; the police who arrived on the scene and investigated the murder; Chuckers's friends, roommate, and coworkers; and the medical examiners and crime scene technicians who analyzed Chuckers's dead body. The prosecution's witnesses also included former police chief Francis Keala, who broke down in tears on the witness stand as he described how close Chuckers had been to his own two sons and how the murder victim, who had grown up in Hawaii without a mother nearby, likely spent more time at the Keala household than his own. Keala admitted that Chuckers had given the police tips about crime in Waikiki and that he "was concerned about who else he was telling."

Cathy Clisby took the stand, too, to tell the court about her boyfriend's paranoia in the days before he died and how Chuckers contemplated staying at his father's house until he felt comfortable again. Chuckers, she said, had confidence that his father and his friends would keep him safe, but Clisby warned him to not underestimate anyone who wished to do him harm.

"I told him he better be careful, whatever he was doing," said Clisby, that "a gun could get him faster than anything."

Marsland was not in the courtroom to hear any of this. Having been subpoenaed by defense lawyers as a possible witness, the prosecutor, like any witness, was forced to remain outside the courtroom until he was called to testify. So Marsland roamed the courthouse halls, gathering with his deputy prosecutors and spokesman, Rick Reed, during recesses to get an update on the trial's progress. The tall, lean, and imposing prosecutor did not escape the attention of jurors as they filed in and out of the courtroom.

"There were times when we saw him outside the courtroom and as we walked by I had the feeling that he was kind of giving the stink eye to the jury," said Jay Melnick, a marketing executive for a bank who was elected by his fellow jurors to be the jury foreman. "He was definitely very emotional . . . I had the feeling that he was staring the jury down as we walked in."

The initial witnesses called by the prosecution—there were twenty-one in all—served to educate the jury as to what type of life Chuckers Marsland led and how it had ended very violently, with bullet holes through his most vital organs. Melnick recalls hearing this testimony, which involved information that Chuckers used and sold cocaine, and feeling sympathy for Charles Marsland. Melnick, too, was a father, and rather than assign blame, his gut reaction was just one of sorrow, that something so unfortunate had to happen, no matter who was at fault.

"The feeling was, 'What's a young kid like this [doing] getting mixed up with these guys?'" said Melnick. "The whole thing was just shocking. It came out that somehow he was involved in drugs, [that] he must have known some bad guys. It was just tragic, right?"

Judging by appearances, Melnick thought the defendants capable of the crimes they were accused of.

"One of the guys, I think, he just looked like a miniature version of a Mr. Clean. He just looked like the kind of guy who would kill somebody. Just physically, he looked like a bad guy," said Melnick. "It became apparent that these were not nice men."

Appearing just as menacing to Melnick was Ching, who came to testify under heavy security. Snipers were posted on the roof, police walked around the courthouse with bomb-sniffing dogs, and Judge Klein encountered undercover officers armed with Uzis as he entered the courthouse that morning through a secure entry. Authorities were taking no chances concerning the security of the hit man turned government witness. At least two threats had been made on Ching's life since he agreed to cooperate, according to the prosecutor's office.

When Ching took the stand, he testified in a flat, matter-of-fact voice, admitting that he had provided cocaine to Chuckers, as did Naone. When Chuckers began talking about these cocaine transactions to the policeman Rezentes, Ching said, there was concern about Chuckers's lack of discretion. Naone, he said, then asked him to help kill Chuckers, to which Ching agreed. Naone was a "very close friend," explained Ching. "In the future, if I needed help, Eric would help me."

Naone allegedly recruited Nee as a driver, which gave Ching pause for concern since he had "socialized" with Nee, but "hadn't committed no crimes with Greg." Dismissing that concern, Ching asked Scanlan, whom he encountered in Don Ho's dressing room, to provide him weapons so he could "do somebody, down somebody."

"It didn't concern you that you were asking a person known to you as a police officer for a weapon to kill someone else?" McGuigan asked the witness.

"Not this police officer," Ching said of Scanlan.

Ching testified that Scanlan fulfilled his weapon request, giving Ching a shotgun and a .38 caliber handgun that was identical to the standard service revolver issued by the Honolulu Police Department. Prosecutors then introduced a police report filed by Scanlan in 1973 that claimed his service revolver was stolen from the glove box of his car. The implication was that Scanlan gave Ching a gun that had falsely been reported as stolen. After he and Naone shot Chuckers, testified Ching, he threw the gun in the Ala Wai Yacht Harbor at the northern end of Waikiki.

Months earlier the prosecutor's office had sought to verify this claim by having two investigators scuba dive in the boat harbor to look for the weapon. The men dove for five days and used an underwater metal detector, but they came up with nothing. Their metal detector, which was popular with hobbyists, could not penetrate more than a foot of silt, the investigators noted. In some places, five feet of silt rested at the bottom of the harbor.

Not to be deterred, the prosecutor's office enlisted the help of the US Navy to look for the gun. Navy divers, who normally searched for explosives underwater, spent twelve days diving in the harbor using more powerful metal detection devices. All they found were pots, cans, and fishing gear. Even if the gun had once been at the bottom of the harbor, theorized the divers, the tide would have likely swept it away long ago.

"They looked so fucking hard, I had heard from another source, that these guys got fungus in their fucking balls because [of] the wetsuits they was wearing in the muck in the Ala Wai looking for that fucking gun," said Christopher Evans, Naone's defense lawyer. "And they never found it."

With Ching's testimony finished, Evans and the defense lawyers who represented Nee and Scanlan quickly went to work to discredit Ching and his testimony. Through their independent cross-examinations, these defense lawyers brought up the discrepancies in Ching's statements to authorities, that he had often changed his story and falsely accused others out of vindictiveness, that he had been convicted for multiple drugs and weapons offenses, and that he was best known for one thing and one thing only in Hawaii: killing people.

Ching admitted to telling lies, but also promised that he was now telling the truth. He looked for sympathy. Becoming a government witness is hard, said Ching, because "being truthful is new."

Once the prosecution rested its case, Ching left the courtroom. Then the lawyers for the three defendants presented their cases. Nee, now living in Washington State with his wife and kids and working as a lumber broker, took the stand to proclaim his innocence. Scanlan eventually did the same.

Naone, however, opted to keep mum. This decision, said his lawyer, was an easy one.

"There was no fucking way I would put him on the stand. Principally, the reason why is because some people do not handle the pressure of being on the witness stand very well. He's one of them," said Evans. "And then his personality, you know. He's been around too many crooks and criminals to sound like a regular human being."

Not that Evans thought his client murdered Chuckers. As Evans recalled Naone telling him, "I'm a criminal. But I didn't do this one!"

Scanlan's lawyer, James Koshiba, was also worried about the impression his client would make on the jury, even though he personally believed Scanlan to be innocent.

"Defense lawyers generally do not put the defendant on the stand because they can be cross-examined and discrepancies, problems can be revealed and often are. Intellectually I understand why you don't do it," said Koshiba.

"But for me it . . . always has been a much simpler problem. And that is if I was sitting on the jury, and the defendant doesn't testify, I always want to know why, what they have to say. And, you know, you're not man enough to get up on the stand, I'm more likely to convict you than I'm not."

Prior to his client taking the stand, Koshiba practiced with Scanlan constantly. Koshiba knew that Scanlan would be cross-examined by prosecutors about his criminal associations and actions, about his checkered career as a policeman, and about giving information to Marsland beside Chuckers's grave and allegedly disclosing the names of his fellow defendants as murder suspects—an accusation Scanlan denied.

"Whatever weaknesses there are I think you should reveal it," said Koshiba. For Scanlan this also might include disclosing his involvement in a heroin deal in Punchbowl Crater; of admitting to many brawls in his life, both in and out of his police uniform; of being, in general, a "kolohe," or rascal, said Koshiba.

[He] had friends on both sides of the fence . . . He knew all of the alleged crooks, criminals, yet was a police officer in the police department," [He] always had that kind of reputation of being a guy who, from one perspective, [could] be terrific because he could move within both circles easily, comfortably, where he was trusted, up to a point.

But it was always up to a point, because police officers being police officers, some were always suspicious and did not like him because he had friends on the other side. On the other side he had friends he had grown up with, but some of them never trusted him as well, because he was a police officer.

In the end Scanlan "did a passable job" testifying, said Koshiba. "After all the work that we did, he still had trouble in areas and places. But I thought generally he did okay."

What was important was that Scanlan denied participating in Chuckers's killing. Just as important, he explained to the jury the circumstances in which he lost control of the police revolver that prosecutors alleged he supplied to Ching to be used in the murder. The truth, said Scanlan, was that he had misplaced his police revolver in 1973 and became "nervous and panicky." Unwilling to accept responsibility for losing the weapon, he reported the gun stolen, claiming it was taken from his car.

The police department issued him a new revolver. But some time later, Scanlan said, he found the original revolver between his couch cushions. Scanlan, now with two police revolvers, found himself in a dilemma: What should he do about the rediscovered weapon?

Rather than admit his lie, Scanlan testified that he telephoned his cousin, fellow police officer Clarence "Rags" Scanlan, and hatched a plan for Rags Scanlan to mail the revolver to the police department anonymously. That way the gun would be returned to the police and Scanlan would not be punished for lying about it being stolen. Rags Scanlan, however, never mailed the gun.

When Koshiba learned the weapon's history as he prepared for trial, the defense attorney was encouraged by this turn of events. If Rags Scanlan would just find the revolver, he reasoned, the prosecution's case would fall apart. Ching, who claimed to have thrown the gun into the boat harbor, would be proven a liar, and Koshiba's client would be acquitted.

Unfortunately it wasn't that easy.

"So naturally, I talk to Rags, and Rags says, 'Ohhh, I vaguely recall it.' And I thought, 'You can't vaguely recall if someone gives you a gun. If your own cousin, or whatever it is, gives you a gun, you don't just say,' 'Well I don't remember, you know,'" said Koshiba.

"I had reservations about the whole story," said Koshiba. "Raymond seemed credible to me, but then when I spoke to Rags, and Rags said, 'Gee I don't remember, you know. Could be, I don't remember,' it just struck me as being disingenuous and, and probably not true."

Koshiba ordered Rags Scanlan to search for the revolver. To Koshiba's dismay Rags came up empty-handed. Koshiba told him to look again.

"[He] kept saying he couldn't find it. And I kept grilling him, because I did believe Raymond. But I had a bit of skepticism as well. I felt he would not lie . . . to me, by that point, because we had enough of a relationship," said Koshiba. "But I always, you know, you're always a little bit cautious and suspicious, and I thought, 'These guys could be lying to me.'"

Koshiba had agreed to represent Scanlan as a favor. The attorney more often practiced civil law, though he had previously served as defense counsel to Alexander Sakamoto, who was accused of being the triggerman in the infamous assassination of State Senator Larry Kuriyama in 1970. Despite Koshiba having helped get Sakamoto acquitted of the murder, the case did not spur Koshiba to seek more accused murderers as clients. High-profile cases required much time, effort, and creativity. The facts were not always on your side. The stakes were high.

Koshiba's friends cautioned him against involving himself in another prominent murder trial. Even without their advice Koshiba was under no illusion that it would be a simple case. Consider the ingredients. The murder victim was the son of a popular politician. The government witness was a notorious hit man who had agreed to tell all. One of the suspects—Scanlan—stood accused of furnishing weapons to the alleged killers when he was a policeman.

"Chuck Marsland was the most popular person probably in the state. And I understood that, and I liked him," said Koshiba, explaining his decision to accept Scanlan as a client. "But I felt that it was my duty as a lawyer, too. I had a responsibility, an obligation, regardless of how afraid, how negative the impact might be of representing Raymond Scanlan . . . I understood this was gonna be a momentous task."

As Koshiba delved into the nitty-gritty of the murder and Ching's confession, he developed a respect for the hit man's mental prowess. Ching was no stranger to Koshiba; they had met previously because Ching, like Koshiba's previous client Sakamoto, had been suspected of involvement in the assassination of Senator Kuriyama. Indeed the acknowledgement of the hit man's participation in that murder was part of Ching's current plea agreement with the prosecutor's office.

To Koshiba, Ching was a masterful liar. He said as much to the jury during the murder trial, calling the government's main witness a "clever, devious," and "streetwise, Akamai crook." Such comments were part of a chorus of attacks on Ching's character. Koshiba's fellow defense lawyer, Richard Hoke, representing Nee, told the jury that Ching was a "master manipulator." Evans, representing Naone, claimed Ching lied to settle scores, and that if he lied previously, he would not hesitate to do so again.

What made Ching so good at lying, said Koshiba, was his ability to integrate details into his confessions. Rather than just tell you he shot someone, Koshiba gave as an example, Ching would pad his statements, explaining how he had been lying in wait for his target, fending off annoying mosquitoes, his palms sweating as he held the loaded gun.

"He embellished it, he makes it real for you . . . It makes the story so much more believable. We're kind of hanging on the chair, man, listening to this guy," said Koshiba. "That is a master liar.

"He's not just an average liar. Shit, if it was an average liar we could pick him out. It's like a little kid, we go, 'Hey, you lying,'" continued the veteran lawyer. "Ronald Ching, you don't ever say he's lying. You don't know, because he's so good at it, you know. That's what he did. He made this whole thing up, man."

Regarding this alleged lie, that Scanlan facilitated the murder of Chuckers Marsland, Koshiba marveled at the tall tale Ching supposedly concocted. Only a criminal mastermind could delight in the perversity of using a police-issue revolver to commit a murder.

"Ronald Ching was a very unusual person. He was not stupid. He could see irony in things. Now whether he could describe it and identify it, I don't know. I doubt it," said Koshiba. "[But] he certainly understood it and he knew how to play it."

"It was a good story, you know. It was a great story . . . That's what a writer might come up with," said the lawyer. "When they told me the story, I thought, 'That is a pretty smart guy, man . . . If he just thought about it, just the idea, wow, you know, this guy is formidable. Don't take him lightly, man.'"

It was a good a story, too, because it was very hard to disprove. Sure, Koshiba and his fellow defense lawyers could label Ching a liar, but there was no guarantee the jury would agree with them. Even liars sometimes tell the truth. Koshiba would need something more. Koshiba needed to find that gun.

The lawyers for Naone and Nee, meanwhile, were busy with their own strategies. For Evans, Naone's lawyer, this included taking advantage of some help from an unlikely source—the federal government.

"What happened, I got a call from [federal prosecutor] Frank Marine, who invited me to his office, said, 'Chris I got some information for you,' that the feds had gathered on Ronald Ching," said Evans. "He suggested to me that I would probably want to have it, and then he suggested ways I could get it."

Through Marine's help Evans "jump[ed] through a lot of hoops" and obtained copies of the results of the polygraph, or lie detector test, that had been administered to Ching the previous year by the FBI in the federal prison medical facility in Missouri. According to Evans these results listed the specific questions asked of Ching, which included queries about the murder of Chuckers Marsland. On these questions and others Ching was said to have shown deception. While a summary of these polygraph results concerning Ching had already been made public through the filing of federal court documents, now Evans was in possession of the original reports and had access to every detail.

Yet there was even more help to come from federal authorities. During the murder trial Evans said he was on a break, walking from the courthouse to Honolulu's federal building for lunch, when he encountered a local FBI agent. To Evans's recollection, this agent stopped him to share some interesting news.

"Hey Chris, what the fuck? What you dig, brah? We got the three, no, two of the three polygraph examiners that took statements from Ronald Ching. They're here on islands!"

"What?" said Evans.

"It's time for you to get them on the witness stand," said the FBI agent.

"Oh, okay!" said Evans.

Again to Evans's recollection, he then walked back across Punchbowl Street in downtown Honolulu and found Judge Klein at the courthouse. Upon Evans's request, the judge granted permission to call the visiting agents out of order. And though the results of polygraph tests are generally not admissible in criminal court, Evans did his best to squeeze what he could from the FBI agents.

"I had a polygraph examiner on the witness stand who basically almost said Ronald Ching failed the polygraph when it came to identifying the individuals who committed Chuckers Marsland's murder," said a triumphant Evans.

Evans was extremely grateful for the assistance from the feds, though it did leave him a bit baffled. He considered the phone call from federal prosecutor Marine "extremely unusual . . . it is rare beyond belief.

"He never did explain his motivation," said Evans. "Apart from perhaps in the interest of justice. It was my hunch and my belief that they, that he, Frank Marine, had reason to believe that Ronald Ching was just lying his ass off to get a deal."

Marine denied making such a phone call to Evans, or any defense attorney. Any information the federal government released regarding Ching, he said, was done according to procedure and was released to prosecutors and defense attorneys at the same time.

In any case, to Evans, the federal government's alleged assistance was not an act of sabotage against the Honolulu prosecutor's office, but instead an attempt to prevent tragedy.

"I would call it in the interest of justice," said Evans. "You certainly wouldn't want three innocent individuals sent to prison for a murder they had nothing to do with."

Nonetheless, Evans did not publicly disclose the help he claimed to have received from Marine and the FBI agent. Had this interaction been known publicly, surely Marsland would have listed it among the examples he cited of federal authorities aiding defense counsel. It would have infuriated Marsland, especially since he and his deputy prosecutors believed Ching was not lying, but telling the truth.

"Ronnie, when he started talking we didn't just accept everything, you know, as gospel. But I was satisfied that when we got to court that he had been briefed and questioned as much as we possibly could. And we believed that he was telling the truth," said deputy prosecutor McGuigan. "I would never put anyone on the stand if I had even the remote idea that they were not being truthful. It's just too much of a gamble."

The revelations made by the FBI agents on the witness stand, however, were soon overshadowed by the deft trial work of Koshiba. He was the last of the three defense attorneys to present his case, and even his fellow defense counsel were not entirely aware of what he planned to do. Though Koshiba would not jeopardize his colleagues' cases to bolster his own, he was not extremely cooperative, either. It was nothing personal, said the lawyer. He just wanted to go it alone.

"I felt like if it was to be won, I had to win it. If it was gonna be lost, I was gonna lose it," said Koshiba. "I just did not . . . want to depend on or rely on other people."

After calling his client, Raymond Scanlan, to the stand, Koshiba called Scanlan's cousin, Rags, eliciting testimony about how Raymond Scanlan, in a panic, had given Rags his supposedly stolen police revolver and asked him to mail it back to the police department. Rags confirmed he received the gun, but said he apparently forgot to mail it. For approximately twelve years it was out of sight, out of mind.

Rags testified he "wasn't sure what I was going to do with it. I apparently tucked it away somewhere and never got back to it . . . I firmly believe I had mailed it back to the department anonymously."

Rags testified that, upon Koshiba's request, he searched his house but could not find the gun. Then, after the murder trial had started, Rags found the revolver. He had been cleaning out his basement when he discovered a manila envelope. Inside was the missing gun.

Koshiba asked what he did with the revolver.

"I've got it with me now," said Rags, pulling from the inside of his jacket a clear plastic bag containing an unloaded revolver.

Nearly everyone in the courtroom was stunned. Days earlier prosecutors had introduced the police report filed by Scanlan claiming the gun had been stolen. Then Ching took the stand and pointed to a map of the Ala Wai Yacht Harbor, telling the court exactly where in the water he had tossed the revolver allegedly given to him by Scanlan. Now that same supposed gun—with a serial number that matched the one listed on the police report— was sitting in the courtroom. It was dry as a bone, too, not underwater, not buried in silt. No one could believe it.

"People fucking freaked. Even the judge flinched," said Naone's lawyer, Evans. "That sneak! That fucking Koshiba. I tell ya, man, that was excellent. I said, 'Wow, brah, ha ha ha. Ooh, that's good.'"

To the jury the presentation of the gun was nothing less than "shocking," said Melnick, the foreman. He wondered how the gun could have possibly been smuggled into the courtroom.

Judge Klein may have wondered the same thing. He couldn't believe his eyes, either.

"That's pretty dramatic you know," said Klein. "I had many, many trials, never seen that kind of demonstration . . . It was pretty freaky."

For the prosecutors any shock quickly gave way to disappointment. They knew instantly the gun's appearance would imperil their case.

"I remember Carlisle and I just sitting there going, 'Shit!'" said McGuigan, who did not object to the gun's presentation. "If we were to challenge it at that point and say it was wrong it just would have crumbled the entire case. We just kind of gritted our teeth and moved on."

Evans didn't blame them for missing the chance to object. He himself had declined to object earlier in the trial when Chuckers's girlfriend said she knew his client to have a reputation as a murderer. Sometimes, the lawyer said, it's better to just ignore others and plow ahead. Besides, it had all happened so fast, and the trial was nearly over.

"The only thing I can tell you is they were so flat footed and so knocked off guard, so flabbergasted they just didn't know what the fuck to do," Evans said of the prosecutors.

Once the excitement wore off, though, even Evans had some qualms about Koshiba's bold tactic. Tossing aside Ching's story about throwing the gun in the harbor, what if a forensic analysis revealed that the bullets found in Chuckers head did indeed come from this revolver?

"Jimmy played roulette with us on that point," said Evans. "We didn't know he found the fucking gun."

"If the prosecutors said, 'Timeout, we want to examine the weapon,' they run ballistics and this fucker comes out a match . . ." said Evans, "that could have been our ass right fucking there, okay."

Yet Koshiba was too savvy to let something like that occur. When Rags Scanlan found the gun, Koshiba says he was still not sure that the revolver was not the murder weapon. So, unbeknownst to his client, Raymond Scanlan, Koshiba arranged for the chief chemist in the Honolulu Police Department's crime lab, who he had met through previous work with the police, to perform ballistics testing. To Koshiba's satisfaction, and relief, the chemist said the bullets fired into Chuckers head came from a different gun. None of this testing was disclosed to the prosecution.

On the day Rags Scanlan was set to testify, Koshiba discreetly marshaled more help from police officers inside the courtroom. To his recollection an officer took the bagged gun into the courtroom and taped it underneath the witness stand. Somehow or another it was smuggled into the courtroom and made its way into the coat of Rags Scanlan. As Koshiba described his maneuvers:

> *I had friends, you know. Around here it's all friends, you know. Like the chemist. I don't think the chemist had to do that for the police department. I think if people found out he'd get fired, because I was representing the defense.*
>
> *But I knew him. I had worked with him. I said, "Ed I have this gun, you know, I'm in the trial. I just want to do a ballistics test. There's no way for me to get a bullet out of this gun. On this island? Get a ballistics test? The only place I know is the police department. Would you do it?"*
>
> *He said, "I'll do it."*
>
> *He took the gun down. He fired it. Retrieved the bullet. Put it in the microscope. Pulled the bullet from the evidence room, put it in the microscope, showed me. Just like that.*

When Rags produced the gun, Koshiba said, the lawyer noticed the surprise of the judge and his fellow defense lawyers. Yet the prosecutors, he said, were subdued, almost as if they had expected to see the gun. He couldn't account for this reaction.

"My initial impression was that these suckers knew somehow," said Koshiba. "They knew I had the gun."

Earlier in the trial Koshiba had worried that he had tipped his hand during his cross-examination of Ching, when he asked the hit man to tell the court specifically where he had dropped the gun in the boat harbor. Koshiba feared that prosecutors might sniff out his ambush.

The lawyer also fretted about the ethical implications of his actions. The fact that he did not share this evidence with his opposition before trial, during what's known as discovery in the legal world, was likely excusable since the gun was allegedly discovered by Rags Scanlan after the trial had started. But, upon its discovery, should Koshiba have informed the judge and his legal colleagues then? Koshiba didn't think so. To disclose it would have allowed Ching, he said, to amend his story, and for the advantage of the gun to be lost.

Koshiba did some legal research to see what precedent might exist for the introduction of such evidence at the last minute, but he did not find any clear indication of what course of action was appropriate. It was a gray area. To Koshiba that meant the gun could be a surprise.

"Ethically I thought I was okay. The worst that could happen is they could sanction me. But too bad, I gotta do it," said Koshiba. "You know I can't risk blowing the case and having Scanlan convicted because I'm worried about, you know, something that might happen to me. The hell with it, I'm going."

When the hubbub over the gun subsided, the trial soon came to a conclusion. Marsland finally came into the courtroom to make a brief appearance on the witness stand. He discussed his meetings with Raymond Scanlan, telling the court that Scanlan had fingered Ching, Naone, and Nee as his son's killers. Also called to testify at the end of the trial were three inmates from the local prison where Naone was being held on account of his failure to make bail. One of the inmates told the court that Naone recently confessed to him his role in the shooting. The other two inmates declared the first inmate a liar, that he fabricated such a conversation with Naone to earn leniency for his own legal problems, which involved kidnapping and sodomizing a sixteen-year-old boy at a Waikiki hotel. Again it seemed impossible to know who was lying and who, if anyone, was telling the truth.

Then the prosecutors and defense lawyers delivered their closing arguments. When deputy prosecutor McGuigan spoke, he did so beside two photographs. On an easel sat the handsome portrait of Chuckers that McGuigan had displayed during his opening statement. Now, too, he exhibited a less flattering image of the young man: Chuckers's blood-drenched corpse lying on the side of the road. As the deputy prosecutor spoke, his boss Marsland and Marsland's eighty-four-year-old mother Sadie, both sitting in the courtroom, listened.

McGuigan claimed Ching and the three defendants on trial formed an "unholy alliance" to execute Chuckers. Each man had a "unique role" and his own motive for participating in the killing. Ching, said McGuigan, was "a tool, an instrument of this boy's death." Nee, through his presence in the car, deceived Chuckers that he was safe, and served as "the hook for this boy to go with these people." Scanlan was a "dirty cop" and "the arsenal, the armorer of the group." Naone was a "strongarm" and "the glue that held the anatomy of this killing group together."

Together they tried to "twist, subvert, disguise and run from the truth."

Each of them "has on their hands the blood of Charles Marsland III," said McGuigan. "I ask you to come back and find each of them guilty of murder."

As for the gun brought into the courtroom, McGuigan claimed there was "no allegation" that the police service revolver that "mysteriously popped up in Clarence Scanlan's basement" was the "one that shot Chuck Marsland."

Defense lawyers countered the prosecutor's statement by deriding Ching, calling him a liar and manipulator nonpareil. When Ching lies, they said, he does so without compunction.

He "won't even bat an eye," said Hoke, Nee's lawyer. "He'll lie, lie through his teeth."

Beyond the lies, Hoke said, there was not "one scintilla of tangible evidence that corroborated Ronald Ching's story."

Koshiba said much of the same. He also questioned why Ching, who was convicted of federal firearms violations in 1976 and 1981, supposedly "didn't have weapons in 1975" and, what's more, decided to ask a policeman, of all people, to furnish them.

"Likely? Make sense?" asked Koshiba.

Koshiba characterized the prosecution as "zealous," claiming Ching and Marsland made for "strange bedfellows" considering Ching's penchant for lying and Marsland's personal interest in the case.

Such remarks irritated the normally reserved McGuigan. He protested Koshiba's remarks against the integrity of the prosecutor's office, claiming it was ludicrous to believe prosecutors would wrongly indict three men for the sake of their own ambitions.

"It becomes personal at this point," said McGuigan. "I find it offensive."

With that, the case went to the jury. After three weeks of listening to statements and testimony, the trial essentially boiled down to one question: Could Ronnie Ching be trusted to tell the truth?

Pity the person who is hunted in Hawaii. It is not a happy existence to be pursued by predators while being penned in by the ocean. Ultimately there is nowhere to hide, at least not forever. It is especially the case on Oahu, the most populous of the Hawaiian Islands. Known as "The Gathering Place," Oahu is an ill-suited locale for those who need to scatter.

The people targeted by Ching and other underworld killers in Hawaii were often terrorized before being killed, privy to the knowledge that somebody wanted them dead. At this point

Hawaii's lush landscapes and sunny days became devoid of appeal. Fear overran all experiences, draining life of pleasure. The unfortunate quarry lived on edge until suddenly, to his horror, the end arrived, signaled by the appearance of somebody like Ching. By then there was no use running. There was no use, either, in appealing for mercy. In Hawaii's underworld, aloha was markedly absent.

Forget the purgative effects of sunshine and trade winds, Hawaii can be a mighty murky place. This is perhaps especially true for the outsider, whose general grounding in life has been developed elsewhere, on some other continent, a world away. Hawaii's murkiness is maintained, too, by those who prefer people to enjoy the islands instead of understand them. In beautiful Hawaii, facilitating enjoyment is easier, and more profitable. And so understanding stays elusive.

No matter how much time spent dissecting the murder of Chuckers Marsland, the jury could not obtain true understanding of this crime. There had been too many lies told, both in the past and during the trial. It could not be determined which things exactly were lies, just that the existence of so many contradictory statements meant lies were being told, by someone, or everyone. Sunlight bathed so many parts of Hawaii—its volcanoes, its valleys, its beaches—but it did not penetrate its underworld.

The jury deliberated for thirteen hours before acquitting all three defendants of murder. According to the foreman, Melnick, the jury was not impressed with the prosecution's case and thought little of Ching's testimony. There was hardly solid proof, the jurors felt, that Naone, Nee, and Scanlan had committed the murder, no matter how criminally predisposed the tough-looking defendants appeared to be.

"By nature you'd think these guys were bad guys, but there was no evidence to show they participated in the way it was described," said Melnick. "My feeling was that Ronald Ching was feeding information for his own self interest, that there weren't enough facts."

The majority of his fellow jurors initially agreed with him, said Melnick, save two or three, who at first favored convicting the defendants. As the jury discussed the case, those in the minority gradually conceded they could not be sure the defendants were guilty beyond a reasonable doubt. The decision then became unanimous: not guilty.

When the verdict was announced in court, Nee and Naone hugged their attorneys. Nee hugged his wife, too, who was crying. Scanlan lifted his lawyer, Koshiba, up into the air, off his feet. Then both men burst into tears. Deputy prosecutors McGuigan and Carlisle left the court stone-faced and silent, avoiding reporters.

Marsland was in his office when the verdict was delivered. He did not want to be in court when the decision was announced, whether the decision was favorable or disappointing. He learned of the verdict from his spokesman, Reed, who called him from the courthouse.

"Chuck, terrible news," said Reed. "All three not guilty."

"Oh, no," said Marsland. "Okay, thanks."

Hanging up the phone, Marsland left his office and got in his car. Within a few minutes the automobile was climbing Puowaina Drive, exposing its driver to magnificent views of Honolulu, the city he patrolled as prosecutor. Then the road banked right, delivering Marsland into Punchbowl Crater and the National Memorial Cemetery of the Pacific. He parked in the back and walked across the lawn of Section T until he reached Site 140, Chuckers's grave.

Ten years earlier Marsland had stood graveside and promised to bring Chuckers's killers to justice. On this day, after a decade's worth of near-daily visits, he came to tell his son he had failed. Though Paul the Apostle and the inscription above the altar in Marsland's church promised, "Love never faileth," the devastated father wasn't so sure. Charles Marsland loved his boy dearly, but he had failed.

Epilogue

Did Charles Marsland fail?

In his own eyes, yes, but it wasn't for a lack of trying. Marsland left the prosecutor's office, and ultimately this world, without accomplishing the two most important goals of his career and life: achieving justice for his son and convicting Hawaii's godfather.

The acquittal of the three men accused of killing Chuckers with Ronnie Ching derailed the prosecutor's attempt to eradicate organized crime in Hawaii. The trial exposed Ching's considerable shortcoming as a witness: that jurors found him unbelievable. The Chuckers Marsland murder trial was slated to be the first of many cases and trials targeting members of the island underworld. Upon its implosion, other cases were abandoned by the prosecutor's office, charges dropped. There would be no ultimate assault on organized crime.

Days after the trial, Ching complained that he was the victim of "bad press" that "portrayed me as a bogeyman, a psychopath." Moreover, said Ching, potential jurors in Hawaii were afraid of being selected for organized crime cases. As a remedy he suggested flying in jury pools from the mainland—two hundred people at a time.

Ching also claimed that Hawaii's underworld was more lucrative and organized than ever before. Leading this underworld was "one specific key figure . . . a conductor." Other gangsters, said Ching, "are out there playing different instruments, they're just part of the orchestra."

Ching would not reveal this conductor's name, but said he anticipated testifying against him in the future. It never happened. Less than two months after the conclusion of the Chuckers Marsland murder trial, Ching's plea agreement with the prosecutor's office was dissolved by mutual consent. Prosecutors had discovered inconsistencies in a number of Ching's fifty-three statements to investigators. Ching himself was becoming reluctant to testify for the prosecution, because he feared for the safety of his family. In August 1985 Ching pleaded guilty in state court to four murders, including the killing of Chuckers Marsland. He was sentenced to four life terms and was required to serve at least forty years in prison before being eligible for parole. He was then sent to prison in Oklahoma to finish his remaining federal prison term for firearm and narcotics violations.

A year later Ching sent a handwritten note to Marsland asking him for forgiveness and lamenting that his brief period of cooperation did not bear more fruit for the prosecutor's office.

"I've tried with all my will to help you in seeking justice but all efforts were shielded by the corruptive influence of Hawaii politics," Ching wrote. "I pray that you not be bitter with that either and please don't lose your perspective so you may continue your work.

"If there is anything that I can do—just ask," Ching wrote in conclusion. "Again I ask your forgiveness and may Akua [god] be with you."

Marsland did not reply to Ching.

After finishing his federal prison sentence, Ching was transferred to a state prison on Oahu. There he spent much of his time in the prison's medical unit, away from the general prison population, suffering from complications of Hepatitis C, a disease he likely contracted from his drug use. By the time Ching died in prison on September 17, 2005, his body weight had dropped in half, to one hundred forty pounds.

Before dying, Ching appealed to deputy prosecutor Peter Carlisle for help getting an early release from prison. Carlisle turned the hit man down.

"He knew I was not willing to assist him," said Carlisle, who followed in Marsland's footsteps in becoming Honolulu's city prosecutor for four terms, then being elected as the city's mayor. "And he said to me he understood, because 'some things can't be forgiven.'

"And I said, 'That's right.'"

Ching remains the only admitted killer of Chuckers Marsland, though some wonder even if Ching's confession is true, given the hit man's penchant for lying. Such mystery still looms, too, over Eric Naone's alleged involvement in Chuckers's murder. Naone's daughter Erica said she recalled her father bidding her farewell when she was three and a half years old, just before police came to arrest him for murder. In the days and hours before the arrest was made, she said, she witnessed her father dumping a car on the other side of Oahu and burning assorted items. It was clear to her that these items did not belong to her father and, if found by the police, might cause him more legal problems. Her father, Erica Naone said, seemed to be aware that his arrest was imminent.

For years Erica Naone wondered about her father's culpability, sometimes applying logic to the question at hand. Such thinking went like this:

I certainly know that he is capable of killing because I know that he killed people in Vietnam. I know that he is capable of being terrifying because I saw him be terrifying—he was terrifying to me, he was terrifying to his friends . . . The question for me has always been: Do these two dots connect? Could he have been terrible to that extent to someone who he was supposed to have been friends with? I guess I don't rule it out. I've never quite been sure, which is why I asked him.

Her father's answer: "Just because I didn't pull the trigger doesn't mean I didn't tell someone to do it."

Though she found this response unsatisfying, Erica Naone did not question her father further. "You just didn't push things with him," she said.

Naone clearly implied he had some kind of involvement in Chuckers's death, yet Erica Naone was not quick to believe him, considering it a strong possibility that her father would falsely claim a connection to the murder to enhance his criminal reputation. However, after her father passed away in 2012, and his ashes deposited in a columbarium at the National Memorial Cemetery of the Pacific, not far from the grave of his alleged murder victim Chuckers Marsland, Erica Naone said she heard some stories from family acquaintances that made it seem likely that her father was indeed complicit in the killing. The murder of Chuckers Marsland remains an open investigation, according to the Honolulu Police Department.

Following the failed prosecution of the three men believed to be Ching's accomplices, the remainder of Marsland's second term was relatively lackluster, though not without controversies. One controversy involved Marsland's aggressive crackdown on pornography in Honolulu, which residents judged as desperately needed or, alternatively, as an assault on personal liberties. Another was his office's entanglement in an investigation of a smear campaign against gubernatorial candidate and former congressman Cecil Heftel. And yet another was a lawsuit against Marsland's office and the City of Honolulu for malicious prosecution, filed by a man who had been charged, and acquitted, of kidnapping and raping two preschool girls on Oahu. The city paid $550,000 to settle the lawsuit without admitting fault. The city also paid about $900,000 in attorney fees to defend the lawsuit. It was an expensive mistake.

Still, Marsland remained popular. In 1988 he campaigned for a third term as prosecutor, still buoyed by his reputation as a hardliner. Some residents, though, were beginning to tire of his inflammatory rhetoric. The nonstop outrage had begun to ring hollow. As *Honolulu* magazine columnist Dan Boylan wrote a few months before the election: "'Sticking people in the can,' 'vicious punks' and 'nailing' criminals are phrases that come easily to Marsland—so easily, so often, and so publicly over the past eight years that he is dangerously close to becoming a caricature of himself: Chuck Marsland, prosecutor incarnate."

Surprisingly, Marsland lost the election to Keith Kaneshiro, the former deputy prosecutor who had once directed the organized crime strike force in Marsland's office. Marsland was not gracious in defeat. He complained that despite the prosecutor's post being made a nonpartisan office two years before the election, Hawaii's Democratic machine acted in full force behind his opponent.

"The old-boy network got together and they got out the vote," said Marsland, who earned 86,552 votes to Kaneshiro's 103,000. The prosecutor said he was flummoxed by an "unusual aspect to this so-called non-partisan campaign. We were non-partisan but the other side was not."

He then denigrated his opponent.

"I don't think he can handle the job. I think he knows it, too. He owes too many people now," said Marsland. "Brother, does he owe."

In response Kaneshiro introduced his vote-getting "machine" at a political rally. It included his parents, brothers, and sister-in-law, as well as other volunteers.

To observers Kaneshiro ran a superior campaign. He also capitalized on Marsland's frequent attacks against assorted political figures and his extreme responses to crime, which, over eight years, slowly poisoned the prosecutor's reputation among assorted ethnic groups on Oahu. Hawaiians might have resented Marsland's continual attacks against Larry Mehau. Japanese Americans might have taken issue with his criticism of Governor

George Ariyoshi. Filipinos were not receptive to his broadsides against State Senator Ben Cayetano, while some Caucasians were concerned with his attacks on civil liberties, and so on. As noted by Boylan, "Marsland offered an almost textbook lesson in how to alienate every voting bloc in Hawaii."

No longer city prosecutor in 1989, Marsland briefly attempted to become Hawaii's top federal prosecutor, or US attorney. Two terms in office had not yet mellowed the sixty-six-year-old. His appointment as US attorney was needed, he said, because the islands were a "cesspool of dope, dishonesty and rottenness."

"Hawaii," said Marsland, "is without a doubt the most corrupt state in the union."

While many regarded this as hyperbole, Marsland had his reasons for such claims. Take the example of Harold Shintaku, the judge who reversed a jury's murder conviction of gangster Charlie Stevens, prompting a public uproar. In June 1989, eight years after overturning the verdict and becoming mysteriously injured in his North Shore cottage, Shintaku slashed his wrists and jumped from the third story of a Las Vegas hotel. The retired judge's death was ruled a suicide, and it was discovered that he had gambling debts totaling twenty-one thousand dollars. Three years later Stevens admitted to having bribed Shintaku to secure the overturning of his guilty verdict.

Marsland exhibited a rare show of restraint when told of Shintaku's death.

"My only reaction is that the guy is gone. What can you say? May he rest in peace," said the recently ousted prosecutor. "You don't go after somebody if they can't fight back."

No matter Marsland's strong anticrime sentiments, he was not appointed US attorney for Hawaii. He did not become governor of Hawaii, either, though he mounted a brief campaign for that position in 1990. By that time, though, his star had faded, the opportunity passed. Some supporters thought it just as well.

"He just was not a politician. His expertise and passion was really limited. I couldn't imagine Chuck talking about education or air pollution," said his former spokesman and aide, Rick Reed. "He was essentially a warrior with a mission. That's what his strength was. I think that's ultimately why he didn't move on to higher office. He would have a hard time being a governor."

Reed left the prosecutor's office in 1986 to campaign for Congress but was unsuccessful. He was then elected state senator from Maui before challenging longtime US Senator Dan Inouye. Reed did not unseat Inouye.

Since Reed had published godfather allegations in the *Valley Isle*, Larry Mehau sued him and others for libel. Some of those lawsuits were settled, others eventually dropped, as was the case with the original lawsuit against Reed. Mehau's lawyer, David Schutter, explained that the suit was dropped because Reed was penniless and could not pay any potential award from a judge or jury. Reed said the lawsuit was dropped because it was obvious he would have prevailed in court.

Then, following a 1985 speech by Reed in which the congressional candidate again named Mehau as Hawaii's godfather, Mehau again sued Reed for libel and defamation as well as invasion of privacy. This time the case eventually went to trial. During the course of the three-month trial, the libel claims were dropped and a jury, in 1992, found that Reed, who represented himself, was not liable for invasion of privacy. Reed felt vindicated by the verdict, claiming he was "going to continue to exercise my freedom of speech and speak out on issues I'm concerned with."

Mehau was discouraged by the failed lawsuit, stating that Reed will "never stop. He has no feelings at all."

Apart from labeling him the godfather of organized crime, Reed did have a few nice things to say about his nemesis, calling Mehau "warm, witty, likable."

Said Reed, "If Larry Mehau were in trouble on the side of the road somewhere, I mean in real trouble, I'd stop and help him. I don't hate him."

In ensuing years Mehau would be subject to more insinuations and accusations about his alleged role in Hawaii's underworld. Mehau, however, has never been indicted or convicted for any major crime.

—◆—

In the two decades after Charles Marsland left public office, the fiery former prosecutor mellowed considerably. His raw anger dissipated as he eased into a quiet life of retirement that featured regular walks with his dogs. He remained devoted to his mother Sadie until her death at age ninety-six, visiting her daily in the nursing home. Sadie Marsland was buried with her husband in Section T of the National Memorial Cemetery of the Pacific within Punchbowl Crater. The grave of Marsland's parents is just a stone's throw from the grave of Marsland's son, which made it easy for the elderly Marsland to commune with his family.

In his twilight years Marsland became somewhat withdrawn and dependent upon the care of his longtime companion, Polly Grigg. He still enjoyed sharing with certain friends the avocados, mangoes, and other tropical fruit he grew at his home. But other friends and acquaintances he encountered about town became unrecognizable to Marsland in his advanced age. Such was the case with former deputy prosecutor Mike McGuigan, who conceded his own appearance had changed since the men worked together.

"I don't think he was senile," said McGuigan, who is now a partner in a Honolulu law firm. "I think he was in his own thoughts."

Though his body slowed and withered, Marsland's legacy remained undiminished. At the very least this legacy included recognition that Marsland drastically expanded the manpower of the prosecutor's office and made sure that victims of crime were as much a focus of the prosecutor's office as perpetrators of crime. Marsland, through his use of the bully pulpit, also made crime a topic of considerable public discussion in Hawaii. He did his best to bring the underworld out into the open.

Even Marsland's political opponent Kaneshiro, who succeeded him as city prosecutor, deems these accomplishments laudable and desperately needed, considering the former inadequacies of Hawaii's legal and law enforcement infrastructure.

"He opened up the criminal justice system to the public. He talked about issues of crime. He brought attention on the criminal justice system, the judiciary, the court, the prison," said Kaneshiro. "Attention was focused on the criminal justice system which was I think rightly so. I think the public needed to know about what was going on."

Yet Marsland's critics regarded him as a dangerous man insistent on not only dismantling organized crime, but also American standards of justice.

"The Hawaiian tradition is to treat people with aloha and there's still some semblance of that in our legal system," said Honolulu defense attorney Brook Hart. "He was into bringing something that was more akin to what the Third Reich sponsored and changing the rules to move toward being a police state."

The man could not be reasoned with, said Hart, and Marsland's rage interfered with the responsible discharge of his duties as a prosecutor. As many judges complained to Marsland's face in court, the prosecutor sometimes cut corners (both figuratively and literally, as Marsland was a notorious jaywalker), which weakened his cases.

"Marsland was not a capable trial lawyer . . . He was driven by emotion. He didn't prepare," said Hart. "His focus was so one-sided that you could never get him to objectively look at a matter that had serious consequences."

Even Marsland's friend, Reed, conceded his former boss could be hardheaded.

"Chuck would get a real firm opinion on scant information and it became really strongly held," said Reed. "If he was told something by somebody he respected he'd believe it really strongly."

Despite these shortcomings, many credit Marsland for severely crimping the operations of organized crime in Hawaii and for tackling the community's most violent criminals. Honolulu lawyer David Bettencourt said this legacy may not be fully appreciated because Marsland's reputation for vigilance stopped much criminal activity before it occurred, especially in the realm of public corruption. In other words, the prosecutor only got credit for convicting criminals, not for intimidating people from becoming, or ceasing to be, criminals.

To be sure, the diminished influence of violent and organized crime in Hawaii was also attributable to the efforts of other local and federal law enforcement groups, as well as increased intolerance on the part of the local community. Yet Marsland was the very public face associated with this fight against crime, and the magnitude of his vigor and outspokenness was simply astonishing, especially for an older, otherwise sedate gentleman who most preferred to be in the company of his dogs, walking to and along the beach. Marsland was a crusader, and his inspiration was derived almost entirely from the grief and fury associated with the murder of Chuckers.

"He would have led a kind of uninteresting, unmentionable, forgettable, I think, kind of superficial life had it not been for that tragedy and the focus it gave him," said Reed.

"The silver lining in the cloud that befell Chuck the day his son died was that his life from that moment took on real meaning and purpose," he said. "As devastating as it was, the death of his son altered Chuck's life in a positive way. All of a sudden, Marsland's warrior nature was in harmony with his life's purpose. Organized crime had messed with the wrong guy."

The fact that Marsland was so blunt and impolitic in Hawaii is noteworthy because such behavior seems to fly in the face of aloha spirit. Though Marsland proudly boasted of his family's long-time kamaaina status, to many his law-and-order mentality did not jibe with the relaxed, live-and-let-live attitude that permeated the Hawaiian Islands. Marsland believed that the permissive and indulgent aspects of Hawaiian culture threatened island society as a whole. His personal mission was to save Hawaii from fostering a culture of fear and violence, as much as it was to achieve justice for his son.

Reed lived in Hawaii for about two decades. He spoke fondly of the islands, but was critical of Hawaii's insularity:

> *Hawaii is a unique state. Partly because of its geographic isolation, and also because of the culture . . . you could end up with a Senate president, police chief and leader of organized crime who all grew up with the same aunties and uncles.*
>
> *There's a tolerance for corruption. There's a provincial mindset that is hostile toward outsiders that contributes to that. So you end up with a tolerance for corruption that . . . to talk about it, or to try to root it out is disloyal, is not local.*
>
> *That's what Charles Marsland flew in the face of and said, "Fuck you. I don't care if it kills me, I don't care if it destroys me, you guys can all fuck yourselves." That's why he was so dangerous to them and why he was so attractive to people.*
>
> *That was really refreshing. You just didn't see that. You know how politicians are so careful, everything they say is crafted, you can't believe a word they say? Marsland was just the opposite. He didn't even have a sense of what was good for him to say or not say. He would say whatever he believed was true.*

Federal prosecutor Frank Marine described, too, the challenges posed by Hawaiian culture when it came to law enforcement. "Hawaii juries are more difficult to convict than a lot of places in the mainland," said Marine. "They're reluctant to stand in judgment of somebody."

Both Reed and Marine are haoles. But late Hawaiian State Representative Kinau Kamalii, who served as a trustee of the Office of Hawaiian Affairs and chairwoman of the Native Hawaiian Studies Commission, shared these men's sentiments. When Hawaii was in the throes of its crime wave in the 1970s and early 1980s, Kamalii, who was once sued with Reed and others by Mehau for making godfather allegations, believed the only solution for solving corruption on the islands was outside help from the US government:

> We need federal help because for so long our state has been under the control of certain individuals. Because Hawaii is unique in the way we have been raised. We intermarry. We have cousins, uncles and friends and the whole scene. It's amazing.
>
> People I talk to say, "I'm related to that one. He's in the Syndicate, but he's auntie's boy and you know how it is. Too bad he went wrong." Nobody is going to finger anybody. Their relationships here are so close that the only way that they're going to be broken is by the federal government. That is my sincere belief. That is the only way.

Local boy Marsland, of course, was not in agreement that federal intervention was necessary. He believed that with enough willpower and determination, residents of Hawaii could clean up their islands themselves, restoring a paradise and eradicating fear. If he failed to achieve certain specific objectives, namely obtaining justice for his son and convicting the leader of the Hawaiian underworld, as much as such a person might have existed, he was successful in a broader sense, helping Hawaii to combat runaway crime.

"He did what had never been done here before and I don't think has been done since, and I think that says something about the man," said McGuigan. "He brought a sense of law enforcement to this community that had not existed before."

More narrowly, said the former deputy prosecutor, Marsland transformed the Honolulu prosecutor's office into a meaningful organization devoid of cronyism and political patronage.

"It was a place where people were proud to come to work every day and proud of what they accomplished," said McGuigan. "They didn't shy away from doing what they thought was right."

Charles Marsland died on April 11, 2007, his eighty-fourth birthday. He was laid to rest in the National Memorial Cemetery of the Pacific within Punchbowl Crater. His body lies above that of his son.

Acknowledgments

Though research and writing often feel like solitary work, the completion of a nonfiction book is only possible thanks to the help and efforts of many people. Especially deserving of my gratitude is each person who agreed to be interviewed regarding his or her memories of Charles Marsland and the Hawaiian underworld. I would also like to thank the *Honolulu Star-Advertiser*, *Honolulu* magazine, *Hawaii Free Press*, Punahou School Archives, and others who permitted me to reprint photographs. Also, the staff of the University of Hawaii at Manoa Library was extremely kind and helpful during my visits.

Jessica Papin of Dystel & Goderich Literary Management and editor Keith Wallman at Lyons Press provided me crucial support. Each displayed much enthusiasm and encouragement for the book. I am so very grateful for all their help.

Mark Berry and the College of Charleston were generous to me. So was Tim Wellesley, who alerted me to the existence of the Hawaiian underworld. Marvin Scharosch was a fine host and tour guide on Oahu.

My greatest debt, though, is owed to Elizabeth, Iris, and Lou. Since writing is such a solitary process, time filling pages means time away from those I love. My family should know their sacrifices do not go unnoticed or unappreciated. I'd always rather look at their smiling, gorgeous faces than a bunch of words.

Sources

I might be the only person to visit Hawaii for its libraries. I certainly hope so. Hawaii is too beautiful a place to spend a trip there within the stacks. Better to train your eyes on the green mountains, the massive waves, the incredible flowers . . . almost anything other than the screen of a microfiche machine.

When you tell people you're heading to Hawaii for work, you don't get much sympathy, just the rolling of their eyes. Lucky for me my work required sometimes venturing beyond the archives to explore Oahu. If I spent much time at the beach or cruising the North Shore, I could legitimately claim it was for research purposes, considering the number of gangland executions that took place on the sand.

I began researching this story after hearing offhandedly from a former law-enforcement source about one of the islands' more notorious gangsters, Henry Huihui. I remember Googling Huihui's name, guessing at the spelling, and, upon seeing the results, being introduced to the Hawaiian underworld that had previously been unknown to me. My mind was blown. Hawaii, which I had never visited, had always seemed a pleasant and relaxing place courtesy of its common depiction in our culture as a vacation destination. I was surprised to learn the islands once supported such an extensive underworld, especially one so violent.

Before long I learned of prosecutor Charles Marsland and his quest to avenge his son's death and destroy the Hawaiian underworld. Marsland, who died three or so years before I began my research, eventually became the focus of this book. I thought his fiery personality, controversial attacks on Hawaii's political and judicial establishment, and personal anguish made him the most compelling person on which to build a story. This was a man obsessed, as evidenced by his near-daily visits to the National Memorial Cemetery of the Pacific to commune with his son. Marsland, for all his faults, had a passion I found remarkable. It was attractive to me that his quixotic struggle occurred in Hawaii—exotic, lush islands with a tragic and complicated history.

Because Marsland and a number of other people mentioned in these pages, including Ronnie Ching, died before I began this book, I relied on news and magazine archives to supply their voices. All dialogue in the book is reprinted verbatim from news accounts and court documents or, alternatively, is presented as recalled by those I interviewed. In other words, none of the dialogue is invented, at least not by me. Like any journalist, I am at the mercy of my sources to be told the truth. Knowing that recollections of the past are sometimes distorted, whether intentionally or not, I have done my best to verify assorted accounts of events related to me and to obtain a multitude of perspectives.

Many people agreed to speak to me for this book, and many people did not. A handful of politicians Marsland once antagonized did not respond to my communications. The same goes for a number of criminals who once ruled the Hawaiian underworld, which perhaps was not surprising, considering these men were suspected of many vicious crimes, though not always charged, and even more rarely convicted. Given that I am not from Hawaii, I was also a stranger to these men, perhaps hurting my chances of engaging them to discuss sensitive subjects. Luckily, however, in many cases their lawyers were at least willing to talk.

On the other side of the law, there was much sensitivity, too. One person I tried to reach responded to my interview request by paying nearly twenty dollars to express mail me a single piece of paper asking me to leave his/her family alone.

To my disappointment I was unable to interview Larry Mehau, as my calls to his security firm were not returned. But of the many people whom I did speak to, almost all agreed to go completely on the record and have information attributed to their names. There are few anonymous sources quoted in the book.

I have fond memories of my time in Hawaii. I enjoyed the hospitality of friendly people, took incredible hikes, toured Doris Duke's magnificent home Shangri-La at the foot of Diamond Head, waded among sea turtles, spied spouting humpback whales from cliffs, spearfished for octopus, and got walloped on the North Shore by a massive wave that soaked my clothes and swept away my sandals. At the same time, I was cautioned by a number of people that I was putting myself in danger by researching this story, poking my head into dangerous matters. It is not a pleasant feeling to be told repeatedly that you are bound to be cut into pieces and dumped in the ocean. Yet so much time had passed, and I was unsure of how seriously I should take these warnings. Complicating things was my introduction to a woman who claimed to have witnessed the murder of Chuckers Marsland but had repressed this memory for nearly forty years. I was unable to verify her account, but was bewildered that her claim should surface just as I happened to research an unsolved murder four decades old.

I attempted to interview as many people as I could for this book. But no matter how thorough my reporting, many of the mysteries and whodunits described in this book remain unsolved. Some secrets, people have decided, will never be shared. Yet it is my hope that this book offers the most complete picture to date of a fascinating period of Hawaiian history and the bold men on both sides of the law who shaped the island underworld.

Selected Bibliography

Newspapers
Boston Globe
Honolulu Advertiser
Honolulu Star-Bulletin
Las Vegas Review-Journal
Los Angeles Times
New York Times
Rocky Mountain News
Valley Isle (Maui, Hawaii)

Books
Ariyoshi, Jean. *Washington Place: A First Lady's Story.* Honolulu: Japanese Cultural Center of Hawaii, 2004.
Carson, Doug. *Punchbowl: The National Memorial Cemetery of the Pacific Aiea.* Hawaii: Island Heritage Publishing, 1992.
Chaplin, George. *Presstime in Paradise: The Life and Times of the* Honolulu Advertiser *1856–1995.* Honolulu: University of Hawaii Press, 1998.
Cooper, George, and Gavan Daws. *Land and Power in Hawaii: The Democratic Years.* Honolulu: University of Hawaii Press, 1985.
Daws, Gavan. *Shoal of Time: A History of the Hawaiian Islands.* Honolulu: University of Hawaii Press, 1989.
Ho, Don, and Jerry Hopkins. *Don Ho: My Music, My Life.* Honolulu: Watermark Publishing, 2007.
King, Samuel P., with Jerry Burris and Ken Kobayashi. *Judge Sam King: A Memoir.* Honolulu: Watermark Publishing, 2013.
King, Samuel P., and Randall W. Roth. *Broken Trust: Greed, Mismanagement & Political Manipulation at America's Largest Charitable Trust.* Honolulu: University of Hawaii Press, 2006.
Singletary, Milly, *Punchbowl: National Memorial Cemetery of the Pacific.* Honolulu: Sunset Publications, 1977, revised 1981.
Vowell, Sarah. *Unfamiliar Fishes.* New York: Riverhead Books, 2011.

Magazines, Journals, and Essays
Borreca, Richard, "Jaws II," *Honolulu*, August 1983.
Borreca, Richard, "Looking-Glass Judge," *Honolulu*, November 1983.
Boylan, Dan, "It's Always High Noon for Chuck Marsland," *Honolulu*, July 1988.
Boylan, Dan, "Okinawan Power," *Honolulu*, December 1988.

SOURCES

Chapman, Don, "Larry Mehau: The Man Behind The Myth [Part I]," *Mid-Week*, January 25, 1995.
Chapman, Don, "Larry Mehau: The Man Behind The Myth [Part II]," *Mid-Week*, February 1, 1995.
Jones, Bob, "The Real Story of David Schutter," MidWeek, July 27, 2005.
Kim, Marilyn, "Danny Kaleikini," *Honolulu*, March 1987.
Kotani, Roland, "Hawaii's Criminal Justice Furor," [Part I], *Hawaii Herald*, March 19, 1982.
Kotani, Roland, "Hawaii's Criminal Justice Furor," [Part II], *Hawaii Herald*, April 2, 1982.
Lipman, Victor, "Charles Marsland," *Honolulu*, February 1981.
Lipman, Victor, "Hayden Burgess," *Honolulu*, January 1986.
McCall, Cheryl, "Used to Crowds in His Act and His Private Life, Don Ho Is the Man Who Put the Blue in Hawaii," *People*, July 2, 1979.
Nicol, Brian, "Lunch with a Killer," *Honolulu*, March 1985.
Richardson, John, "The Curse of the Syndicate," *Islands Business*, January 1984.
Shaplen, Robert, "Islands of Disenchantment–I," *New Yorker*, August 30, 1982.
Shaplen, Robert, "Islands of Disenchantment–II," *New Yorker*, September 6, 1982.
Trask, Haunani, "Lovely Hula Hands: Corporate Tourism and the Prostitution of Hawaiian Culture," 2008.
"You're a doll," *Honolulu*, June 1974.

Government Reports
Organized Crime in Hawaii, Volume I: A Report to the Hawaii State Legislature, by the Hawaii Crime Commission, August 1978.
Drug Abuse and Trafficking in the State of Hawaii and the Trust Territory of Guam: A Report of the Select Committee on Narcotics Abuse and Control, US House of Representatives, 95th Congress, 2nd Session, 1978.

Notes

Prologue

4 "belonged to a fraternity": Interview with G. E. Castagnetti, April 5, 2013.

Chapter One: They Took Everything

7 "As soon as I saw": letter from Charles Marsland to his daughter, May 1, 1975.

8 "the sand beneath his toes": Interview with Rick Reed, March 13, 2013.

10 In 1982, native Hawaiians comprised: Shaplen, Part I.

11 "Chuck's dead!": Interview with Alexander Pedi, April 5, 2013.

11 "They took everything away": Interview of Eric Naone by Honolulu police, April 18, 1975.

16 "We looked down to pray": Ho, p. 79.

17 Just halfway through the year: *Star-Bulletin*, June 19, 1975.

18 victims in Hawaii's criminal underworld: Organized Crime in Hawaii.

19 "The crime syndicate is here": *Advertiser*, July 16, 1970.

20 "The only way": *Los Angeles Times*, June 5, 1977.

20 "bruddah": *Star-Bulletin*, January 30, 1974.

20 "to make things good": Ryder's description of the Syndicate's origin are from court testimony reported in the *Star-Bulletin* on January 23, 1974, and July 2, 1974.

21 "gave him the bone": *Star-Bulletin*, July 2, 1974.

21 "wild hatred for Negroes": *Advertiser*, July 20, 1970.

21 "If you guys had come": ibid.

22 "You are one of the worst": ibid.

23 "Delicious, send more": *Los Angeles Times*, June 5, 1977.

23–24 These women charged: *Advertiser*, July 22, 1970.

24 Heroin seized: *Drug Abuse and Trafficking in the State of Hawaii and the Trust Territory of Guam.*

25 heroin . . . stashed inside the cadavers: Interview with David Bettencourt, March 21, 2013.

27 "If no pay, shake 'em down": *Star-Bulletin*, January 18, 1974.

27 "I only went to one class": *Advertiser*, December 16, 1978.

27 "I give up my family": *Star-Bulletin*, January 25, 1974.

28 "Nappy was the quiet but deadly": Interview with anonymous source.

28 "They used to say": Interview with Ray Hamilton, February 2013.

28 "their roots in Hawaii": *Drug Abuse and Trafficking in the State of Hawaii and the Trust Territory of Guam.*

29 "A lot of the organized crime": Interview with David Bettencourt, March 21, 2013.

30 "a very nice man": Kim.

30 In perhaps the greatest example: Cooper, p. 251.

31 "At this point, the syndicate": *Advertiser*, July 19, 1970.

33 "of notorious and unsavory reputation": Petition for Final Order of Exclusion, Nevada State Gaming Control Board, January 14, 1975.

33 "This Hawaiian Syndicate": *Advertiser*, August 23, 1974.

33 "five local boys": King, p. 7.

34 "second family": *Advertiser*, January 25, 1974.

34 "crime lord": *Star-Bulletin*, February 15, 1974.

35 "are a little unusual": *Advertiser*, November 29, 1979.

36 Nery "gotta go": *Star-Bulletin*, January 13, 1979.

36 "Monte is no damn good": *Star-Bulletin*, December 19, 1978.

37 "Just tell them": *Advertiser*, June 25, 1974.

37 "haole wahines": *Star-Bulletin*, July 1, 1974.

37 "just beat the hell": ibid.

37 "Put 'em here": ibid.

38 "You make this one": ibid.

39 "We're happy about it": *Advertiser*, July 12, 1974.

40 "They must like me": *Star-Bulletin*, May 7, 1975.

40 "Because," Pulawa said, "he remembered": ibid.

40 "Oh well": Interview with Brook Hart, March 21, 2013.

41 "Since grade school": *Star-Bulletin*, May 7, 1974.

41 "the community is afraid of you": *Star-Bulletin*, May 20, 1975.

41 "There were people saying": *Star-Bulletin*, July 2, 1979.

42 "Mister Nappy Pulawa": *Advertiser*, July 13, 1975.

Chapter Two: Vicious, Mad Dogs

44 "bristled at any questioning": Eulogy for Chuck Marsland by Rick Reed, April 30, 2007. Parentheses in original.

46 "No announcer": *Daily Boston Globe*, January 26, 1957.

48 "Campbell and his radio station employee": *Boston Globe*, November 26, 1963.

49 "commando style": *Advertiser*, July 23, 1972.

49 "He was a good, caring dad": Interview with Mark Keala, February 15, 2013.

50 "It was wonderful": Interview with Phil and Joan Hester, March 26, 2013.

50 "As he got older": Interview with Mark Keala, February 15, 2013.

50 "just so full of himself": Interview with Rick Reed, March 13, 2013.

51 "From an awkward, raw-boned teenager": Letter from Charles Marsland to his daughter, May 1, 1975.

51 "wise guy": Interview with Jon Andersen, March 6, 2013.

51 "changed from a real nice guy": *Advertiser*, April 18, 1975.

51 "I adored him": Interview with Cathy (Clisby) Galka, April 19, 2013.

52 "Him and Cathy were sweethearts": Interview with Alexander Pedi, April 5, 2013.

52 "He had a lot of potential": *Star-Bulletin*, April 18, 1975.

52 "He liked the situations": Interview with Alexander Pedi, April 5, 2013.

53 "perch"... "bunny dip".... : "You're a doll."

53 "It was a cowboy show": Interview with Alexander Pedi, April 5, 2013.

53 "Here lies Waikiki": Shaplen, Part II.

54 "swarthily handsome"... "I kiss grandmas": McCall.

54 "She was the most beautiful": Ho, p. 90.

55 "One night, I felt": Ho, p.91.

55 "second to the State Capitol": Ho, p. 104.

56 "Eric Naone was not": Interview with Christopher Evans, April 12, 2013.

56 Having a friend as strong: Naone described his fights with Samoans in an interview with the Honolulu police, April 18, 1975.

57 "He said, 'Next time'": Interview with Paul Bowskill, March 24, 2013.

57 "devastating consequences": Letter from Charles Marsland to his daughter, May 1, 1975.

58 "Chuck, he wanted": Interview with Mark Keala, February 15, 2013.

58 "You really didn't think": Interview with Cathy (Clisby) Galka, April 19, 2013.

58 So normal . . . Naone killed people: *Advertiser*, May 31, 1985.

59 "He sort of felt": Interview with Paul Bowskill, March 24, 2013.

59 "Like a Greek god": Interview with Alexander Pedi, April 5, 2013.

59 Declaring Ching to be too "rowdy": *Advertiser*, June 1, 1985.

59 "He looked like a guy": Interview with Paul Bowskill, March 24, 2013.

59 As Ching left … "get" Chuckers: *Advertiser*, June 1, 1985.

60 Calling the murder "completely senseless": *Star-Bulletin*, April 18, 1975.

60 "A lot of the underworld people": *Advertiser*, April 18, 1975.

60 "[Chuckers] would get up": Interview with Alexander Pedi, April 5, 2013.

60 "Everybody interacted really well": Interview with Cathy (Clisby) Galka, April 19, 2013.

60–61 "a likeable kid": *Advertiser*, April 18, 1975.

61 "That's when he popped it out": *Star-Bulletin*, June 1, 1985.

61 According to Ching: *Star-Bulletin*, June 5, 1985.

62 "If he was, I didn't know": Interview with Alexander Pedi, April 5, 2013.

62 "The rumors were": Interview with James Koshiba, March 26, 2013.

63 "favor economy" . . . "He felt entitled": Interview with Erica Naone, April 7, 2014.

65 "knows that Ching": Interview of Eric Naone by Honolulu police, April 18, 1975.

65 "Although being very cordial": Interview of Ronald Ching by Honolulu police, April 18, 1975.

67 "You could tell": Interview with Jon Andersen, March 6, 2013.

67 "It was the worst thing": Interview with Alexander Pedi, April 5, 2013.

67 "He looked great": Interview with Cathy (Clisby) Galka, April 19, 2013.

67 "Chuckie's casket was the same": Letter from Charles Marsland to his daughter, May 1, 1975.

67 "If it had been strictly": *Star-Bulletin*, June 11, 1985.

68 "devastated" . . . "I never saw": Interview with Cathy (Clisby) Galka, April 19, 2013.

68 "Everything had been knocked": Interview with Phil and Joan Hester, March 26, 2013.

68 "savage, senseless insanity": Letter from Charles Marsland to his daughter, May 1, 1975.

69 "one of the finest": ibid.

70 "His father was obsessed": Interview with Alexander Pedi, April 5, 2013.

70 "take care" of these people: *Advertiser*, June 30, 1985.

70 "obsessed" . . . "Prolonged grief": Interview with sister of Polly Grigg, September 5, 2011.

72 "We were acting": Interview with Frank O'Brien, April 11, 2013.

73 "Somehow, some way": Letter from Charles Marsland to his daughter, May 1, 1975.

Chapter Three: He Will Stop at Nothing

74 "sovereign nation of Hawaii": *Advertiser*, October 25, 1978.

75 "This court is the creation": *Advertiser*, June 16, 1978.

75 "Eh brah, why me?": Lipman, January 1986.

76 "Does this happen frequently?": Interview with Peter Carlisle, March 22, 2013.

76 "I, Wilford Kalaauaia Pulawa": *Advertiser*, October 25, 1978.

76 "It's all take, take, take": Cooper, p. 254.

77 "less than honorable": *Advertiser*, October 25, 1978.

78 "It's bullshit": *Star-Bulletin*, December 7, 1978.

79 "This is it, pal": *Advertiser*, December 22, 1978.

79 "The more I talked": *Star-Bulletin*, December 21, 1978.

79 "incredible and bizarre lie": *Star-Bulletin*, January 31, 1979.

80 "Nappy is always his happy self": *Advertiser*, February 2, 1979.

80 "I feel like I just kissed": ibid.

80 "The only comment I have": *Star-Bulletin*, February 26, 1979.

80 "street fighters": *Advertiser*, September 8, 1975.

81 "The fighting goes on": *Star-Bulletin*, June 6, 1978.

81 "The situation falls": *Organized Crime in Hawaii.*

83 "With every known make": *New York Times*, July 2, 1922.

85 If true, however, Shirai's report: The existence of a long-standing rumor regarding the identity of the alleged Godfather of Hawaii was reported in the *Advertiser*, June 24, 1977.

85 "You'd better stop talking": The *Valley Isle*, June 15, 1977.

86 "Even though we didn't": *Advertiser*, June 24, 1977.

86 "wild charge"… "no questions about": *Star-Bulletin*, June 23, 1977.

86 "Anybody who grew up": *Advertiser*, June 24, 1977.

86 "Larry always did have": ibid.

87 "[Keala] described Larry's position": ibid.

87 "If that isn't aiding": ibid.

88 "I was stupid": Chapman, Part I.

88 "He was like [Arnold] Schwarzenegger": Ho, p. 10.

88 "I loved being a cop": Chapman, Part I.

88 Mehau was quite good at this: Mehau's arrest statistics were reported in the *Star-Bulletin*, October 9, 1958.

89 "They wouldn't break cleanly": *Advertiser*, October 3, 1957.

89 "Do you intend": *Advertiser*, April 27, 1964.

90 "I really used to feel": Chapman, Part I.

90 "I'm not saying": Chapman, Part II.

91 "Police sergeant Larry Mehau": *Star-Bulletin*, September 11, 1960.

91 "outstanding" . . . "loose handling" . . . "unduly familiar": *Advertiser*, October 9, 1958.

91 "zealous efforts to achieve": *Star-Bulletin*, October 9, 1958.

91 "In weighing the factor": ibid.

93 "He's basically a good kid": *Advertiser*, September 8, 1975.

93 "preposterous" . . . "That's incredible": *Star-Bulletin*, October 20, 1976.

93 "When someone with": ibid.

94 "We the only U.S. citizens": Nicol.

94 "a significant pattern of isolation": Navy personnel records of Ronald Ching.

94 "wanted to be free": ibid.

94 "wrong crowd": ibid.

95 "tear something (or someone)": ibid.

95 "I can't smile": ibid.

95 "reason of unsuitability": ibid.

95 "immaturity, impulsivity, irresponsibility": ibid.

96 "crawling with prostitutes": *Advertiser*, April 28, 1982.

96 "People were afraid of him": Interview with Keith Kaneshiro, April 2, 2013.

96 "made his bones": Nicol.

96 "cold-blooded": Interview with Keith Kaneshiro, April 2, 2013.

96 "reptilian": *Star-Bulletin*, September 18, 2005.

96 "stone killer": Nicol.

98 "If I had anything to do": Interview with Peter Carlisle, March 23, 2013.

99 "thumbed his nose": *Advertiser*, August 25, 1984.

99 "would be dead": *Star-Bulletin*, August 8, 1981.

99 "really down to earth guy": Ching's commentary on the methods and pleasures of killing all were reported by Nicol's article.

102 "I shoot him right here": Interview with James Koshiba, March 26, 2013.

102 "There are people": Interview with Peter Carlisle, March 22, 2013.

102 "He had a warped sense": Commentary on Ching's drug use, romantic life, and sex appeal come from an interview with an anonymous source.

104 Together they cruised: Details of Ching and Scanlan's interactions come from an interview with James Koshiba, March 26, 2013.

105 "As long as I'm around": *Advertiser*, November 20, 1981.

106 "He felt like": Interview with Erica Naone, April 7, 2014.

108 "vendetta": *Star-Bulletin*, March 13, 1981.

108 "Marsland believes Ron Ching": *Advertiser*, March 13, 1981.

108 "Marsland has been after him": *Star-Bulletin*, March 13, 1981.

108 "He will stop at nothing": *Advertiser*, March 13, 1981.

Chapter Four: Enemies in Common

111 "spooky" and "Satanic-looking": Interview with Peter Carlisle, March 22, 2013.

112 "I could not sit": *Star-Bulletin*, April 29, 1983.

112 "I know that there are": ibid.

112 "I have to protect": ibid.

113 "When somebody steps up": Lipman, February 1981.

113 "gross and ugly": *Advertiser*, June 15, 1979.

114 "wouldn't take no": *Star-Bulletin*, June 27, 1979.

114 "take care of" her new "punk": *Star-Bulletin*, June 14, 1979.

115 "devastating": *Star-Bulletin*, June 16, 1979.

115 "immaculate ejaculate": *Advertiser*, June 27, 1979.

115 "Are you saying I lie?": *Star-Bulletin*, June 26, 1979.

116 "That message was, 'You're dead'": *Advertiser*, June 27, 1979.

116 "Marsland's a colorful figure": *Star-Bulletin*, June 11, 1984.

116 "a cold-blooded attempt": *Advertiser*, June 27, 1979.

117 "bad judgment" and "ridiculous": *Advertiser*, July 4, 1979.

118 "I'm just happy": ibid.

118 "I don't even know": Lipman, February 1981.

118 "couldn't even go": *Advertiser*, November 6, 1980.

118 "Questionable"..."asinine": *Advertiser*, August 23, 1979.

119 "You drop something": ibid.

119 "I want you to be": *Star-Bulletin*, August 23, 1979.

120 "gathering force" and poised to "crash ashore": *Advertiser*, July 24, 1979.

120 "lock 'em up": ibid.

120 "bullshit"... "You're faced with": ibid.

120 The Hawaiian crime statistics: Kotani, Part I.

120 In 1980 the state's murder count: The Disaster Center.

120 Sixty-five of those murders: *Star-Bulletin*, January 7, 1981.

121 "We are a community": ibid.

121 "The criminal justice system": *Hawaii Herald*, March 19, 1982.

121 "Everything right now": ibid.

121 "intercession by do-gooders": *Advertiser*, July 24, 1979.

122 "there had been no single word": *Advertiser*, September 29, 1979. Parentheses in original.

122 "very fragile asset"... "without a shred": *Star-Bulletin*, September 27, 1979.

122 "The front office": *Advertiser*, October 3, 1979.

122 "The only thing": *Advertiser*, January 15, 1980.

123 "Deputies are used to working": *Advertiser*, October 3, 1979.

123 "normal differences that you find": *Advertiser*, September 28, 1979.

124 "he couldn't have anybody": *Star-Bulletin*, September 29, 1979.

124 "paranoid little man": ibid.

124 "The arguments from": Interview with Peter Carlisle, March 22, 2013.

124 "brutal, senseless and cruel": *Advertiser*, January 3, 1980.

124 "troubled by the quality of evidence": *Advertiser*, October 3, 1980.

124 "serious questions" . . . "criminality is so extensive": *Advertiser*, January 3, 1980.

125 "When he did that": Interview with Peter Carlisle, March 22, 2013.

125 "the most gutless ruling": *Advertiser*, October 3, 1980.

125 "the final straw": *Star-Bulletin*, March 11, 1980.

127 "Anybody who has been": *Rocky Mountain News*, February 6, 1945.

128 "You don't know me": Details of Rick Reed's first meetings with Charles Marsland are from an interview with Rick Reed, March 13, 2013.

131 "bare-knuckled": *Advertiser*, October 30, 1980.

132 "swing down from": ibid.

132 "Perhaps," he said, "our concentration": *Star-Bulletin*, October 28, 1980.

133 "I was born and raised": ibid.

133 "I don't have a personal": *Star-Bulletin*, September 3, 1980.

134 "It's a mandate": *Advertiser*, November 5, 1980.

Chapter Five: If You Looking for Trouble

135 "There are so many cases": *Advertiser*, November 21, 1980.

136 Fifteen hundred charges of sexual assault: Shaplen, Part II.

137 "I feel very sorry": ibid.

137 "stilted language": *New York Times*, March 22, 1981.

137 "I doubt very much": *Star-Bulletin*, April 9, 1981.

137 "judicial atrocity book": *Star-Bulletin*, September 28, 1981.

137 "When you have cases": ibid.

138 "You've got a real mixed bag": Interview with David Bettencourt, March 21, 2013.

139 "jackass": *Star-Bulletin*, July 10, 1981.

139 the case of Warren Miller: Details of Miller's crimes can be found in *State of Hawaii v. Warren David Miller*.

140 "positively absurd and a travesty": *Advertiser*, September 17, 1981.

141 "This one really bothered me": *Advertiser*, September 1, 1981.

141 "These are people": Richardson.

141 "Here we have a major": *Advertiser*, September 17, 1981.

142 "fucking shithead" ... "the worst appointment": *Advertiser*, September 25, 1981.

142 "utterly stupid": ibid.

143 "inconsistency in any case": *Star-Bulletin*, September 28, 1981.

144 "You know what": Interview with Peter Carlisle, March 22, 2013.

145 "wasn't that dissimilar": *Advertiser*, October 20, 1981.

145 "I hate to be vicious": ibid.

145 "I'm sure he didn't graduate": ibid.

146 "a calculated campaign": *Star-Bulletin*, October 21, 1981.

146 "organic brain dysfunction" ... "that freed": *Las Vegas Review-Journal*, April 1, 2000.

147 "Carry your own fucking briefcase": Jones.

147 "He had an almost photographic": Interview with Frank O'Brien, April 11, 2013.

147 "God, he was brilliant": Interview with David Bettencourt, March 23, 2013.

147 His auto fleet: *Star-Bulletin*, July 12, 2005.

148 "David would overpay you": Interview with Frank O'Brien, April 11, 2013.

148 "Version of how he got married": Interview with David Bettencourt, March 23, 2013.

148 "Towards the end": Interview with Mike McGuigan, March 21, 2013.

148 "[Schutter] is going to tell us": *Star-Bulletin*, July 10, 1981.

149 "you'd applaud your fool heads": *Advertiser*, July 24, 1979.

149 "They hate you": ibid.

150 "To watch them": Chapman, Part I.

150 "The large home": *Advertiser*, June 13, 1972.

151 "These ohia logs:" ibid.

151 "No sense they ruin my door": Chapman, Part I.

151 "No wonder Larry never locks": *Star-Bulletin*, May 1, 1980.

151 One of the shepherds: *Advertiser*, June 13, 1973.

151 "What are you gonna do": Chapman, Part II.

152 "It's a good life": *Mehau v. Reed*.

153 "Larry Mehau is my friend": *Star-Bulletin*, January 9, 1975.

154 "[I] was his friend": *Advertiser*, September 22, 1980.

154 "I know I'm controversial": Ariyoshi, p. 45.

154 "I've known you": ibid.

155 "[Mehau] knew all the entertainers": ibid.

155 "We started at nine o'clock": Ariyoshi, p. 52.

156 "That's a bunch of malarkey": *Los Angeles Times*, July 15, 1979.

156 "I was the one": Ho, p. 104.

158 "old man": *Los Angeles Times*, July 10, 1979.

158 "He was more strict": *Mehau v. Reed*.

158 "Along the way": *Los Angeles Times*, July 15, 1979.

158 "OK, you better start calling": Chapman, Part II.

159 "There's tensions and headaches": ibid.

159 "If it weren't for Larry": *Los Angeles Times*, July 10, 1979.

160 "[I] told them whatever": *Mehau v. Reed*.

161 "I don't know how many": *Advertiser*, September 22, 1980.

161 "there were people strolling": ibid.

161 "I had six hundred": ibid.

161 "That's the last thing": ibid.

162 As Moku, the wooden dummy: *Star-Bulletin*, January 17, 1985.

162 "Hawaii's official man of mystery": *Star-Bulletin*, January 17, 1980.

Chapter Six: No Rock Da Boat

163 "I keep hearing": *Advertiser*, May 9, 1981.

164 "police state": Kotani, Part II.

164 "Anyone on the outside": Kotani, Part I.

164 "If a police state": *Star-Bulletin*, January 29, 1982.

164 "Chuck Marsland has taken it": Kotani, Part II.

164 "manufactured": Kotani, Part I, p. 4.

165 "blowing smoke out": Kotani, Part I.

165 "who don't want to pass": *Advertiser*, April 22, 1982.

165 "a bunch of half-assed": *Advertiser*, April 28, 1982.

165 "I rock the boat": Richardson.

165 "a few arrogant, imperious": *Advertiser*, April 28, 1982.

165 "If we do": *Star-Bulletin*, April 21, 1982.

166 "Every man has a role": *Star-Bulletin*, April 22, 1982.

166 "Cool it"… "Hey, Chuck": ibid.

166–67 "Waipahu special" . . . "unlike the typical": *Star-Bulletin*, April 24, 1982.

167 "just trying to hide": *Star-Bulletin*, July 7, 1982.

167 "Acoba's indirect and gutless": ibid.

167 "If they were truly interested": *Advertiser*, July 17, 1982.

167 "total scum": *Advertiser*, April 28, 1982.

168 "My uncle is Alema Leota": *Advertiser*, August 13, 1982.

168 "We going off you": *Star-Bulletin*, August 14, 1982.

168 "right down his throat": ibid.

168 "that I didn't get to": *Star-Bulletin*, April 30, 1982.

168 "When he gets out": *New York Times*, July 16, 1984.

168 "My mom always gets sick": *Star-Bulletin*, August 14, 1982.

169 "The silence that has followed": *Advertiser*, May 14, 1982.

169 "He was just passionate": Interview with Mike McGuigan, March 21, 2013.

170 "He had really come in": Interview with Peter Carlisle, March 22, 2013.

170 "He surrounded himself": Interview with Mike McGuigan, March 21, 2013.

171 "Sometimes he really wanted": Interview with Rick Reed, March 13, 2013.

172 "Do that which will help": *Star-Bulletin*, June 12, 1984.

172 "[He] forgot us": *Advertiser*, April 1, 1986.

173 "We were happy": Interview with Rick Reed, March 13, 2013.

173 "You gotta be careful": ibid.

173–74 "two pets" . . . "It's hard": Interview with Keith Kaneshiro, April 2, 2013.

174 "Basically he wanted": ibid.

175 "Don fit a role": ibid.

176 "Ronnie is a smooth guy": ibid.

176 "It's not going to look": ibid.

177 "You cannot give this guy": ibid.

177 "You're making a mistake": ibid.

178 "With all that": Interview with Mike McGuigan, March 21, 2013.

178 "It was very interesting": Interview with Peter Carlisle, March 22, 2013.

178 "When it came": Interview with Mike McGuigan, March 21, 2013.

179 "He was just a wonderful man": Interview with Phil and Joan Hester, March 26, 2013.

180 "This time I remember": Interview with Rick Reed, March 13, 2013.

180 "Whatever Sadie says, goes": ibid.

180 "so full of himself": ibid.

181 "divorced him at least fifteen": Eulogy for Chuck Marsland by Rick Reed, April 30, 2007.

181 "She was one to fly": Interview with Phil and Joan Hester, March 26, 2013.

181 "I thought I told you": Interview with Rick Reed, March 13, 2013.

181 "It was really bad": ibid.

182 "party hack": *Advertiser*, August 12, 1983.

182 "Wakatsuki is neither": *Star-Bulletin*, August 30, 1983.

183 "I don't know whether today": *Star-Bulletin*, April 25, 1983.

183 "The jury had no problems": *Star-Bulletin*, June 28, 1983.

183 "That's what gripes me": *Advertiser*, March 13, 1983.

184 "Our prosecutor is running amok": *Star-Bulletin*, March 9, 1983.

184 "Reporters can't resist": Borreca, August 1983.

184 "We must guard against mistaking": *Advertiser*, May 1, 1983.

184 "reckless and intemperate": *Star-Bulletin*, September 18, 1981.

185 "poor loser". . . "implausible excuses": ibid.

185 "Many lawyers see Marsland": Boylan, July 1988.

185 "If we just keep": political campaign commercial for Charles Marsland, circa 1984.

186 "sworn duty to prosecute": *Advertiser*, September 28, 1983.

186 "seek justice, not merely convict": ibid.

186 "To Mr. Marsland": *Star-Bulletin*, September 28, 1983.

186 "are going to have": *Advertiser*, May 22, 1983.

187 "One does not refuse": *Advertiser*, May 23, 1983.

187 "The only thing that bothers": Richardson.

187 "I wouldn't miss it": *Advertiser*, March 20, 1983.

187 "I kind of like": *Star-Bulletin*, January 13, 1984.

Chapter Seven: My Bare Hands

188 "Hey, brah, can I cash": *Advertiser*, January 19, 1984.

189 "Gee . . . they're all my friends": ibid.

189 "you better not sue anyone": *Advertiser*, December 30, 1983.

189 "He can take care of himself": *Mehau v. Reed*.

190 "the conclusion among the people": ibid.

190 "It was a guilt by association": Interview with Keith Kaneshiro, April 2, 2013.

191 "Are you going": Henry Huihui's statements regarding this alleged conversation with Larry Mehau were recounted by former FBI agent Ray Hamilton, who read from an FBI report, during an interview with the author in February 2013. Also, Huihui testified about this conversation in court, as reported in the *Advertiser*, December 5, 1984.

191 "It was more important now": *Advertiser*, December 5, 1984.

192 "I had serious reservations": Interview with Frank Marine, February 24, 2014.

192 "How's it, Chuck?": *Star-Bulletin*, May 9, 1984.

193 "The people of the state": *Advertiser*, June 2, 1984.

194 "Dan Bent advised me": Frank Marine recalled his interactions with Charles Marsland during an interview on February 24, 2014.

196 "I WILL FUCKING KILL YOU": ibid.

196 "Gee, maybe we can find": ibid.

196 "Frank would shake his head": Interview with Ray Hamilton, February 2013.

197 "We just had different approaches": Interview with Mike McGuigan, March 21, 2013.

198 "The wrong word": *Star-Bulletin*, June 4, 1984.

198 "honey of an opportunity": ibid.

198 "For him, it wasn't the big": Interview with Peter Carlisle, March 22, 2013.

198 "I would not have done": Interview with Frank Marine, February 24, 2014.

198 "monumental pissing match": *Star-Bulletin*, July 16, 1986.

199 "We have entered": *Star-Bulletin*, January 26, 1984.

200 "Those who run our legislature": *Star-Bulletin*, March 30, 1984.

200 "If Chuck didn't get": Interview with Peter Carlisle, March 22, 2013.

201 "I respect what he stands for": *Star-Bulletin*, October 23, 1984.

201 "There was a real rift": Interview with Mike McGuigan, March 21, 2013.

202 "It was supposed to be": *Star-Bulletin*, February 3, 1983.

202 "He's probably the most truthful": *Advertiser*, January 30, 1986.

202 "If they didn't have laws": Chapman, Part I.

203 "I don't know how many": *Mehau v. Reed*.

204 "operating thesis": ibid.

205 "Marsland has also helped": *Star-Bulletin*, November 1, 1984.

206 "Ching felt like a cold serpent": Interview with Rick Reed, March 13, 2013.

208 "We talk face to face": Nicol.

208 "I could see": *Star-Bulletin*, June 26, 1985.

208 "I realize what I've done": ibid.

209 "I don't want to say": *Star-Bulletin*, August 2, 1984.

209 "There isn't a prosecutor": Interview with Frank Marine, February 24, 2014.

209 "Why in God's name": *Star-Bulletin*, July 31, 1984.

209 "The worst personal sacrifice": *Advertiser*, August 3, 1984.

209 "It was hard to swallow": ibid.

210 "the only entrée we have": *Star-Bulletin*, August 2, 1984.

210 "This vendetta BS": ibid.

210 "We spent a lot of time": Interview with Peter Carlisle March 22, 2013.

211 "An indelible moment": Interview with Mike McGuigan, March 21, 2013.

211 "instructed by another": *Star-Bulletin*, August 1, 1984.

211 "There's a whole cabal": *Advertiser*, July 31, 1984.

211 "I have been feeling": *Star-Bulletin*, July 31, 1984.

211 "liar" . . . "I have told this": *Star-Bulletin*, August 1, 1984.

211 "complaint department": *Advertiser*, June 15, 1984.

212 "fill in the blanks": Interview with Keith Kaneshiro, April 2, 2013.

213 "If you hadn't had this opportunity": Interview with Rick Reed, March 13, 2013.

Chapter Eight: Love Never Fails

215 "You going": testimony of Ronald Ching in *State of Hawaii vs. Eric Naone, Greg Nee, and Ray Scanlon* (sic), as reported in the *Advertiser*, June 4, 1985.

217 "The police department": *Advertiser*, April 13, 1985.

218 "out of revenge": *Star-Bulletin*, May 11, 1985.

218 "That information is truthful": Interview with Frank Marine, February 24, 2014.

219 "I gave them bits of truth": *Advertiser*, June 5, 1985.

221 "Whenever you're dealing": Interview with Mike McGuigan, March 21, 2013.

221 "I remember thinking": Interview with Robert Klein, March 27, 2013.

222 "fiercely loyal and close": *Star-Bulletin*, May 25, 1985.

222 "he was concerned": *Star-Bulletin*, May 30, 1985.

223 "I told him he better": *Advertiser*, May 31, 1985.

223 "There were times": Interview with Jay Melnick, March 24, 2013.

224 "very close friend"... "in the future": testimony of Ronald Ching, as reported in the *Advertiser*, June 4, 1985.

225 "They looked so fucking hard": Interview with Christopher Evans, April 12, 2013.

226 "being truthful is new": *Advertiser*, June 5, 1985.

226 "There was no fucking way": Interview with Christopher Evans, April 12, 2013.

226 "Defense lawyers generally do not": Interview with James Koshiba, March 26, 2013.

227 "nervous and panicky": *Star-Bulletin*, June 13, 1985.

228 "So naturally, I talk to Rags": Interview with James Koshiba, March 26, 2013.

230 "clever, devious": *Advertiser*, June 15, 1985.

230 "streetwise, Akamai": *Star-Bulletin*, June 15, 1985.

230 "master manipulator": *Advertiser*, June 15, 1985.

230 "He embellished it": Interview with James Koshiba, March 26, 2013.

231 "What happened, I got a call": Interview with Christopher Evans, April 12, 2013.

232 "Hey Chris, what the fuck": ibid.

233 "Ronnie, when he started talking": Interview with Mike McGuigan, March 21, 2013.

233 "I felt like": Interview with James Koshiba, March 26, 2013.

234 "wasn't sure what": *Star-Bulletin*, June 13, 1985.

234 "I firmly believe": *Advertiser*, June 13, 1985.

234 "I've got it with me": ibid.

234 "People fucking freaked": Interview with Christopher Evans, April 12, 2013.

234 "shocking": Interview with Jay Melnick, March 24, 2013.

235 "That's pretty dramatic": Interview with Robert Klein, March 27, 2013.

235 "I remember Carlisle and I": Interview with Mike McGuigan, March 21, 2013.

235 "The only thing": Interview with Christopher Evans, April 12, 2013.

236 "I had friends, you know": Interview with James Koshiba, March 26, 2013.

238 "unholy alliance": *Star-Bulletin*, June 14, 1985.

238 "has on their hands": *Advertiser*, June 15, 1985.

239 "won't even bat an eye": *Star-Bulletin*, June 14, 1985.

239 "one scintilla of tangible evidence": *Advertiser*, June 15, 1985.

239 "didn't have weapons in 1975": *Star-Bulletin*, June 15, 1985.

239 "It becomes personal": ibid.

240 "By nature you'd think": Interview with Jay Melnick, March 24, 2013.

241 "Chuck, terrible news": *Star-Bulletin*, June 19, 1985.

Epilogue

242 "bad press" that "portrayed me": *Advertiser*, June 26, 1985.

244 "He knew I was not": *Star-Bulletin*, September 18, 2005.

244 "I certainly know": Interview with Erica Naone, April 7, 2014.

246 "Sticking people in the can": Boylan, July 1988.

246 "The old-boy network got together": *Advertiser*, September 18, 1988.

247 "Marsland offered an almost": Boylan, December 1988.

247 "cesspool of dope": *Advertiser*, April 7, 1989.

247 "My only reaction": *Star-Bulletin*, June 2, 1989.

248 "He just was not a politician": Interview with Rick Reed, March 13, 2013.

248 "going to continue": *Star-Bulletin*, February 5, 1992.

248 "never stop. He has no feelings": *Advertiser*, February 5, 1992.

248 "warm, witty, likable": ibid.

249 "I don't think he was senile": Interview with Mike McGuigan, March 21, 2013.

250 "He opened up": Interview with Keith Kaneshiro, April 2, 2013.

250 "The Hawaiian tradition": Interview with Brook Hart, March 21, 2013.

251 "Chuck would get": Interview with Rick Reed, March 13, 2013.

251 "He would have led": ibid.

251 "The silver lining": Eulogy for Chuck Marsland by Rick Reed, April 30, 2007.

252 "Hawaii is a unique state": Interview with Rick Reed, March 13, 2013.

253 "Hawaii juries are more difficult": Interview with Frank Marine, February 24, 2014.

253 "We need federal help": *Valley Isle*, June 29, 1977.

254 "He did what had never": Interview with Mike McGuigan, March 21, 2013.

Index

Acoba, Judge Simeon, 139–43, 167, 183, 184
Ala Wai Yacht Harbor, 225
American Civil Liberties Union, 184
Andersen, Jon, 51, 67
Anderson, Eileen, 167, 199
Anderson, Senator D. G., 86, 87
Arashiro, George I. "Fat Man," 78
Ariyoshi, Governor George, 85, 86, 152, 153–56, 188, 204
Ariyoshi, Jean, 155, 166

Bailey, F. Lee, 146–47
Baker, Arthur, 96–98, 159, 204
Barenaba, Randy, 42
Batman (TV show), 54
Bayonet Constitution in 1887, 16
Bender, Ruth, 96
Bent, Daniel, 189–90, 194, 204
Bettencourt, David, 29, 108, 138–39, 147, 198, 251
Bingham, Hiram, III, 8
Bixby, Lydia, 4
Blue Hawaii (movie), 12
Bowskill, Paul, 53, 57, 59, 61–62
Boylan, Dan, 184, 246
Brady Bunch, The (TV show), 12, 54

Brando, Marlon, 91
Bumatai, Andy, 151
Bureau of Alcohol, Tobacco, and Firearms, 156
Burgess, Hayden, 75, 80
Burns, John, 85, 154
Burns International Security Forces, 152–53
Butler, Chris "Jagad Guru," 172

Campbell, Jack, 47
Campbell, Kamokila, 161
Capone, Al, 41, 157
Career Criminal Units across the Hawaiian Islands, 111, 122–23
Carlisle, Peter
    on Chuck Marsland as a manager, 170, 200
    defense prosecutor at retrial of William "Nappy" Pulawa, 169
    deputy prosecutor in Chuckers Marsland's murder investigation and trial, 220–21, 241
    elected as Honolulu's city prosecutor for four terms and then elected mayor, 244
    and Frank Marine, 198
    on Judge Harold Shintaku, 143–44

as one of Chuck Marsland's
    favorites, 173
on Rick Reed, 200
on Ronnie Ching, 102
and the Vernon Reiger Sr.
    case, 111, 124–25
Carstensen, Don, 99–101, 169,
    174–75, 201–2
Cayetano, Ben, 148, 166–67,
    182, 184
Central Union Church in
    Honolulu, 7–8, 66
Ching, Ronnie
    abduction and murder of
        Arthur Baker, 96, 207
    admits to killing Bobby
        Fukumoto, 207
    admits to killing Chuckers
        Marsland, 206, 207,
        214–16
    admits to killing Senator
        Larry Kuriyama, 207,
        229–30
    as an independent gangster,
        separate from the
        Syndicate, 96
    appearance of, 102
    arrested for firearms and
        narcotics offenses and sent
        to federal prison, 108, 243
    attempt at suicide, 95
    birth of, 94
    at Chuckers Marsland's
        funeral, 67
    death of, 243
    discusses the ins and outs
        of killing with Don
        Carstensen, 99–102, 175
    and drugs, 61, 103
    as employee of the Hawaii
        Teamster Production
        Unit, 105
    fails lie detector tests on plea
        deal information and he
        is deemed unreliable, 217,
        218–19, 231–32, 242
    in federal penitentiary,
        93–94, 175–76, 177, 206
    girlfriends, 102–4
    given plea deal in exchange
        for information regarding
        unsolved crimes, 176–77,
        207–12, 214–16, 243
    at the Infinity Club, 56, 57,
        59, 62–63
    and the murder of Arthur
        Baker, 96–98, 159, 176
    and the murder of Bobby
        Fukumoto, 98–99, 176
    and the murder of Ruth
        Bender, 96
    and the murder of
        State Senator Larry
        Kuriyama, 96
    in the Navy, 94–95,
    physical appearance, 95
    pleaded guilty to four
        murders and sentenced to
        four life terms, 96, 243
    testifies at the trial for
        Chuckers Marsland's
        murder, 224–26, 229–32
Chung, George Soon Bock
    "Yobo," 18, 22
Clisby, Cathy, 11, 51, 58, 67,
    68, 222–23

cockfights, 17–18, 139
Cohen, Mickey, 41
Cook, Captain James, 14–15
Crosby, Bing, 11–12

Day, Jane. *See* Marsland, Jane
Defries, John, 55
DeLima, Frank, 155
Department of Justice,
    Washington, D.C., 197
Diamond Head, 9
Drug Enforcement
    Administration, 156, 204

Echeverria, Peter, 33
Eisenhower, President
    Dwight D., 90
Ekita, George, 34
Entin, Hershey, 92–93
Evans, Christopher, 56, 225,
    226, 230, 231–33, 234, 235

Fanene, Penrod, 159, 168
Fasi, Mayor Frank, 85, 120, 121
FBI, 156, 190
Federal Aviation
    Administration, 153
Fellezs, Sherwin K.
    "Sharkey," 34
Fong, Harold, 33, 39
Fukumoto, Bobby, 98–99

Giancana, Sam, 33
Gibb, Police Chief Doug,
    199, 200
Girls! Girls! Girls! (movie), 12
Golden Triangle, Asia, 24–25

Great Plymouth Mail
    Truck Robbery trial in
    Massachusetts, 146
Grigg, Polly, 49, 50,
    180–81, 249

Hamilton, Ray, 28, 196–97
Hanauma Bay, 9
Handa, Clarence "Japan," 36–38
Harrington, Al, 155
Hart, Brook, 34–35, 41, 250
Hawaii
    1778 arrival of English
        explorers, 13
    changes to property laws in
        the nineteenth century, 16
    crime and organized crime
        and statistics, 19–42,
        81–82, 119–20, 120–21,
        242–43
    drug trafficking and
        distribution, 20, 24–25
    earns statehood, 13, 16
    gambling, 17–18, 26–27,
        31–33
    merchants and trading, 15
    population of, 13
    Protestant missionaries from
        New England, 15, 16
    racial tension and anger
        over the alleged culture-
        corrupting influence of
        mass tourism, 17
    sugar plantations, 29
    tourism, 13, 29
    trees, 14

as a United States territory,
2, 16
and the US government,
16–17
written language and the
printing press, 15
Hawaii, HI "Big Island," 14, 15
Hawaii Five-O (TV show), 12,
13, 119
Hawaii Crime Commission,
81–82
Hawaii Kai neighborhood of
Honolulu, 6, 8, 9, 214
Hawaiian Homes Commission
Act of 1920, 150–51
Hawaiian Syndicate, 20–42, 80,
81–82, 165, 186
Hawaiians
decline of native population,
15–16
and disease, 15
immigrant population
increases, 16
people introduced to
Christianity, 15
Haycock, Clair, 33
Heen, Judge Walter, 38
Heffron, Corrine, 92
Heftel, Cecil, 245
Helm, Adolph, 84–86
Helm, George, 84, 85
Helton, William, 53–54
Hester, Phil and Joan, 48,
49–50, 68, 178
Hilo International Airport,
159–60

Hiram, Police Chief
Roy K., 86
Ho, Don
business relationship with
Marcus Lipsky, 157–58
career in entertainment,
54–55
on day of Chuckers
Marsland's death, 203–4
and Eric Naone, 56, 88
on Hawaiian history, 16
and Larry Mehau, 158–59
performs for George
Ariyoshi's campaign,
155, 156
at the Polynesian Palace,
54, 55
Hoke, Richard, 230, 239
Honda, Judge Edwin, 112, 115,
124–25
Hong, Attorney General
Tany, 186
Honolulu, HI
Chinatown, 95–96
nightlife, 53–54
prostitution and narcotics,
20, 23
skyline, 1
Honolulu Advertiser
(newspaper), 19, 31, 150,
153, 168
Honolulu City Council, 199
Honolulu International
Airport, 25
Honolulu magazine, 184, 246
Honolulu Police Department,
19, 33, 48, 90, 156, 217–18

Honolulu Star-Bulletin
(newspaper), 81, 121, 205
Hope, Bob, 54
House Judiciary
Committee, 164
Huddy, Judge Wendell, 183
Huihui, Henry
charged with murder,
kidnapping, and
conspiracy, 35–39
as a cooperating witness for
the federal government,
190–93, 194–95, 196, 218
and Nappy Pulawa, 26–27,
29–30
retrial in murder, kidnapping,
and conspiracy case,
77–79, 190–91
and tax evasion, 33–35
Hunter, Gene, 31

I Dream of Jeannie (TV show),
12, 54
Iha, Dennis M. "Fuzzy," 31, 32,
35–38
Infinity Club, 43, 52–53, 54, 59
Infinity Dolls, 52–53
Inouye, Senator Dan, 248
insanity defenses in Hawaiian
courts, 135–36
Internal Revenue Service, 33
IRS, 156

Johnson, President Lyndon
B., 90
Johnson, Richard "Dickie," 23

junkets to Las Vegas from
Hawaii, 31–33

Kahala neighborhood of
Honolulu, 9, 147
Kahale, Cyril, 211–12
Kahanamoku, Duke, 9
Kahoolawe, HI, 14, 30,
82–84
Kai-shek, Madame Chiang, 91
Kailua, HI, 10
Kalakaua, King of Hawaii,
2, 16
Kaleikini, Danny, 30
Kalua, Bernard, 188
Kama, Joseph, Jr., 61
Kamalii, Kinau, 85, 86, 87, 253
Kamehameha the Great,
15, 30
Kaneohe, HI, 10
Kaneshiro, Keith, 96, 173–74,
176–77, 190, 212,
246, 250
Kaohu, Alvin "Blue Eyes"
accused of killing Benny
Madamba, 80
charged with murder,
kidnapping, and
conspiracy, 35–38
as one of Pulawa's gang
of lieutenants in the
Syndicate, 27, 32–34, 40
paroled from prison, 193
tax evasion, 33–35
Kapu, Sam, 55
Kauai, HI, 14, 30, 42, 159, 204
Kauhane, Charles, 30

Keala, Mark, 49, 50, 58
Keala, Police Chief Francis,
    6, 19–20, 61, 64, 86–87,
    177, 222
Kealoha, Moses, 86
Kennedy, Jackie, 54
Kennedy, President John F., 48
KHON-TV, 87
Kim, Earl K. H., 21, 159
Kim, John Sayim, 18
King, Judge Samuel, 33–34, 40,
    41, 93
Kiyota, Rodney, 125, 146
Klein, Judge Robert, 221, 232,
    234–35
Koko Crater, 10
Koolau Mountains, 9, 10
Koshiba, James, 62–63, 101–2,
    226–31, 233–37, 239
Kuriyama, State Senator Larry,
    96, 229, 230

Laie, HI, 20, 21, 37
Lanai, HI, 14
Lanham, Judge John C.,
    74–79
Leota, Alema
    ascent into the underworld,
        22, 23, 31
    his role in Charles Nelson's
        murder, 21–22
    and pension from the
        Syndicate, 80
    referred to as "total scum" by
        Chuck Marsland, 167–68
    and tax evasion, 33–35

Leota, Dannette Beirne, 35, 36,
    37–38
Leota, Reid, 21–22, 35
Lii, Josiah, 191–92
Liliuokalani, Queen of
    Hawaii, 16
Lincoln, President
    Abraham, 4
Lipsky, Marcus, 157–58
Lockheed Corporation, 160
Lord, Jack, 13
Lovely Hula Hands (essay), 12

Madamba, Benny, 80
Mafia, 165
Magnum P.I. (TV show), 12,
    13, 105
Makapuu Point, 10
Marine, Frank, 192, 193–96,
    198–99, 231–33, 252–53
Marsland, Charles F.
    (grandfather), 44
Marsland, Charles F., III
    "Chuckers" (son)
    appearance of, 8
    birth of, 47
    changes to a tough-guy
        type, 51
    and drugs, 61–62, 223, 224
    education of, 8, 52
    ejects Ronnie Ching from
        the Infinity Club, 59, 62
    at Erhard Seminars Training
        course, 49–50
    gravesite at the National
        Memorial Cemetery of
        the Pacific, 3, 68

job as doorman and host for the Infinity Club, 8, 52–53, 56, 57, 59
murder and funeral of, 7–8, 66–67, 214–16
and Ronnie Ching and Eric Naone, 56
talks to authorities about underworld crimes, 61
as a teenager, 50–58
tendency to exaggerate and boast, 50
Marsland, Charles F., Jr. "Chuck" (father)
as an assistant attorney general, 45–47
assaulted by Penrod Fanene, 168
begins own investigation into his son's death, 69–71, 177
birth of, 44
campaign and election and reelection for Office of Prosecuting Attorney in Honolulu, 132–33, 204–5, 212
death of, 254
death of father, 6
as a deputy attorney general for Hawaii and later as a deputy corporation Counsel for the City and County of Honolulu, 48–49
as a deputy prosecutor, 72, 74, 92, 111
divorce from Jane Marsland, 46, 47
education, 44, 45
files wrongful death suit against then unknown defendants in his son's murder, 72, 146
fired as a deputy prosecutor, 119, 122, 125
first campaign for Office of Prosecuting Attorney in Honolulu as a Republican, 130–32
frustrations concerning crime in Hawaii, 74, 120–24, 135–41
grand jury on Oahu to issue indictments for those believed to have participated in his son's death, 205–6
his get-tough-on-crime policies, extreme responses to crime, and frequent attacks against political figures, 131–32, 135, 163–64, 182, 246–47, 251
his legacy, 249–50
and the Honolulu Police Department, 217–18
and insanity defenses, 135–36, 139–43
and invasion of the Philippines, 6
on the judicial system, 121–24, 125, 163–66

as lawyer for the city of
    Honolulu, 6
loses election for third term
    as city prosecutor, 245–46
management style, 169–70
married to Jane Watts, 46
in Massachusetts, 6, 44, 45,
    46–47
in the Navy Reserve Officers
    Training Corps, 44–45
not content with police
    investigation of his son's
    death, 69
at the Outrigger Canoe Club
    to voice frustration over
    crime in Oahu, 120–24,
    125, 149
personality and traits,
    130–31, 178–79
physical appearance of, 116
promoted to director of the
    Career Criminal Unit in
    Honolulu, 111–12, 122
as the prosecuting attorney
    for the City and County
    of Honolulu, 135–41
prosecutor in case involving
    Vernon Reiger Sr., 111–19
rapport with judges, 137–46,
    163, 167, 182, 183
relationship with
    daughter, 47
relationship with Frank
    Marine, 193–99
relationship with Judge
    Edwin Honda, 112,
    115–19, 121
relationship with son,
    49, 60
retirement of, 249
and retrial for Nappy Pulawa
    and other underworld
    thugs for the murder of
    Nery and Iha, 74–80
runs for term as Hawaii's top
    federal prosecutor or US
    attorney and governor of
    Hawaii, 247
sets up a private practice, 47
son's death, 6–7, 177–78
suggested making the
    prosecutor's office a
    nonpartisan elected
    position, 132
testifies at his son's murder
    trial, 237
as a trust officer for First
    Hawaiian Bank, 48
visits psychic, 71
visits to his son's gravesite, 1,
    4–5, 126, 206, 241
in World War II, 44–45
Marsland, Jane (ex-wife), 44,
    46, 48
Marsland, Laurie Jane
    (daughter), 44, 47
Marsland, Sadie (mother), 44,
    60, 179–80, 238, 249
Maui, HI, 14, 15, 85, 172, 248
Mauna Kea, 154
McCoy, Jim, 81
McGuigan, Mike
    as an inner circle advisor to
    Chuck Marsland, 169–70

on Chuck Marsland, 178, 254
on David Schutter, 148
deputy prosecutor in Chuckers Marsland's murder investigation and trial, 197, 220–22, 233, 238, 239, 241
on Don Carstensen, 201
and favoritism by Chuck Marsland, 173–74
McLachlin, Chris, 52
McLaughlin, Judge J. Frank, 22
McNeil Island Federal Penitentiary, 75, 76
Mehau, Beverly, 150, 189
Mehau, Larry
appointed to the State Board of Land and Natural Resources in 1970, 154
and Arthur Baker's death, 204
birth and childhood of, 87–88
campaigned for election and reelection of George Ariyoshi for governor of Hawaii, 155–56, 188, 189, 204
campaigned for George Ariyoshi for lieutenant governor of Hawaii, 154–155
and Don Carstensen, 202–3
and Don Ho, 157–59

invested in and then ran a private security company, Hawaii Protective Association, 152–54, 159–60
investigated for alleged interactions with gangsters, 156–57, 159–60, 192
and John Burns, 154
named the Neighbor Islands coordinator, 155
as a policeman, 88–92, 154
ranch and ranch life, 150–51
retired from police force, 92, 149
and Rick Reed, 202–3
suspected godfather and leader of Hawaiian organized crime, 85–87, 149, 189–90, 201, 249
suspicions of involvement in Chuckers Marsland death, 203
and the Valley Isle newspaper, 85–86
Mele Kalikimaka (song), 11–12
Melnick, Jay, 223–24, 234, 240–41
Miller, Warren, 139–43
Miranda rights, 147
Mitchell, Kimo, 84
Molokai, HI, 14, 15
Moon, Eric, 205
Morris, Freddie, 162

Nabors, Jim, 161
Nakagawa, Togo, 122, 123, 124, 125, 169
Nakamura, Yoshiro, 164–65, 166
Nam, Kenneth, 142, 167
Naone, Eric
  acquitted of Chuckers Marsland's murder, 240–41
  Army exploits in Vietnam, 107
  arrested as part of a failed plot to kidnap Corrine Heffron and robbery charge, 92–93, 220–21
  attended Chuckers Marsland's funeral, 67, 213
  confrontation with Samoans, 56–57
  death of, 245
  and Don Ho, 55, 56
  in federal prison, 103
  friend of Chuckers Marsland, 11
  and the Hawaii Teamsters, 92, 105
  his temper, 63–64
  and Larry Mehau, 159
  as member of the criminal underworld, 58, 92
  pleaded guilty to buying ammunition as a felon, 93
  strength of, 55–56
  suspected of Chuckers Marsland's murder but denies being at the scene, 64–65, 212–13, 214–16, 219–20, 244–45
Naone, Erica, 63–64, 106–7, 244–45
National Memorial Cemetery of the Pacific
  and Chuck Marsland's gravesite, 254
  and Chuckers Marsland's gravesite, 1–2, 68, 126
  gravesite for reporter Ernie Pyle, 126–27
  gravesites for soldiers who fought in World War II, Korean War, and Vietnam, 3, 126–28
  and human sacrifices, 2
  opened on July 19, 1949, 3
  positioned hundreds of feet above Honolulu, 1
  and Sadie Marsland's gravesite, 249
  and statue of Lady Columbia, 3–4
Native Hawaiian Studies Commission, 253
Nee, Gregory, 65, 67, 213, 214–16, 226, 240–41
Neighbor Islands, 28, 40, 155, 182
Nelson, Charles, 21–22
Nery, Lamont C. "Monte," 31, 32, 35–38
Nevada Gaming Commission, 32
Niihau, HI, 14
Nixon, Pat, 91

Nixon, Vice-President Richard, 90

Oahu, HI
  conquest of, 9–10, 14, 15
  and gambling, 17–18, 26–27
  geology of, 9–10, 14
  Kalama Valley, 29
  known as the "Gathering Place," 239
  population of, 10, 14, 239
Obama, President Barack, 8
O'Brien, Frank, 72, 146, 147, 148
Office of Hawaiian Affairs, 17, 253
Ogawa, Kaoru, 160
Omidyar, Pierre, 8
Operation Firebird, 156, 159, 189–90, 204
Osano, Kenji, 160
Otake, Harry, 31–32, 35
Outrigger Canoe Club, 8, 50, 120

Palmer, Reverend Albert W., 66
Paradise, Hawaiian Style (movie), 12
Pavey, Judith, 144–45
Pearl Harbor, HI, 44
Pedi, Alexander, 51, 52, 59, 62, 67, 70
Peters, Henry, 165
Pirics, Carmen, 53
Polynesian Palace, 54, 55
Presley, Elvis, 12, 54
Preston, Kelly, 8

Protect Kahoolawe Ohana, 84
protection payments, 18
Pulawa, Wilford "Nappy"
  charged with murder, kidnapping, and conspiracy, 35–39
  charged with tax evasion, 33–35, 39–42
  convicted and jailed for tax evasion, 41–42
  found guilty of unlawful imprisonment at the retrial for kidnapping and murder but verdict was voided, 79–80
  and the Hawaiian Syndicate, 21, 22, 23, 26–31, 32–34
  involved in small businesses, 30
  and Larry Mehau, 159
  at McNeil Island Federal Penitentiary, 75–76, 80
  retrial for kidnapping and murder, 74–80, 191
Punahou School, 8
Punchbowl Crater. *See* National Memorial Cemetery of the Pacific
Puowaina Volcano, 1–3
Pyle, Ernie, 126–27

Reed, Rick
  on Chuck Marsland, 248, 251
  as Chuck Marsland's right-hand man, 149, 168, 169, 200–201

elected as state senator from
Maui, 248
on the Honolulu Police
Department's failure
to break murder cases,
217–18
marriages and children,
172–73
meeting with Chuck
Marsland in regards to
Marsland's campaign for
Office of Prosecuting
Attorney, 128–30
publisher of the *Valley Isle*
newspaper, 86, 172
relationship with Chuck
Marsland, 170–71,
173, 201
and Ronnie Ching,
206–7, 208
spiritual philosophy, 172
sued by Larry Mehau for
libel and defamation, and
invasion of privacy, 248
Reiger, Vernon Sr., 109–19,
124–25
Resnick, Ash, 160
Rezentes, Manny, 217, 218,
220, 224
Rubin, Barry, 183–84
Rutledge, Art, 105
Ryder, Roy, 20–21, 27, 34,
35–39, 77–79

St. John, Jill, 91
Sakamoto, Alexander, 229

San Diego, Police Chief
John, 86
Sandy Beach, 10
Scanlan, Rags, 228–29, 233–34,
235–36
Scanlan, Raymond
acquitted of Chuckers
Marsland's murder,
240–41
charged with murder of
Chuckers Marsland, 213,
216, 220, 224–25
as a felon, 105
meeting with Chuck
Marsland, 108
as a policeman, 104–5
testifies at trial for Chuckers
Marsland's murder,
226–29, 233–34
Schutter, David, 144–45,
146–49, 189, 209
Schutter Foundation, 148
Scott, Clifford, 35
Scott, Shannon, 114–15, 116
Selleck, Tom, 13
sexual assaults in the
Hawaiian criminal justice
system, 136
Sherman, Eddie, 150
Sherman, Shawn, 151–52
Shintaku, Judge Harold,
142–46, 165–66, 247
Shirai, Scott, 84–85
Sinatra, Frank, 54
societal taboo or *kapu*, 2
Spencer, Lee, 132–33

Sterrett, Michael, 39–40, 41
Stevens, Charlie, 142–43,
    166–67, 247
Surfers, 155–56

Tarbell, Deputy Chief Arthur,
    89, 91–92
Trask, Haunani-Kay, 12
Trask, Tommy, 161

US Customs, 156

Valley Isle (newspaper), 85–86,
    87, 128, 129, 189, 201, 208
Vericella, Tony and Dana, 161

Wagner, Robert, 91
Waianae, HI, 17, 142
Waianae Mountains, 9
Waikiki, Oahu, 8, 18, 23–24,
    53–54, 57, 61, 222
Waikiki Beach, 1, 49, 120
Waikiki Wedding (musical), 11

Waimanalo, HI, 10, 17–18
Wakatsuki, Judge James,
    139, 182
Ward, Michael, 191
Wie, Michelle, 8
Wilson, Bobby
    among Pulawa's gang of
        lieutenants, 27, 30
    charged with murder,
        kidnapping, and
        conspiracy, 35–39
    retrial in murder, kidnapping,
        and conspiracy case,
        77–79, 191
    and tax evasion, 33–35
Wilson, Pierre "Fat Perry," 97
Wong, Richard "Dickie,"
    188–89

Yakuza, 160, 165, 174
Yamamoto, George, 76, 78–79

Zulu, 155

About the Author

Jason Ryan is a journalist living in Charleston, South Carolina, and is the author of *Jackpot: High Times, High Seas, and the Sting That Launched the War on Drugs*, a nonfiction account of the daring exploits of the South's "gentlemen" smugglers and the innovative, President Reagan-era federal investigation that brought them to justice. *Publishers Weekly* praised it as a "thoroughly researched account . . . Ryan re-creates the era with a vivid, sun-drenched intensity." *Kirkus* hailed it as a "A well-told tale of true crime," while *GQ* called it "meticulously documented and lucidly spun . . . part *New Yorker* feature–part Jimmy Buffett song . . . the result is adventuresome, lavish, informative fun. Try it. You'll like it." Ryan was previously a staff reporter for *The State* newspaper in South Carolina's capital, Columbia.